THE
WORLD
OF
RELIGIONS

T0124898

THE WORLD OF RELIGIONS

SAMARPAN

PAPER
MISSILE

NIYOGI
BOOKS

Published by
NIYOGI BOOKS
Block D, Building No. 77,
Okhla Industrial Area, Phase-I,
New Delhi-110 020, INDIA
Tel: 91-11-26816301, 26818960
Email: niyogibooks@gmail.com
Website: www.niyogibooksindia.com

Text @ Samarpan

Editor: Jayalakshmi Sengupta
Cover: Misha Oberoi
Design: Shraboni Roy

ISBN: 978-93-86906-46-5
Publication: 2018

Printed at: Niyogi Offset Pvt. Ltd., New Delhi, India

In memory of

Srimat Swami Chandrananda ji Maharaj
a great mentor and a great monk

Contents

Each soul is potentially divine. The goal is to manifest this divinity within, by controlling nature, external and internal.

Do this either by work, or worship, or psychic control, or philosophy—by one, or more, or all of these—and be free. This is the whole of religion. Doctrines, or dogmas, or rituals, or books, or temples, or forms are but secondary details.

—Swami Vivekananda

Foreword

Religion has been interpreted differently in different ages and countries for people to adopt it as a tool to equip themselves in the social and transcendental space, in the ways best suited to them. So, avatars, saints, sages, *muni-rishi*s, and prophets have taught *dharma* (religious way of life) through different modes and languages for easy comprehensibility by their people.

It is a common belief that one has to follow and be true to one specific religion, say, Hinduism, Islam, or Christianity—the religion to which one was born or got converted. This limited idea of religion was challenged by Sri Ramakrishna when he came into the spiritual scene in the 19th century. He, unlike others, practised every spiritual path available to him and then taught how truth can be achieved through any spiritual path; that faiths were mere paths for evolution for which one need not quarrel with others. He also taught that religion did not mean confinement. Rather, it implied emancipation through its practice. Thus, one learns from his teachings that Truth and God are one. Hence, dharma too, cannot be compartmentalised; God is single, lone, and next to none. Sri Ramakrishna showed that this fact was not hypothetical. It can be realised by any sincere seeker; one can transcend the dividing line between any two religions through direct realisation, where theoretical knowledge fails.

Scholarly attempts to understand dharma (to mean, religion) invariably result in many theoretical questions that bring to fore unending doubts and debates, leaving one more confused than before. But, if the subject is discussed by someone who lives and leads a religious life, in conformity with the prime codes of dharma, one can provide a clear picture of the spiritual world. I am convinced of this fact after going through the draft of the book *The World of Religions*, by Samarpan, whom I know well.

The scheme of the book is designed to provide an overview of the eight major religions, out of which four are Indic and others are West Asian, covering all the major religions of the world. Chapter–1, titled 'The Art and Science of Religion' is divided into major sub-themes, like The Science of Knowing, Religion and Spirituality, Common Bases of Religions, and Religion and Rationality. This chapter provides a guideline to the readers to logically understand the process of accumulation of knowledge and the process of knowing religion. In this context, the three stages of knowledge—*shabda*, *artha*, and *jnana*, as accepted in Yoga philosophy, voice the treasures of Sanatana Dharma. The four essential aspects of religion—philosophy, ritual, ethics, and myths are also discussed with adequate technical reference. The inclusion of 'Religion and Rationality', with special reference to Vedanta (Pramana), seems highly consistent with the logical axis of the entire thought process of the work.

The next eight chapters discuss Hinduism, Buddhism, Jainism, Sikhism, Zoroastrianism, Judaism, Christianity, and Islam. All maintain a uniform structure of presentation that covers the background—Prophets, Major Texts, God-consciousness, Philosophy, Ethics, Rituals, and Sects of each of these religions. Through all these discussions, the spiritual core of that religion stands out in bold relief.

The author being a Hindu monk, it is natural that he will use Hinduism as the base to understand and explain different religions, as is invariably done by the Western scholars when they discuss religions of other lands. One thus finds comparative appreciation with reference to Hinduism in all the chapters. While this may not be liked by some, it will surely help people from Indian traditions to understand different religions.

Discussion on Semitic religions (Judaism, Christianity, and Islam) makes us realise how Judaism occupies the position of the source from where Christianity and Islam have evolved with their exclusive features. To know more about Christianity and Islam and to explore their past and perspective, one has to understand Judaism too, something that is usually given a miss.

To me, this book appears highly reader-friendly in which one gets a brief but clear picture of the religions of the world. The gist of all religions, including their technical details, have been clearly pronounced. In a sense, this volume will take part in creating 'religion awareness' and 'spiritual consciousness' among the common readers. I really appreciate this goal.

Who is a true citizen in the world of religion? The answer is, 'He who translates dharma in his life'. One who is dedicated to the religious way of life is its *insider*, while others stand at the doorsteps of religion as interrogation marks. In recent decades, the world has witnessed how some people have brought bomb blasts and bloodshed, fire and tear, tyranny and terrorism in the name of religion. In the past, one religious community was attacked by 'the others', but now we find enough instances to conclude that even the followers of a religion attack their own people who belong to different sects. Communalism is traditionally explained as inter-community conflict, but in this e-age, it has become an intra-community conflict. It simply means that some people are doing harm to their own people in the name of 'doing religion'! Qualities like 'acceptance' and 'tolerance' are going beyond the reach of followers of religions day by day. This is a real threat to human civilisation.

Great intellectual works on religion—their myths, literature, and practices, do indicate how much of labour has gone in producing those works, but rarely do such work help people take the path of dharma and spirituality. Worse, some of these works are even misleading. This results in a break of continuity of God-consciousness from the hearts of a common man. The modern age is lacking the nectar, which dharma is capable of bestowing. Inner peace, brought about by dharma, is the only way to bring tranquillity in the lives of people and those around a practitioner.

Due to a lack of understanding of different religions, our intolerance can only lead us to more destruction, pushing our souls into nothingness. Those who understand the crises looming over the human civilisation suffer in silent agony. Amidst this vacuum, this book is like a silver lining. It shows how spirituality and devotion, as the alphabet of all religions, can recreate some more lines of love and affection to live in this world.

Here I wish to appreciate Samarpan's vast research in writing this book. More than that I want to offer my deep respect to him for spelling out the message of 'oneness' through all the chapters. Being a monk for the most part of his life, he is a true insider in religion, which has helped him understand well the nuances of religion and spirituality. His hold on the subject and his vision find expression through simple words in this book—simple words that hide his scholarship.

I believe this book is an excellent attempt to talk about dharma to the generation of this e-age, who seem to be far removed from the essence of religions. To live a meaningful life in the age of globalisation, it is not only important to know one's roots, it is also important to know the roots of others. Inner peace demands inner engineering, and external peace demands a good understanding of the beliefs and convictions of others. I am definite, this book will be one of the bricks in the bridge that needs to build the right connections with people.

After completing the book, I feel each page of this book opens the threshold of the major religions by way of information and also by allowing us a peep into the sacred message that each of these religions has to offer. Like me, I think many more readers will become curious to know more about other religions. Words are not enough to express the delight I experienced after reading this valuable book.

Professor Sheikh Makbul Islam

Ph.D; D.Litt.;

Associate Professor, Calcutta University;

Ex-Dean, Students Welfare, University of Kalyani, Nadia;

Principal Investigator, Major Research Project on Sri Jagannath Consciousness, UGC

Preface

The desire and ability to acquire knowledge distinguish the human society from every other species. It is through knowledge that human beings control nature, both external and internal. Seen historically, European races have been more inclined towards gaining knowledge of the outer world, while Asian countries devoted themselves more to the knowledge of the inner world—the science of religion. It is fascinating to see how every major religion has originated in from Asia—Hinduism, Buddhism, Zoroastrianism, Judaism, Christianity, and Islam. Whatever the material achievement of other countries, Asia will always remain the masters and teachers of inner engineering.

Over millennia, religion has been the strongest bonding force and also the most divisive factor of communities. People have used, abused, and mostly misused religion to advance their own concerns that range from the mundane to the profane. This has made religion a suspicious idea to many, which in turn has led to a loss of understanding of its true character and its capability in transforming human nature.

Every religion has two aspects—its spiritual essence and its popular practices. The first comes from the intuitive knowledge of God by the spiritual masters, who pass on their wisdom to their disciples and followers. The later generation of disciples add the practices and trivial acts of their masters to frame the mould in which a devout need to cast oneself to be perfect. With time, myths and ritual are added to the corpus of spiritual truth, and practices. All this gives birth to a new religion or a sect.

Depending on the topological and psychological differences of human beings, religious practices are bound to vary. This results in serious differences in the outlook of religions. The spiritually challenged followers of a religion take these differences seriously and fight over them with those belonging to other religions. The resultant quarrels and bloodbath put off the less religiously inclined who start condemning religions, even though they may have respect for spiritual personalities. This gives rise to comments like 'be spiritual and not religious'. However, the fact remains that both the external and the internal aspects of religions are intertwined; one cannot survive without the other.

This work presents an overview of the spiritual core and the essential philosophy and practices of the eight major religions of the world. Ways of life as Taoism, Humanism, etc., and prehistoric religions have been left out of narration.

There are remarkable works on every religion, comparative religion, and world religions, but nearly all of them are quite voluminous, presenting a wide range of subjects. Indeed, to do justice to the study of any religion, one needs a book, if not volumes. However, there are many who want to have a ringside view of the basics of different religions. This book is a modest attempt at doing this. It is hoped that first-time readers of religions will find it useful.

Care has been taken to present the religions the way they are, without getting into any controversial issues. In spite of all the care, the possibility of inadvertent mistakes remains. The author apologises for any such oversight.

Samarpan

The Art and Science of Religion

THE SCIENCE OF KNOWING

Historians and analysts have theories about how religion made its first footfall in the human society. Freud believed that it was rooted in man's libido and mortido; Marxists found the play of class struggle in it, and most others link it with ancestor worship and the worship of nature. A study of early religions of Greece, Egypt, China, and Rome clearly reveals this link, sometimes with strange information like the deity of faeces or manure, Sterquilinus, in the Roman pantheon of gods. However, a student of religion would know that no matter how convincing the proponents of these theories may be, the truly living religions are only those that have transcended such elemental beginnings, and are rooted firmly in the knowledge of the Divine. These religions have continued to be with us for centuries, while the minor ones that were rooted in greed, fear, or ignorance, slowly withered away.

One thing common to these religions is that they all have their sacred books, which are essentially the records of the spiritual realisations of their masters/prophets. It is on the basis of these scriptures that the followers of a religion lead their lives. A large number of books and rituals flowing out of them confuse the beginners in the study of religions. However, the world of religion is not as mysterious or chaotic as many presume. It does not run on blind beliefs, inane rituals, or on irrationality as is made out to be by the untrained. There are also no major contradictions between the fundamentals of any two religions, often used as a fecund ground for a bloodbath. Yet, most people shrug at the mention of the 'R' word, blaming it precisely for these reasons.

One reason for the chasm between the believers and the indifferent is the lack of good works on the science of religion. Such works are few, and even those have not been updated to suit the current mindsets. One of the rare works, which present the science and techniques of spiritual knowledge in a comprehensive format, is Yoga Sutras by Patanjali (c. 300 BCE), popularly known as Yoga philosophy. This small book of four chapters, leads a person from the ground level to the highest state, by describing the working and control over the mind in a systematic manner. It assumes nothing, accepts no beliefs, and tolerates no hocus-pocus in its practices. Intensely practical and rational, it is absolutely non-sectarian. Anyone desirous of understanding spirituality can do so by practising the steps and methodology described in it.

According to Yoga, a person takes in the world through his five senses, which send impulses to the brain, making it react variously. The reactions, taken collectively, are known as the mind. The ensuing knowledge, born of the reactions in the mind, can be compared with the oyster that throws a reaction in the form of enamelling to an external irritant entering its body. Depending on the intensity of this reaction by the oyster, the formation of the pearl inside it is good, bad, large or small. Similar is the case of the mind that throws a reaction to the impulse that it encounters, and the resulting knowledge, intense or weak, is like the formation of the pearl. Yoga philosophy begins from this stage of mind becoming active due to impulses. It does not discuss the role and importance of the brain and its neural channels since they are mere organs and belong to the realm of physical sciences.

The process of acquiring knowledge involves three stages—*shabda* (the external impulse), *artha* (meaning of that impulse), and *jnana* (the knowledge arising out of that impulse). When impulse hits a sense organ, it sends the signal to the brain, which tries to understand its meaning by comparing it with past experiences. In the final act, the mind throws out its individualised reaction towards the object from which the signal came. This is jnana, knowledge.

These three stages are distinct processes but get mixed up in such a fashion as to stay indistinct to a common man. One perceives only their combined effect. The first aim of a practitioner is to control his mind so that he can distinguish between these three stages. Depending on how well a yogi can distinguish these three stages, he is considered that much advanced. The final aim is to reach the stage when he can hold back his mind completely from throwing out reactions to any stimulus external or internal. It is then that spiritual knowledge dawns upon him.

What one experiences in that state of no-mind, where the mind completely stops taking in the impulses, is difficult to describe. Yoga philosophy simply says that 'in that state, the spiritual reality appears the way it is'. The further explanation to this is that one experiences the Divine, devoid of anything worldly. The seers are venerated as the incarnation of God, Son of God, Prophet, or Sage.

Since the transcendental reality (God) is experienced only when the mind stops working through proper *sadhana* (spiritual discipline), it is impossible to know (through the mind) the nature of God. Hence, it can never be described satisfactorily in words. This may sound absurd, nevertheless, it is true. God (call it by any name) is infinite (non-finite, to be more precise), as described by every scripture of the world. This infinity is different from the idea of infinity in physics, mathematics, or as commonly understood. Ordinarily, infinite implies hugeness like ocean or sky, largeness as with numbers, incomprehensibility or absurdity as in physics. However, the infinity of God is different from all this and has no imagery from this world to convey it, leaving the untrained bewildered as to its connotations. Spirituality is to experience the infinite in the transcendental state. There is no other definition of it.

Although the nature of the transcendental reality cannot be described, the masters who have experienced this hint at it variously, which has been summed up in the Hindu tradition as: 'Reality (God) alone exists. It is of the nature of consciousness, and is blissful (called Sat-Chit-Ananda in the vedic tradition)'. To some, reality (which is non-finite) appears, as if, with the mask of the finite, known as Vishnu, Kali, etc., while to some others it appears as the formless, or impersonal.

After realisation, one sees everything in this world either as pure consciousness, or as a manifestation of God, or as controlled and run by God. These three worldviews are known as Advaita, Visishtadvaita, and Dvaita. In all of these perceptions, the superiority of matter and mind in this world ceases to exist for the spiritually realised person. He now sees the Divine as supreme, and therefore fears none, craves nothing, hates nobody, and wishes all well. His journey from passion to compassion being complete, he becomes the universal benefactor of the world—he becomes the world teacher. When a critic calls religion an opiate or a sham, he tends to overlook the fact that these sages had no ulterior motive to fool the public. Nay, they even gave up all that a person holds dear in this world—Buddha gave up his kingdom; Jesus gave up his life, and saints give up all that they have in the name of God.

RELIGION AND SPIRITUALITY

After realisation, every master acquires special powers to preach and make disciples. A saint or a scholarly person also preaches, but his effectiveness is nowhere near the power of the words of the master, who can turn a sworn atheist into a confirmed believer by a mere glance, touch, or a word. The Bible talks about this power as:

> And Jesus came and said to them, 'All authority in Heaven and on Earth has been given to me. Go therefore and make disciples of all nations…' *(Matthew.28.18–20)*

Awed by the power of such a personality and the immensity of the truths that he preaches, the masses start following him and emulating his acts in the hope that they too would be able to replicate the realisation. Sometimes it is also done as a mark of respect to the master. With the passage of time, these practices, some of which may be trivial and unnecessary, crystallise as core beliefs like ethics, rituals, and myths of a new religion.

It is worth mentioning here that any description demands observation, analysis, and expression. Since God is a subjective experience, the idea of describing him correctly is absurd. Again, prejudices related to theology, temperament, need, and capacities of the listener, as also the suitability of time and localities add to variations of outlooks of different religions.

Every religion has four essential aspects—philosophy, ritual, ethics, and myths that differentiate one religion from the other. But are religions and their pillars truly different? The answer is a big 'No'. When the search for the Divine is made within oneself, it is known as spirituality; and when this search is through a society, it is called religion. Similarly, this search for the Divine through one's intellectual ability is known as philosophy; through one's actions is rituals; through stories is myths, and through one's conduct is known as ethics. Although these four aspects appear different, in reality, these all are paths leading to the Divine alone. The list of paths does not end here. In our own times, Gandhiji famously said that he wanted to realise God through politics, and he strove towards that. Indeed, the path to the Divine can never be limited.

When a religion is in full play, its philosophy is taken up as the central way of life by the higher minds, while rituals, codes of conduct, and mythologies sustain the ordinary followers of that religion. The practitioners of any religion are usually unillumined persons, and so they confuse the myths, codes, and rituals as true spirituality, and also confuse scriptures with historical truth. It is at this point that differences and quarrels erupt between religions.

It is well known that followers of most religions carry intolerance towards others, but if one can imagine Buddha meeting Jesus and the resulting conversation that they might have, one will understand how true spirituality works, and how the followers of religions behave.

COMMON BASES OF RELIGIONS

Despite all the differences that one can conjure up between any two religions, certain fundamental ideas run through all of them. Some of these are discussed here.

Every religion preaches that a person is much more than what he appears to be. They all accept that there is the spark of the Divine in everyone, which when experienced, can take him away from the sorrows and grief that surround him at every step of life. How and why this divine nature was lost, remains a mystery. Hindus call it *avidya* (ignorance); Christians call it original sin; Islam calls it *gaflah*, and some others call it God's will.

A religion stands on its core belief that the Divine is truer than the ephemeral world, which one sees all around. For them, a person is not a mere body-mind complex but, in essence, divine. The corollary to this is that there has to be a continuation of the present life in some form or the other after a person is dead to this world. Following this, Indic religions believe in rebirth, while West Asian religions believe in the continuation of life in heaven or hell.

Every religion stresses the importance of the present life since the attainment of a better world depends entirely on the present. For this reason, no religion permits suicide, nor do they permit immorality of any kind. The onus of one's action and its consequences lie with the individual. Religions do talk about God's will, but it essentially means that one should accept the results of one's actions as the Lord's will. This does not allow any kind of passivity, least of all moral passivity.

Ethics and morality are defined and described differently in religions. However, it should not be seen as a contradiction. The idea is that once a person accepts a particular mould in the form of a religion to cast oneself into, he cannot allow his mind to play tricks and make him go astray after that.

Every religion agrees that the Divine is unknowable, and beyond description, and so they assert that scriptures alone can give an idea about Him since these are the records of His own words through various channels. If one leaves out the greed of the unscrupulous, and a misunderstanding of these scriptures, it will be seen that every religion strives towards the spiritual well-being of its adherents. The only goal of every religion is to make a man fit to be accepted as divine; everything else in religion is secondary.

Most importantly, they all stress upon the importance and growth of the inner life. They agree that a well-balanced external life is needed, but the goal of every religion is to take its followers towards a spiritual life, away from the swings of worldliness.

RELIGION AND RATIONALITY

People often wonder if religion is rational the way science is because spiritual truths can neither be demonstrated nor can one argue about them. The answer is yes. Every religion is absolutely rational, although their practices may not be.

The crucial difference between the approaches of science and religion lies in science being reductionist—the whole is equal to the sum of its parts. Religion is holistic—the whole is more than the sum of its parts. Who is right, is a big debate that has been raging on since the times of Aristotle, or even earlier.

Science depends on models, which it keeps fine tuning from time to time to adjust the new data and findings. It is through this process that science evolves from good to better models. Religion, on the other hand, talks about the spiritual truths that can be attained by following a systematic path, as explained earlier. Religion is not a model, and so there is no scope of evolution of its core ideas.

Religions in general, and Vedanta in particular, rely on the validity of *pratyaksha pramana* (sense perception), and *anumana pramana* (reasoning)—the two tools that are essential for scientific growth. Every religion has contributed immensely to the growth of logic and sciences of its land through its methods of acquiring knowledge. *Syadvad* (which leads to a probabilistic outcome) of Jainism, and *neti-neti* (the process of negation) of Vedanta, are two very powerful tools of reasoning in mathematics, although they have developed independently. In the Vedas, one comes across the mantra '*purnasaya purnamadaya purnam eva avasishyate*'—infinity taken away from infinity is infinity. This fact about infinity was realised by the sages thousands of years ago!

The third method of knowledge is known as *shabda pramana*, which is about the knowledge gained through the words of scriptures. The ideas about God, soul, rebirth, creation, etc. cannot come through direct perception, or through reasoning. Hence, one must depend on what the sages have said about these. In order to benefit from these perceptions, it is sufficient for an individual to be open to the view that, after all, the sages had no ulterior motive to mislead people, and that they had the purest of character, along with a supremely incisive and brilliant mind. The real strife between science and religion lies exactly on this point. Neither science will accept scriptures as the valid source of knowledge, nor would religion give up the scriptures when it comes to transcendental truth.

To be rational means to be consistent. Religions are fully consistent in their own way and do not suffer from inner contradictions. They bring meaning to life and are universally applicable. If this is not being scientific, then what is? A tree is judged by the best fruits it produces, and not by the rotten ones. This applies to every branch of knowledge. Religion must be judged for its rationality by the greats produced by it, and not by the tinkerers of rituals.

The problem with religion lies with its four pillars—philosophy, mythology, ethics, and rituals. Since a religion's philosophy is based on the intuitive truths, these cannot be defended against the onslaught of the worldly-wise. Myths are worse; their goal is to present spiritual truths to crude minds through fantastic creatures and their unbelievable feats. The followers take them as facts and the critics attack these to undermine the spiritual truths that are embodied within them. Same with codes of conduct and rituals; these need regular updates to suit the changing times, but one rarely dares do that. Thus, the life-giving truths of religions are ignored because one finds the myths and rituals irrational.

In passing, it should be mentioned that Greek philosophers had come up with certain ideas about God and the world that shaped the outlook of Judaism, Christianity, and Islam; although these religions did not accept all of their premises. According to the Greeks, the universe is without a beginning and end. God, the creator, is one, but has general and particular qualities. He is all pervasive, is bodiless, knows Himself, and knows everything else too. The soul is material but is independent of body and matter. Nothing unnatural happens in the world, and so every phenomenon of the world can be explained.

Hinduism
The Religion of Inclusiveness

SACRED TEXTS

The great Indian subcontinent, with its cloud-piercing mountains, wide rivers, stretching for miles, gestating plains, green valleys, monsoon rains, and bright sun, has been the land of plenty. Here flora, fauna grew in abundance, effortlessly. So, when the Aryans appeared in this land, thousands of years ago, indigenously or otherwise, they found an idyllic life, unlike many others who were compelled to roam, rampage, and spill blood for a living.

The peace born of plenty led the race to cultivate finer tastes in music, art, literature, etc., due to which they named themselves Aryan, meaning 'cultured'. In addition, these people were contemplative. To be meditative is the privilege of the calm. It is only amidst tranquillity that philosophy, poetry, and spirituality are born. The restless, at the best, have a brush with them without touching their depth.

The external nature of the land and the internal nature of its inhabitants set a resonance, which led to great spiritual truths, the likes of which were not seen in the world. These truths, when applied to the Indian way of life, crystallised as Hindu dharma, or simply, Hinduism; its influence spread over the land whose boundaries touched from Iran to Indonesia, from China to Sri Lanka.

Some of the great introspective minds of this race, who lived along the banks of Indus, now in Pakistan, transcended the realm of words to reach the depths of silence. In that state of 'no-mind', when the mind is no more the medium of knowledge, a person stands face to face with truths concerning the creator, created, and creation. In this state of intuitive wisdom, Buddha attained enlightenment, Jesus realised himself to be the Son of God, and Prophet Muhammad became the Messenger of Allah.

From the standpoint of an onlooker, the spiritual teachings of these masters appear to have come from them, but the masters knew that those truths were not thought-out by them. They treated them as words of God. In turn, the scriptures revealed by them were venerated as divine oracles and commandments by their followers.

The great minds of the Aryan race, who had dedicated themselves to contemplation, came to be known as *rishi*s (lit. seers, sage). It is difficult to say when exactly they appeared on the Indian soil—some say 4,000 years ago; others claim, it happened tens of thousands of years ago. In any case, they were, perhaps, the first of the humans to realise the importance of the internal nature of man, and how everything was secondary to the Divine. These sages also realised that the only way to overcome one's fear, sorrow, grief, and death was to get out of the snares of the external and internal worlds and by surrendering to the Divine, the infinite, conscious, and blissful. This idea has been beautifully expressed in the prayer:

Tameva viditva ati mrityumeti, nanyah pantha vidyate ayanaya
(The path to immortality lies in knowing the Divine)

Depending on how well and in what form one knows the Divine, the worshipper is blessed accordingly. When one worships God as the provider of favours, or destroyer of fear, He ends up being like a divine milch cow; when He is seen as life's essence, He becomes the God that He is. The Aryans viewed God in both these aspects. For example, when the Divine was seen as the bestower of rains, He was called Indra; and when Indra was seen as the face of the Divine, He was known as the adorable God. This was same with every single God, like Vayu (Wind God), Agni (Fire God), Varuna (Water God), etc. This practice of seeing God as the controller of nature and also as the face of the infinite continues even today, and it is this practice that makes Hinduism what it is—the religion of inclusiveness.

The tradition of great sages did not end or wane but continued for a long time. There were joined by female sages (*rishika*) and child prodigies, who made their contributions to the existing spiritual wisdom. What these sages realised in their meditative state, they passed on to their disciples, who most often were their children. With time, these truths and thoughts were set into a poetic metre. Traditionalists believe that the truths have been recorded exactly the way they were realised.

Poetic metres of a single line came to be known as mantras, and if they comprised stanzas, they were called *sukta*s (hymns). These revealed truths were strictly maintained through an oral tradition by the family of the sages. They were considered sacred and Aryans believed that one could achieve or acquire everything by reciting them properly and by performing *yajna*s (making offerings into the sacred fire).

The mantras could be used to produce different results through a corresponding intent. For example, there is this famous Gaytri mantra recited every day by millions of Hindus:

> *Aum bhur bhuvah svah/ tat savitur varenyam/ bhargo devasya dhimahi/ dhiyo yo nah prachodayat*
>
> (We meditate on the effulgent Lord, who is the creator of the universe; who is worthy of worship; who is the embodiment of knowledge and light; may He enlighten our intellect)

This is a meditative prayer for spiritual enlightenment. This can also be interpreted as a prayer to get riches, as well as a prayer to Sun God, to wash away one's sins. In the same way, practically every mantra could/can be used at three different levels— for worldly gains, for pursuing a righteous way of life, and for spiritual illumination.

The idea of using the same prayer for different purposes paved the way for the Hindu way of life that defined the goal and purpose of life. These came to be seen as four—*dharma* (righteous life that would lead to a better afterlife), *artha* (worldly prosperity), *kama* (enjoyment), and *moksha* (liberation from the cycle of life and death). Hindu religion prescribes both worldly enjoyment, as also attainment of heaven, and going beyond here and hereafter, as valid goals of life. Its scriptures, literature, philosophy, art, sculptor, etc. focus on one or more of these goals.

The mantras and the hymns came to be collectively known as Vedas (knowledge), since these described the spiritual principles behind external and internal nature, and also what lies beyond them. Herein lies a major difference between Hinduism and other religions. Hinduism is based entirely on spiritual principles that can be realised by anyone, anywhere, and at any period of time, whereas other religions run on acceptance of the words of their masters. Irrespective of how great a spiritual master may be, he is bound to behave according to the norms of the period in which he is born. This results in mixing up of spiritual truths and localised practices that need careful sieving as time passes, without which a religion becomes time warped, with deadly consequences. Hinduism is completely different that way. It does not depend on any personality, howsoever great, for its survival. It is so impersonal in nature that sages did not even leave their names behind to indicate who the seer of a particular mantra or work was. What we get by way of their authorship is mostly a family name or a mere pen name.

The Hindu traditionalists, however, believe that whenever God creates, He first lets out the Vedas, the sum total of knowledge, from which creation fans out. This implies that creation is not a random process; It follows a set pattern even though God is beyond any reasoning or pattern.

Thus, Hinduism is eternal, since truth is eternal; the vedic sages only discovered them, the way Archimedes realised the laws of buoyancy in moments of silent contemplation in the bathtub. This makes Hinduism a non-sectarian and an inclusive religion that respects every religion and accepts them as valid paths to reach God, as long as the principles taught by those religions are verifiable by anyone.

Usually, there are four kinds of people who pray to God— seekers of favour, those in crisis, the inquisitive, and those who have realised God. Personalities like Moses, Jesus, and Zarathustra belong to the fourth type, who knew God and loved Him. There is, however, a fifth type that has been prevalent only in India—the Brahmins. People belonging to this class, which later came to be equated with a caste, were trained since their childhood to take the path of God and scriptures. This created a situation where a Brahmin was neither as competent as the sages to contemplate upon God, nor was he interested in the worldly matters. So, many of those Brahmins took a ritualistic way of life to stay God-centric, without being contemplative. These Brahmins should not be confused with the priestly class one encounters in present-day Hinduism or in other religions. They were not priests, nor were they great spiritual personalities; they were simply dedicated to religion without being spiritual masters. These Brahmins fine-tuned the science of *yajna* and popularised these throughout the subcontinent. It was they who maintained different portions of the Vedas in their families through an oral tradition. Some of these families continue to do so.

Vedas

With time, as the vedic corpus grew to a mammoth size, the fear of losing parts of this precious spiritual wisdom also grew. If a family died out or failed to maintain its portion, for some reason, it could be lost forever. Around 2000 BCE, Vyasa began the process of collecting available vedic literature and started to organise them into four books; *Rig Veda, Sama Veda, Yajur Veda,* and *Atharva Veda.*

Rig Veda became the collection of all the *rik* mantras, a particular kind of chant used as prayers during yajnas (sacrifices). *Sama Veda* was another collection of mantras from the *Rig Veda,* also meant to be sung, but used only in certain special sacrifices. *Yajur Veda* comprised *yaju*s or prose mantras, used while pouring oblations in sacrifices. The remaining portion of were consolidated as *Atharva Veda*.

Each of the four Vedas can be broadly divided into two sections that deal with rituals and core spirituality respectively. Each of these sections has two sub-sections. Separately, these are known as Mantra or Samhita (the prayers), Brahman (the process of ritualistic yajna), Aranyak (contemplative hymns), and Upanishads (spiritual truths).

The four Vedas are the fountainhead of Hinduism. Everything of this grand old religion flows out of these sacred books that contain the four aspects of religion—philosophy, mythology, rituals, and ethics. The sages of the post-Vyasa period took up each of these four aspects and created dedicated literature without compromising with the vedic truths.

The Vedas and consequently the Hindus, perceive existence as a complete whole, in which nothing is compartmentalised. The objects change form only to find a new body and a new place in the universe, which has both visible and non-visible spheres. The difference between the lower and the higher existence, as between humans and gods, is not fundamental but due to the difference in their manifested power. Hence, a lower being can reach a higher plane of existence through right kind of work and acquisition of knowledge.

There are obviously many ways to gain this power. The sages preferred the performance of yajnas and offering prayers to gods for the purpose. Over the period, sages and their disciples came up with innumerable yajna for different goals, and soon there were prayers and chants for everything that a person may want in this life or the next.

Yajna is performed by pouring oblations to the gods, who are not definitive personalities, but mere masks of the infinite consciousness. God is infinite. So, how to contemplate upon Him or pray to Him? Since mind can think of only what it can grasp, i.e. the finite, one way to circumvent the problem is to put a finite mask, howsoever ineffective or temporary, on the infinite. To do so, the sages took up various aspects of nature, gave them a divine personality to make contemplation easy, and then tried to express the infinite through that personality. This general principle of expressing the infinite through a personality differentiates the vedic gods from the Greek gods, and also from the angels of the Abrahamic religions.

This simple principle of expressing the infinite through a personality trait, or the power of nature, gave rise to hundreds and thousands of gods. Since there cannot be multiple infinities, there is no way that there can be a real existence of multiple gods; whatever the appearance, the reality had to be one. This truth has been beautifully presented in this mantra:

Ekam sat vipra bahudha vadanti
(That, which exists, is One; sages call it by various names)

To the sages, the being perceived was one and the same; the perceiver was different. Hence, the perception of the Divine too was different. This gave birth to the idea of unity in diversity, which has been the core of Indian religion, philosophy, and the Hindu way of life. Hinduism is thus neither an idolatrous religion, nor monotheistic, polytheistic, or pantheistic religion. The running theme through all the scriptures of the Hindus is that God alone exists.

The relationship between a devotee and the gods was not limited to one or a mere few. In the Vedas we find the gods being adored and worshipped as father, mother, friend, guest, lover, and many more. Depending on the predominance of emotion in a person, one could build a particular relationship with his chosen God, knowing all the while that in truth, all gods were the face of the same Divine.

To perform the sacrifices properly, the scholarly Brahmins came up with auxiliary vedic literature, known as Vedanga. These are six and deal with the art of pronunciation, manual of rituals, grammar, vedic dictionary, prosody, and astrology. It was mandatory for a vedic Brahmin to master at least one Veda, and these six.

The vedic gods and the yajnas were great spiritual outlets for those interested in gains and glory. However, they were inadequate for those rare minds that craved for truth and truth alone. These sages stopped looking at the infinite through the finite masks of gods like Indra and went all out for the infinite the way it was. Their realisations are known as the Upanishads.

Upanishads

The Upanishads form the last sections of the Vedas and are considered to be the spiritual essence of the Vedas. So, these are also known as Vedanta (lit. end/essence of the Vedas). In spite of being sections of the Vedas, the Upanishads have a distinctive character of their own, away from gods, heavens, and yajna and its ritualistic traditions of the Vedas. These are treated as independent literature, and along with Gita, they form the foundation of the philosophy of Hinduism. It is not known how many Upanishads there are; eleven of them, on which Shankaracharya wrote his commentary, are more popular.

The Upanishads discuss the nature of atman, world, and God. However, their central theme is the supreme reality, Brahman, which alone exists; everything else is a mere play of names and forms. The way the same clay is used to make different items with varied names and forms, what one sees as the world, may appear to have a distinct reality, but it is not so.

When perceived through the world of mind, this supreme reality (i.e., Brahman) appears as the creator and controller of the universe; and when perceived without the medium of the active mind, it is experienced as formless. Thus, God is perceived in Hinduism as both formless, and with form.

The conscious principle present in every living being is known as *atman*. In its pristine aspect, it is pure consciousness, and identical to Brahman, the supreme reality. Being of the nature of consciousness, it knows everything and is pure, infinite, and ever-existent. Due to *maya* (divine ignorance that cannot be explained), it gets identified with the world of the mind to behave like any other object of the world. In that state of identification or bondage, it is known as *jivatman*, or simply *jiva* and is equivalent to the English word soul. It transmigrates and takes up different bodies and forms, till it attains its natural state of freedom through spiritual practices.

When a spiritual aspirant makes an effort to get out of this existence, he slowly disentangles himself internally from what he held dear in the world and starts moving towards self-knowledge through the calmness of his mind. As the realisation dawns upon him, he knows himself to be atman that lies within himself. If he continues with his spiritual practices, he comes to realise that the same atman that is within him, is in others too. And finally, he may come to realise that atman alone exists and that it is non-different from Brahman, the ever-existent reality.

This last state of self-knowledge is known as *advaita*. It is sometimes referred to as monism, but that is an incorrect interpretation. Monism implies the presence of one, single entity; advaita means non-dual, implying that there are no two separate realities like consciousness and inertness, or mind and matter. Advaita implies that there is no way of knowing if it is one, or beyond the idea of one–two, because the mind itself ceases to exist in that state. The best way to describe the state of advaita is 'What is, is'; one cannot say anything else about it in defining terms.

The Upanishads talk of these three stages of self-knowledge. However, their speciality lies in the universality of advaita, expressed in statements like '*sarvam khalu idam Brahma*' (Brahman is everything), and '*aham Brahma asmi*' (the individual and the universal are same), etc. The great spiritual aspirants, who realise these truths, are known as *jivanmukta*, free while living, which is the highest spiritual state that can be conceived of. Hinduism thus talks of achieving blessedness here and now, in this very life, as opposed to waiting to die to go to the heavens.

The idea of advaita, although quite incomprehensible by the common minds, is the highest realisation by the Hindu mind and is its greatest contribution to the world of religion.

At times, the Upanishads take help of conversations and simple stories to elaborate the spiritual truths that they want to preach. One of the popular Upanishads, *Katha Upanishad*, discusses the nature of spiritual reality through a discourse between Yama, the God of death, and Nachiketa, a young Brahmin boy who was cursed in anger by his father to go to death. Yama was not at his abode when the young boy reached there, and so he waited for three days without food and water. On his return, Yama felt sorry to see the young Brahmin wait for him like that, and so he offered him three boons for each day that he had waited there. Nachiketa first asked for his father's anger to subside (i.e. worldly gain), then he wanted to know the secret of a yajna that could take one to the high heavens (i.e. taking care of afterlife), and as the third boon, he wanted to know the secret of atman (i.e. *mukti* or freedom that lies beyond here and hereafter).

The discourse that follows is a masterpiece in spiritual literature in which Yama shows how ordinary minds get ensnared in the pleasures of this world that makes them forget their real nature. This results in their being born again and again until they take the higher path of spirituality. It is then that they realise the three stages of self-realisation, as described in the preceding paragraphs.

In the *Brihadaranyaka Upanishad*, there is the story of Yajnavalkya, a great sage, who once gave a discourse to his erudite wife, Maitreyi:

> It is not for the sake of the husband that the wife loves the husband, but for the sake of the atman that she loves the husband. None loves the wife for the sake of the wife, but it is because one loves the self that one loves the wife. None loves the children for the children; because one loves the self, therefore, one loves the children. None loves wealth on account of the wealth; because one loves the self, therefore, one loves wealth. Where there are

two, one sees another, one hears another, one welcomes another, one thinks of another, one knows another. But when the whole has become that atman, who is seen by whom, who is to be heard by whom, who is to be welcomed by whom, who is to be known by whom?

In brief, the Upanishads teach that atman alone exists. Hence, there can be no dichotomy of any kind in this world—there is nothing secular or profane, nothing worth seeking or avoiding.

Itihasas

The Vedas and Upanishads, although great in their vastness, richness, and majesty, suffered from a severe constraint. Brahmins, whose ancestors were the founder sages of the Vedas, were the keepers of these books. They made the books exclusive for those belonging to the upper castes. They probably had a right to do so because of the labour and sacrifice that went into maintaining these sacred books. However, a society cannot thrive without its access to spiritual truths and its practice. The spiritual inclusiveness of the Vedas was thus marred by the social exclusiveness of the Aryans of the period.

Hinduism (or the religion of the Aryans) would have become a highly exclusive religion like Judaism and Zoroastrianism if Valmiki and Vyasa had not opened the spiritual floodgates by their masterly creations of Ramayana and Mahabharata. Hinduism, as understood in present times, has been shaped by Valmiki and Vyasa, who based their works on the spiritual truths of the Vedas. However, they presented them as a poetic story in which they wove spirituality, religious ideals, history, legends, myths, tradition, and local practices of the period. By making use of the format, Valmiki and Vyasa succeeded in presenting the sublime and abstruse spiritual truths to the masses, irrespective of their station in life.

The sacred books discussed in this section are collectively treated as scriptures, of which a Hindu may accept one or many as the guiding book of his life. Scriptures are defined as works that lead a person to attain one of the four goals of life—*artha* (wealth), *kama* (pleasure), *dharma* (noble acts), and *moksha* (spiritual practices). The first two are meant for the betterment of life in this world; dharma is meant to better one's afterlife, and moksha is meant for those who want nothing in this life or in the afterlife.

Not much is known of the great poet-sage Valmiki (c. 4000 BCE), who composed Ramayana. Traditions claim that he was a robber known as Ratnakar, who had a change of heart and went into deep meditation in which he stayed for years. By the time he achieved enlightenment, he had been covered by anthills (*valmik*) around him that gave him the name Valmiki.

To be enlightened is one thing; to impart knowledge unto others is something entirely different. Hence, not everyone who attains enlightenment becomes a teacher. The joy born of knowing God/Truth is so overwhelming that sages go deaf to the world to remain merged in the divine joy until their body falls away. Only in rare cases, an enlightened one comes down from that state, probably out of compassion, to preach the humanity higher truths of life. Or, it may be because they were divinely ordained to do so, as is seen in the lives of Jesus, Muhammad, Sri Ramakrishna and others. Valmiki was surely one of the chosen ones to spread the light of religion to the world. He did that by composing Ramayana, the story of Sri Ramachandra—King of Ayodhya.

Valmiki had an excellent grasp of Indian religious ethos, which he put to great use by weaving them through the story of Sri Rama. He came up with the epic scripture that became a storehouse of religious wisdom, myths, legends, values, and practices. Later, poets took up this story, along with other narrations by the sage, to create their own regional versions of Ramayana, representing their own unique understanding of the spiritual world. There is nothing wrong with it since the infinite world of spirituality can never be squeezed into mere one or two scriptures.

Valmiki's Sri Rama was the epitome of a good human being with an extraordinary character. Poet-sages of later period, however, recreated the personality of Sri Rama as *sopadhik Brahman* of the Upanishads, or God with a personality. With time, Sri Ramachandra, came to be worshipped as a personal God, with all the traits of the infinite as discussed in the Vedas and the Upanishads. This gave birth to works on Rama-literature, popular in most Asian countries. Thus, Lord Rama, who embodied the idea of the infinite God, came to be worshipped in India. In religion, persons, personalities, and divine beings are always secondary; it is the principles representing them that matter.

Valmiki's Ramayana would have sufficed as mass scripture for the Hindus; however, India being the land of spirituality where every minor detail of religion is meticulously worked out, there is always space for more scriptures. Vyasa entered this space, and through his enormous contribution, extending to volumes, he brought to fore every aspect of religion in detail. So much so, practically nothing new has been added in Hinduism after Vyasa. Later sages explained, detailed, and built on what this great sage-poet had bared for all.

Vyasa's authority was so great that he was able to collect the available vedic literature and classify them into the four Vedas, as mentioned in the earlier section. He then created Mahabharata in one lakh verses and is believed to have written eighteen Puranas (to be discussed later), which contain around five lakh verses. One may doubt these claims since it is believed that many later poets too passed off their works in his name. However, there can be no doubt that Hinduism is primarily defined by the works credited to Vyasa.

The story of Mahabharata, as we know, is woven around the royal cousins, Kauravas and Pandavas, vying for the seat of power, finally settled by the great Mahabharata war, where both clans are nearly wiped out. Vyasa took up this event and created his incomparable epic in which he discussed and detailed various aspects of dharma (the way of life) through the innumerable stories and characters that have left their indelible mark on the Indian psyche. Like Valmiki, he stayed true to the Vedas, although he relegated gods like Indra to a secondary position and made the personal aspect of God more important.

Indian society has been in a constant ferment throughout its history. It must have been more so during the time of Vyasa when various philosophies, outlooks, values, castes, tribes, and religious faiths were floating around loosely and needed to be set like a mosaic; not as a palimpsest for the original to get lost in its reinterpretations.

Vyasa left out nothing; nor did he ignore, dishonour, or erase anything. This way he made Hinduism an inclusive religion. In the process, Vyasa covered everything that a man of religion may require—psychology, philosophy, rituals, ethics, social conduct, religious stories, etc. The best way to describe the work is a quotation from it:

> Whatever is there in this world to be known, concerning the various ways and goal of life, is there in this book; and whatever is not here is nowhere to be found.

The defining element of Mahabharata, however, is the introduction of the personality of Sri Krishna, who is treated as the Lord of the universe, incarnated on this earth to guide humanity towards perfection. The multifaceted personality of Sri Krishna helped later philosophers and devotional poets to create innumerable spiritual works centring him.

Over millennia, these two scriptures, Ramayana and Mahabharata, along with the auxiliary books based on them, came to represent the urges, inspirations, strivings, and purpose of the Hindu race, along with its spiritual prowess and religious catholicity.

Gita

The Gita, a poetic work of mere seven hundred verses, is a small but important section of Mahabharata and is the sacred book of the Hindus. It is presented as the discourse by Lord Krishna to Arjuna—the lead warrior of the Pandava clan—in the battlefield of the Mahabharata war. Arjuna had gone to take part in the battle but was overcome with despondency at the sight of near and dear ones, ready to kill each other for worldly gains and honour. Instead of performing his duty of a warrior, Arjuna wanted to escape the war. Sri Krishna would not permit it. He placed before Arjuna the realities of life, world, creation, and God, to guide him out of the ocean of grief and sorrow, which are at the root of human existence.

Gita describes the Divine in its both aspects, personal and impersonal, and the way to realise it. The natural way to attain the Divine is the path of renunciation, in which one gives up every kind of attachment as practised by Sufi saints, Christian mystics, Buddhist, and Jain monks. The second path is that of *karma* (action), in which one performs an action in an unselfish way or offers the results of the action to God, thereby remaining untainted. In this way, Gita teaches the two paths of spirituality, popularly known as *pravritti marg* (path of action) and *nivritti marg* (path of renunciation). As will be seen in the following pages, every religion ultimately follows one of these two paths.

Seen objectively, the Upanishads present the spiritual gist of the Vedas, whereas the Gita is the gist of the Upanishads, thus making it the distillate of Hindu religion. Indeed, in its brevity and content, it is a handbook of Hindu religion, philosophy, and spirituality—in short, life itself.

Puranas

The story goes that Vyasa was not satisfied with his creation of Mahabharata since it did not discuss *bhakti* (devotion). Mahabharata centres on performing one's duties unselfishly to attain spiritual upliftment. There were many who wanted to give up everything for the sake of God, but Vyasa did not have anything tangible to offer to these aspirants. So, he took up his pen once again to express the nuances of devotion in all its aspects, through the stories of Puranas (lit. old stories that remain ever new). He poured his heart out at the feet of three aspects of God—Brahma (creator), Vishnu (sustainer), and Shiva (destroyer)—who are in essence one but appear as three, due to the different roles superimposed on them. Mahabharata was woven around a clan, with divinity thrown in good measure; whereas the eighteen Puranas, composed in nearly five lakh verses, were woven around the Divine, with generations of kings supporting the text. The innumerable stories of the Divine in these scriptures make many refer to them as 'mythology', which is not correct. Unlike a mythological narrative, the Puranas are religious texts, like the Bible, in which spiritual truths are presented in the story form. Symbolic stories like Adam's fall from heaven, which one gets in Christianity or Islam, are found in abundance in the Puranas; however, they were written without losing sight of the spiritual truths taught by the Vedas. The goal of the narratives in the Puranas is to lead a person towards enlightenment through mythological stories, philosophy, ethics, and rituals—in that order of importance. When this order of priority changes, the name of the class of literature changes as well.

Although the Puranas are secondary in importance to the Vedas, they have a tremendous importance for the followers of different sects, particularly for those who do not have access to the Vedas. Of the eighteen Puranas, *Srimad Bhagavatam* is very famous. Centring the life of Sri Krishna, it is a complete sacred text that contains everything that a spiritual aspirant may need.

Taken conjointly, Ramayana of Valmiki, Mahabharata, and the Puranas are known as Itihasa–Purana literature. A Hindu may not know the content of the Vedas and the Upanishads, but every Hindu knows some part of Itihasa–Purana.

Tantras

Then there is another class of literature, known as Tantra, devoted to Shakti, the female principle of God. The origin of the Tantras is not known for certain; probably these grew independent of vedic traditions.

Mother worship is a vital aspect of Hinduism, whose origin is in the Vedas, and which has been occasionally mentioned in some Puranas. Mother worship has been elaborated and specialised in the Tantras. Like other classes of religious literature discussed above, these texts form a complete system of thought woven around Siva-Shakti, with a distinct philosophy, mythology, and rituals. Tantra makes a free use of *mantra* (sound equivalent of God) and *yantra* (geometric representation of God), to attain spirituality.

It was earlier mentioned, how the yajnas of the Vedas were performed exclusively by the Brahmins, who slowly made these books exclusive only for the upper class, leaving out the majority of the Indian people who had been absorbed in the religious system now known as Hinduism. With the appearance of Itihasa–Purana literature, many aspects of religion were thrown open to the masses, but the all-prestigious vedic yajnas eluded them. It is believed that this gave rise to the unmapped growth of secretive rituals; they included vedic practices in a completely unrecognisable format. The controlling mechanism of the Vedas and the Brahmins missing from this system, the sages of these practices worked out their own formats to present the spiritual truths, where they used baser elements of life (like wine and sex) that are usually abhorred by the cultured. Since Hinduism is an inclusive religion, it ultimately absorbed this stream too, with additions and alterations. In the present times, a large number of rituals practised by the Hindus have directly descended from the refined form of the Tantras.

Smritis

The sacred books mentioned above contain the entire spread of Hindu dharma, but a common man wants to know the dos and don'ts, duties, objectives, and way of life in clear terms, which these books lack. This gave rise to the class of literature known as Smritis, the book of laws, which are based on the principles of the Vedas but have been written as a set of codes of conduct and ethical practices. The rules laid down in these books discuss the entire gamut of right conduct, starting from the most trivial daily acts of an individual, through the duties of people stationed at various stages of responsibilities, to the highest philosophical wisdom that one may aspire to attain. These books also discuss philosophy, aspects of creation, goal and purpose of life, etc., making them a religious text, unlike the constitution or the penal code of a country.

Hinduism believes that the spiritual truths are eternal, as recorded in the Vedas, but with the changing times, their application in the form of religious practices, ethics, values, etc. have to change. Hence the need for a new law book for every age. The first of these is believed to be the *Manusmriti.*

Like Valmiki and Vyasa, almost nothing is known about Manu. He might have been a great sage (c. 300 BCE), or it might be simply a pen name since he is quoted in the book to be the first human on this earth. Whosoever he might have been, Manu collected the existing practices of the society, sieved them to check for their alignment with the vedic principles, and then codified them as the law book to be followed by all.

One important aspect of Smritis is their emphasis on caste because of which they have come under severe attack in recent times. What people fail to realise is that the sages who wrote the Smritis are not at all responsible for this, since they only codified what was current, and what should have been considered as correct practices in those times. Also, caste as a social practice, although sanctioned by the religion, plays no role in spirituality or religious practices. After all, there are no separate heaven, hell, and state of liberation for different castes.

The discussion on these sacred books brings the all-important question, who is a Hindu? It is easy to define a Christian, Muslim, or a Parsee by the sacred book to which he owes his allegiance, but what about the Hindus? How can one point them out?

A Hindu is one who accepts one of the four *purusartha* or goals of life—dharma, artha, kama, moksha—as his own, and strives to attain it through the spiritual truths as preached in the Vedas, or in any of the texts based on the vedic principles, as true. The truths preached by these texts (and any other text that may come in future) may differ in their detail but are in essence absolutely the same. Thus, if a person accepts any of the many versions of Ramayana, as the guiding scripture, to attain one of the four goals, he is then a Hindu.

CONCEPTS

The scriptures of the Hindus detail the truth about God, and the resulting ideas about the soul, world, and life. This section gives a brief overview of these.

God

God, the Divine, is infinite, pure consciousness, and blissful. By its very nature, the infinite cannot be limited to a definition or a description within set parameters, and so a defined God is no God. He can be hinted at in certain qualifying terms that vary according to one's culture and mindset. However, that can never be the end of knowledge about God. Hindu religion learned this fact early in its tryst with the Divine, and therefore rarely discarded any facet of God, accepting every description of the infinite as yet another facet.

God in Hinduism is seen in multiple forms—a limited divine being (in the lower forms of religion), personalised God, like Indra (in the Vedas), Virat the World Soul (in Vedas and Upanishads), impersonal Brahman without any defining qualities (in the Upanishads), Brahman with defining qualities (in some sects), and personal God (in popular Hinduism). This list is not exhaustive. There are many more aspects discussed in the Vedas and the Upanishads.

The most important ideas about God in these texts are—He alone exists,

> Thou art woman, Thou art man; Thou art boy, Thou maiden
> Thou art the old man tottering with the staff; Thou exists
> in all forms *(AV.10.8.27)*

God being so, one can have any kind of relationship with Him. Every religion, other than Hinduism, works out one relationship with God (e.g. Judaism), or a few relationships (e.g. Christianity), whereas Hinduism relates the individual with the universal in every possible way, and also works out ways to attain Him through a number of paths. More importantly, it leaves room for a relationship that may crop up in future. The Puranas used this truth about God to its full advantage and came up with descriptions of how God can be worshipped as a son, friend, lover, husband, master, etc.

He is the most important one. Nothing in this world can be traded in exchange for Him, i.e., one must strive to God and God alone.

> O, God! I will not sell Thee for the highest price,
> Not for a thousand, nor for ten thousand, O mighty one,
> Nor for an infinite amount, O Lord of countless wealth!
> *(RV.8.1–5)*

The second aspect of the Divine, popular in the Upanishads, is the impersonal omnipresent God. He is infinite, ever free, without a form, and beyond the grasp of the human mind. This aspect of God is also known as *nirguna nirakara* Brahman (without any qualifying traits and form). He cannot be called a knowing being because knowledge belongs to the human mind. He cannot be called a reasoning being because reasoning is a sign of weakness. He cannot be called a creating being because none creates except in bondage. He cannot be called good since nobility is a state of mind.

> He, the self-existent One, is everywhere—the pure one, without a (subtle) body, without blemish, without muscles (a gross body), holy and without the taint of sin; the all-seeing, the all-knowing, the all-encompassing One is He. *(Isa Upa.8)*

> There is One who is the eternal Reality among non-eternal objects, the one (truly) conscious entity among conscious objects, and who, though non-dual, fulfils the desires of many. *(Katha Upa.2.2.15)*

The third aspect is known as *sopadhik* Brahman, God with qualities and attributes. It is also popularly known as *saguna sakara, saguna* Brahman, Isvara, personal God, God with form, or simply God. He is the highest manifestation of the infinite that can be perceived by the mind. It is this aspect of God that is worshipped by the devout, and with whom they form a relationship of love, adoration, and expectation.

God, the eternally free, cannot be imagined to get into the act of creation since every action is preceded by desire, which is a form of bondage—something unimaginable for God. So, the Hindu outlook attributes creation to the power of God, which is distinct, but dependent on him. This creative principle is usually referred to as maya, prakriti, shakti, etc. and is worshipped variously as Durga, Kali, Lakshmi, and others. God and His creative power, shakti, are unified like fire and its burning power. However, depending on one's beliefs and family traditions, one accepts them as same, or as two separate entities.

When God is perceived through this power of maya or shakti, he appears to have become three. He, therefore, has three different names—Brahma (not to be confused by Brahman, the supreme reality, the creator); Vishnu, the sustainer; and Shiva, the destroyer. These three are one and the same in essence, but due to the intervening medium of the individual and collective mind, they appear different.

In addition to these, there are millions of gods and goddesses, who represent various aspects of the Divine. According to some, three hundred and thirty million of them. This allows a Hindu to choose a God of his liking.

The concept of personal God in Hinduism is different from monotheism (the doctrine of one and only one God—*Ekeswaravada*) of Zoroastrianism, Judaism, Christianity, and Islam. When a Hindu claim that Krishna is God, he simultaneously accepts the divinity of Rama, Shiva, Vishnu, and others too. This makes Hinduism a non-proselytising religion. For them, God of every religion is a particular mask of the infinite Brahman.

Avatar

In the Vedas, some gods like Indra and Vishnu were described as capable of taking up various forms by the power of maya, or through their inherent powers. In later times, this power was attributed to Lord Vishnu, the God, who came to be believed to have incarnated for the consolidation of good and destruction of the unrighteous whenever the need arises. God is beyond good and bad and has no favourites. But his creation is maintained in a fine balance, in which the cancerous powers tend to overwhelm the noble. So, God takes up different forms, including that of animals to bring back the balance.

Whenever God incarnates, religion gets a fresh strength and there is a push forward in the spiritual evolution of all. The number of possible incarnations is believed to be ten, twenty-four, and also innumerable, since any final statement about God and His acts cannot be made—that would mean limiting the limitless.

Aum

Mention was made of the importance of silence in meditation that leads to God-realisation. It has been narrated by the mystics of every religion that in the state of deep silence one goes beyond every kind of sense perception before merging one's mind in the Divine. The last object that one remains aware of, before letting go the world entirely, and also the first thing one becomes conscious of after the meditation is over, is a deep gong-like sound. The sages of the Upanishads named it *Aum*, which later came to be identified as the sound equivalent of God. The symbol is so expressive and universal that it was accepted by the Buddhists, Jains, and Sikhs too.

Aum is the symbolic representation of both personal and impersonal aspects of God, the way, say H denotes Hydrogen element in its entirety. When one looks at the created world, one realises that every object has three aspects: a physical manifestation, a verbal representation, and the idea behind both. Thus, every object in this world, seen and unseen, has a name that requires sound produced by the vocal system, which begins with the guttural 'a', through velar 'u', and ending at the lips with 'm'. By combining these three sounds one gets 'Aum', which is the symbolic matrix of all sound, the basis for all names. Since name and objects are non-different, and because God is the matrix of all objects, 'Aum' is respected as the verbal representation of God. The silence that follows after one pronounces Aum, denotes the impersonal aspect of God, implying that it cannot have any attribute.

In spite of all the differences in the various sects of Hinduism, as also between Hinduism and other Indic religions, Aum retains its universality through all of them. Thus, every Hindu accepts Aum as the universal symbol of God.

In later times, Tantras added many more sound equivalents like *hrim* to denote the various aspects of Shakti. These came to be known as *beeja* (seed) to imply the source of power through which one can attain anything in this or the other world.

Creation

'Who am I; wherefrom have I come; what is my destiny?' are puzzling questions asked by all. Answers to these are as varied as the creator himself. There are a number of popular theories that explain the origin of life—a chance product of matter (rationalists), comes from nothingness (physics), appears from the universal mind (philosophy), a play of creative principle (Hindus), and the will of God (most religions), etc.

Hinduism refutes most of the popular theories of creation. For example, to say that creation is caused due to the Lord's will is to say tactfully that he does not have the answer. To say that the dead matter produces patterned life is to stretch one's imagination too far. To say that creation comes out of nothingness is to contradict the very fundamentals of sensibility.

There are two popular theories in Hinduism to explain the process of creation described in the two hymns of the Vedas, Purusha Suktam *(RV.10.90)* and Nasadiya Suktam *(RV.10.129)*. The first one takes up creation as having come out from, and by Purusha (God). According to it, when God wishes to create, his very thought manifests Brahma, the creator God. Brahma then gets down to the job of creation by meditating on the principles and process of creation that was there in the previous cycle. With time, the creation blooms in all its majesty.

The second theory is that energy was produced by the pure consciousness (God) as the first product through his divine power. This was known as *prana*, which acted on itself (energy hammering energy) to create fine matter, known as *akasha* (the finest first particles).

This concept was later elaborated. The sum total of energies is also called Prakriti, the universal Mother Nature, which is composed of three qualities: *tamas* (inertness), *rajas* (activity), and *sattva* (equanimity) in balance. For a divine mysterious reason, whenever there is an imbalance in this triad, they start combining with and also overpowering each other. In the process, the qualities convert into very fine particles, which with time become gross objects. The subtle aspects of space, air, fire, water, and earth, are at the root of everything in the universe. The creation of every single object proceeds from the combination of these five elements in a set order. Thus, every object of the universe we live in contains these five elements in varying proportion.

Why the idea of five elements, when anyone can see the variety of material around? The answer is that whatever the number of fundamental particles and element in the world, ultimately, they will have to be grasped by the five senses to know them. The subjectivity involved in this model may not be acceptable to many, nevertheless, being a model like any other scientific model, it has its own ground.

In spite of the models to explain the universe, its perception and its creation, the sages believed that the mystery of creation is too deep to be explained satisfactorily. An act cannot be explained unless there are possibilities of explaining it through one of the various methods of knowledge, which in this case, does not exist.

After staying in a balance for a period, the creation moves towards dissolution, only to emerge again as creation. This cyclic creation–dissolution–creation is going on eternally in an infinite number of gross and subtle universe or, better still, in various multiverses. God is not finite and cannot be associated with a finite universe, in finite time, with finite objectives; hence, Hinduism treats creation as an eternal act. However, while talking of creation, the scriptures always mean the particular cycle for a particular universe; they never take into account the entirety of creation.

Soul

Religion is the search for permanence amidst the fleeting nature of existence, and so it refuses to accept that one's existence is an accidental flux of matter amidst the cosmic chaos. This leads religion to the search of self—the permanent entity behind the human life.

The self is the real individuality, the true 'I' of a person, which is formed by one's awareness of oneself depending on his mental evolution and cultural bias. Even the same person may have different ideas about his self at different stages of his life.

The idea of the self as being one with the body-mind-ego complex has been popular in the Vedas and with non-philosophical people. Being embodied (in any conscious being) performs good and bad actions that leave subtle impressions on its psyche. To work out these impressions (*samskara*), one has to take up another body after the destruction of the former. This reincarnation is guided and goaded by the forces of what one deserves and desires. These forces are collectively known as *karma*. Humans are born again and again until one takes the spiritual path to get rid of one's inherent desires and the samskaras one carries. To do so, one needs to surrender oneself completely to the God.

The other idea of self, popular with the vedantins, is that it is infinite, ever pure, and ever free. The bondage and limitations that it experiences are not absolute but are imaginary in nature.

> It (the Atman) moves and moves not. It is far and likewise near. It is inside all this and it is outside all this. *(Isa Upa.5)*

The Upanishads stress that the infinite consciousness cannot be two and that atman (individual self) and Brahman (the supreme self) are non-different. This can be realised only by a few great souls in their depth of meditation. For the rest, the self is embodied, whose master is God, and which moves from existence to existence according to what it acquires by way of merit, demerit, and knowledge.

PRACTICES

Svadhrama

Hindu religion accepts that sameness can be attained only in a spiritual state since inequality is the law of life. Hindu practices and way of life are based on this premise.

Diversity and human limitations being a matter of fact, Hinduism suggests different goals for different mentalities, which are popularly known as dharma (righteous living), artha (acquisition of wealth through rightful means), kama (enjoyment), and moksha (liberation). Of these, the first three are for the householders, while the fourth one is for the monks. However, it is expected that every Hindu would give up the world at some point in time, in order to devote themselves fully to spirituality and attainment of moksha.

Inequality in social life, born of capacity and attitude made Hindu sages evolve the *varna* (caste) system, according to which everyone was assigned a place in the social hierarchy from where one could move towards one of the four goals of life by staying true to one's duties. However, caste is essentially a social system that got the hue of religion.

The inequality born of a person's age resulted in *ashrama* system, which expects people of various age groups to have different kinds of duties. There are four ashramas: Brahmacharya, Garhastya, Vanaparastha, Sannyasa.

These two systems, varna and ashrama, were used to work out the *svadharma* (the duties) of a person for his spiritual evolution. There are six kinds of duties, which constitute svadharma: Varna dharma—professional duties; Ashrama dharma—duties connected with one's age; Varna-ashrama dharma—duties of a particular profession related to his age, e.g. a senior member of business community should train the next of the generation; Nimitta dharma—noble actions that purify one's mind, like regular study of scriptures, Guna dharma—duties born of a particular position, e.g. a king's duties, and Samanya dharma—duty as a human being.

The idea of svadharma has been very strong in Hindu religious life, due to which no one was allowed to transgress it easily. Gita goes to the extent of saying that it is better to die performing one's svadharma than to take up the dharma of others.

Every Hindu is also expected to perform five-fold daily duties called Pancha-Mahayajnas (five great sacrifices). This is based on the principle that a person owes his existence to many beings, both dead and alive. To repay their debts, one must practise these daily sacrifices. The first of these is Brahma-yajna (also known as Rishi-yajna), dedicated to sages and is performed by a daily study (*svadhyaya*) of the holy scripture. Deva-yajna is dedicated to the divine beings and is performed by the daily ritualistic worship at home and the temple. Pitri-yajna is meant for the ancestors and is offered by a ritualistic offering to them at the time of noon food. Manushya-yajna is for the humanity and is performed by feeding guests. Bhuta-yajna is for the animals and is performed by feeding the birds and animals. The scriptures go to the extent of condemning a non-performing person of these five daily sacrifices as 'living dead'.

Samskara

Every religion practices purification rites and consecration ceremonies to cleanse oneself of the worldliness as opposed to the sacred nature of the religious life. In Hinduism, these are known as *samskara*s (lit. purification) that cover the entire gamut of a Hindu's life—from the moment he is conceived in the mother's womb, till his death. The sages realised that an artful life requires constant care, culture, and refinement, without which one would degenerate and become a savage. All the samskaras and allied ceremonies are based on the philosophy that life is a progressive cycle, which required sanctification at every stage.

In the vedic period there were sixty-four samskaras, but later it was reduced to sixteen: Garbhadhana—prayer to gods to get a good baby; Punsavanam—prayer during pregnancy for a healthy child; Simantonnayana: prayer in advance stage for a beautiful child; Jatakarma—birth ceremony; Namakarana—naming ceremony; Niskramana—first taking out of the baby; Annaprashana—the first feeding of cooked rice to the new-born; Chudakarma—first shearing of the head; Karnavedha—the piercing of the child's ear; upanayana—sacred thread ceremony; samavartana—graduation ceremony at the teacher's place; Vivaha—marriage; Grihasthashrama—entering the life of a householder; Vanaprastha—leaving for the forest in the old age; Sannyasa—monkhood; Antyeshti—the last rites of the dead.

In addition to these ethical and social practices, there are innumerable religious practices that depend on locality, culture, and the sect to which one belongs. These include mode of worship, fasting, pilgrimage, etc., which is beyond the scope of this work to detail.

Bhakti

The practice of svadharma and samskara would have remained the mainstay of Hinduism if Ramanuja (11th CE), had not opened the floodgates of *bhakti* (devotion) as the only way and goal of life. Prayers and devotion to God had been in vogue since the earliest vedic period in India. The Puranas popularised those concepts, but it was left for Ramanuja to bring bhakti to everyone's door.

When Ramanuja was growing up, there was the glory of Advaita Vedanta for the great minds, but the common man had to remain satisfied with only the pomp and show of the ritualistic religion, which were considered to be of no importance by the wise. Ramanuja changed all that. He not only challenged Shankara's standpoint, but, apparently defeated it, and established his own system of thought known as Visistadvaita in which devotion and rituals got more importance than philosophy and realisation of advaita. His teaching centred *sharanagati* (surrender) to God as the means to moksha, and he was so firm about it that he interpreted Upanishads and Gita entirely from the standpoint of bhakti, and also popularised it everywhere.

Later some more great minds like Nimbarka (12th CE) Madhava (13th CE), Vallabha (15th CE), and Chaitanya (16th CE) took up bhakti as the way of life and preached the masses to surrender oneself to God, unconditionally. The movement gained much momentum through the contribution of Alvars and Nayanars from Tamil Nadu, Namdev and Tukaram in Maharashtra, Mirabai from Rajasthan, Tulsidas and Kabir from Uttar Pradesh, and many more. Soon the songs composed by them were being sung all over, making Bhakti movement the prime force of Hinduism.

These sage poets talked of God in all his aspects. God was seen as beyond form, and also with form, as Rama, Krishna, Shiva, Vishnu. The prime moving force was intense devotion to one's ideal.

Hinduism, the highly individualistic religion, had finally become the all-inclusive religion that it is today.

WORLD VIEW

Two apparently irreconcilable facts in every religion, the permanence of the soul and the impermanence of life, demand that there be a world view that will make fit these two, and also everything else arising out of their frictional rubbing. It is due to this that no religion can ever live without heaven and hell where the permanence of the soul will have to enjoy or suffer for its interactions with the impermanence of the world.

Heaven and hell—These are places of temporary residence just like earth, where the soul (subtle body/embodied self) goes to enjoy the fruits of all the virtuous acts it performed during its human life. The idea of heaven later gave rise to the belief in the existence of seven higher spheres of existence, and seven lower one. In the higher regions, only the religious could go, while the lower ones were reserved for people who were great achievers, but not religious. The later poets changed the idea of *patala* (lower spheres) to hell. Since no one had ever seen heaven, hell, or patala, the poets had a licence to fly free with their imagination, and thus the later Hindus came up with every kind of heaven and hell. However, no Indian philosophy pays any attention to these. Their focus is always on how to make the embodied self-conscious of its nature, and then to make it give up every worldly connection to move towards *mukti* (liberation).

Karma—What one sows, one reaps—is the law of life on which Hinduism and every other Indic religion run. What one does, utters, and thinks, constitute one's action, which after its completion leaves an impression on the psyche of the person. When a similar situation arises in future, the person is impelled (not compelled) by these impressions, lying dormant in his psyche. If he repeats his acts, then the impression becomes stronger. Thus the impelling force in the future becomes stronger, to become compelling forces, as seen with hardened criminals.

The powerful acts performed in life have to fructify. But not every act performed by a person can be worked out in just one life. Also, certain exceptionally meritorious acts or nefarious activities need different spheres of existence to be worked out. For example, an extremely vicious person would need the body of a demon to work out his tendencies. These ideas, partly thought-out and partly observed by the sages, through their intuitive powers, made the theory of karma one of the important pillars of Hinduism. This also led to the idea of rebirth.

Rebirth—The Vedas propound the idea of cycles, according to which creation takes place on the same principles as it had been in the previous cycles. The permanence of soul (the embodied self), and the world view, along with the idea of cyclic creation, automatically leads to the idea of transmigration of the soul. While every West Asian religion talks about one-time creation—a single rebirth in some place after the death—every Indic religion talks about metempsychosis—where a soul transmigrates into lower and higher beings, depending on its actions and knowledge, until it gets moksha (liberation from the cycle of birth and death). Rebirth is an essential component of Hinduism.

The idea of rebirth is a great philosophical concept by the Hindus to the world. According to it, a person is himself responsible for his state of affairs, and fate. What he did in the past, he reaps in the present, and what he does now he will reap in the future. God is in no way responsible for the disparity and the injustice seen in this world, nor is He partial to anyone in any form.

The idea of rebirth and karma make Hinduism a completely positive religion in which one is forced to take responsibility for everything. True followers of Hindu religion can neither blame God nor their fate or chance for the evil that comes their way.

PHILOSOPHY

Philosophy is the science of knowledge. In its generic aspect, it is used to analyse any branch of knowledge, including mathematics and science, but it is generally used to analyse existence in its entirety. Since every religion delves deep into the mysteries of existence, philosophy becomes an integral part of religion.

Philosophy of any religion centres its chief scriptures, which in the case of the Hindus is the Vedas. Although a storehouse of spiritual truths, these texts need to be analysed, harmonised, explained, and presented coherently to bring out from them a systematic world view and philosophy. This was done by sages of great capabilities, who founded their philosophies based on the vedic texts to explain God, world, and the self. This they called *darshan*, meaning 'to perceive'. Of the many philosophical systems that came up in India, six have come down to us prominently—Samkhya, Yoga, Nyaya, Vaishesika, Mimasa, and Vedanta, founded respectively by Kapila, Patanjali, Gautama, Kanada, Jaimini, and Vyasa. In addition, there were Pasupat, Shakta, and other philosophies that are not as popular as the earlier six.

Discussion on Hindu philosophy is never considered complete till the materialist philosophy of the Charvak is discussed. It is not known if such a materialist school of philosophy indeed existed in India; nevertheless, the arguments used by them were taken up by the six systems of Indian philosophy to counter them.

The six systems of Indian philosophy are not the speculative philosophy that one encounters in the West. Instead, these were ways of life, based entirely on the Vedas, practised by a good number of people, and preached by the sages of the highest order. However, like any philosophy that tries to explain the inexplicable, these philosophies have chinks that make them vulnerable to attack by other systems of thought as well. When Shankaracharya (c. 8th century CE) came on the Indian scene, he picked holes in every philosophy so thoroughly to establish Vedanta that the remaining five lost their sheen forever and are now confined to the textbooks. Since then Hindu religion has been equated with the Vedanta philosophy.

Acharya Shankara is believed to have been born in 788 CE, (many think that he was born earlier) in Kaladi, Kerala. A child prodigy, he left his widowed mother to give up the world and took the path of sannyasa when he was hardly eight years old. The traditions claim that he attained the supreme knowledge by the time he was twelve and then got down to writing commentaries on eleven Upanishads, Gita, and Brahma Sutra, which is an important treatise on Vedanta, for the next four years. By the time he was sixteen, he had completed his major writing work, and then for the next sixteen years, he moved around the length and breadth of India establishing the philosophical supremacy of Vedanta, establishing monasteries to maintain the purity of religion, and concretising Hindu rituals and practices. By the time he gave up his body at thirty-two, he had infused freshness and vigour in Hinduism that had not been done since the time of Vyasa. Modern Hinduism was now born.

Shankara kept the basics of arguments very simple. According to him, any knowledge that came through the five senses was to be treated as perfectly valid, unless contradicted by superior inputs. Similarly, reasoning was to be treated with respect and was to be used to arrive at correct knowledge. However, when it came to super-sensuous knowledge about God, soul, rebirth, etc., these two methods of knowledge could not be relied upon, since one cannot know about these through the senses, nor can one prove or disprove their non-existence through reasoning, since a better mind will always disprove the established conclusion. So, one has to accept what scriptures have to say in these matters. Scriptures being records of sages who were pure, unselfish, noble, and with intuitive wisdom, there is no reason to doubt their words.

What Shankara wrote in his commentaries, and also in his independent compositions, came to be known as Advaita Vedanta. The grandness of his interpretation of the Upanishadic statement, 'atman is Brahman' remains unmatched. In the world of religion, this is the greatest finding by human minds, and it is India's greatest contribution to the world of thoughts.

Later, two great minds, Ramanuja (b. 1017 CE), and Madhvacharya (b. 1238 CE) took the bhakti elements (devotion) of the Upanishads and Gita to come up with the Visishtadvaita and Dvaita philosophies, respectively, that attacked the Advaita of Shankara viciously. The battle continues to rage even today. The rankling issues between these three revolve around the ideas of the soul, God, and their relationship. A devotee of God does not want to accept that in essence, he is one with God—it is a sacrilege to him. Advaita accepts the non-difference of self from Brahman, Visishtadvaita accepts the relationship between God and self as between a tree and its leaf, while Dvaita, like most other religions, accept God as the master and the self as subservient.

The cantankerous issue of the differences of the three philosophies was finally resolved by the Ramakrishna (b. 1836)–Vivekananda (b. 1863) philosophy that presented the three outlooks as perceiving the same reality under three conditions of one's attitude. Hinduism was thus made inclusive once again in which different philosophies and religious outlooks were accommodated as valid.

These three, Dvaita, Visishtadvaita, and Advaita, are now collectively known as the Vedanta since they base their arguments on the truths of the Upanishads. These three philosophies cover the whole of Hinduism.

ETHICS

A practising Hindu has the freedom to choose any of the sacred books to make it the guiding light of his way of life. As mentioned earlier, these sacred books, innumerable though they are, must not contradict the spiritual truths as preached in the Vedas, but in their applied form they do differ substantially with each other. So, there is no single book that can claim to be the ultimate in dictating values, ethics, and practices for a Hindu, nor is there a uniform civil or religious code.

There are, however, two broad principles that govern the Hindu way of life: to give up all for God; and alternatively, to perform worldly duties unselfishly. This second one can be carried out either by staying detached towards the results of one's duties or by consecrating every act, trivial or important, to God. These three outlooks—renunciation, unselfishness, and consecration define the Hindu way of life, along with its values, ethics, duties, morality, and practices.

In the Hindu system, there is no Cartesian divide between the sacred and secular. All that exists belongs to God, who has no opponent to counter him. Nothing in this world can be termed profane by a Hindu. The rightness of an act does not flow from God, nor from any sacred book, but it is treated as an aid to make the spiritual journey of an individual smooth. Similarly, the idea of sin does not play any role in Hinduism. For them, sin is the transgression of a certain code of conduct, which in itself is dynamic. Sin is more like a mistake, which can be corrected easily, and if that is not enough, one can choose any of the penances to absolve oneself.

THE FUTURE

It would be a perfect tribute to Hinduism, the mother of all-inclusiveness, to quote from *India and Its Native Princes—Travels in Central India and in the Presidencies of Bombay and Bengal*, by a French traveller, Louis Rousselet, published in 1876. The author quotes a Christina father:

> Our labours are in vain; you can never convert a man who has sufficient conviction in his own religion to listen, without moving a muscle, to all the attacks you can make against it.

Acceptance is spirituality, and inclusiveness is the sign of having attained its highest level. The open-ended nature of Hinduism allows it to accommodate everything that belongs to the realm of religion. This gave it the resilience to withstand the onslaught of Islam and Christianity for a thousand years, and helped it weather the storm of scientific outlook and materialism, and move on with its message of universal acceptance.

Buddhism
Religion of Compassion

AUTOCORRELATION OF RELIGIONS

There is a saying that a new sect is formed in any religion every thirty years or so. This may or may not be true, but it is a fact that the history of any religion is the story of the fight between its priests and the prophets. Religion is difficult to understand and is much more difficult to practise. This creates spiritual inertia in the minds of the practitioners of any religion after a time. It is then that the priests take over a religion, and due to their own lack of spiritual insights, they go on increasing the weight of rituals, myths, and practices on the devout, who keep panting under it. When greats like Jesus, Krishna, or Buddha are born, they infuse the life-giving strength of spirituality in the religion in which they were born. Sometimes they break free from their mother religion, as in the case of Jesus, and sometimes they continue to be with it, as in the case of Sri Krishna.

Lord Buddha is unique in the sense that he founded a new religion that opposed the popular practices of Hinduism, and yet the Hindus worship him as an incarnation of God.

By 7th century BCE, the vedic religion with all its ritualistic paraphernalia had spread far and wide over the Indian subcontinent. The sweep of Brahmanical values, vedic sacrifices, religious discussions, and caste system were indeed immense. The privileged believed that they could get any favour from the gods by performing yajna, and the non-privileged believed that they could hope to rise higher only in the next birth by serving the privileged *dwija* (higher castes) in the present life.

Rituals, like any fence, protect the beginner but hinder the growth of the great. Every religion is sustained by its rituals, but the true call of the soul lies in spirituality, which demands that one rise above all that belongs to the world, including ritualistic prayers and worship. The Vedas suffered from the excess of everything; there were too many yajnas, priests, books, rituals, castes, etc. There were the Upanishads with their sublime philosophy, which had nothing to do with the rituals, but these were confined to a very small class of people. The conditions were thus ripe for a revolutionary change in the outlook towards religion—it was time for Gautam Buddha and Mahavir Jain to appear on the Indian spiritual stage.

A major departure of Buddha and Mahavir Jain from the Upanishadic outlook was that while the Upanishads were absolutely impersonal in imparting spiritual traditions, the new paths preached by these two great teachers revolved around personality that helped the masses identify themselves with them, the way they had earlier stayed glued to the invisible gods and goddesses of the Vedas and Puranas. Also, these two masters made spirituality the core religion for the masses, which otherwise had remained confined to the Upanishadic teachers and their select disciples.

LIFE AND TIMES OF BUDDHA

It is said that a prophet is not worshipped in his own land. Indeed, among all the prophets, Buddha alone was respected in his own lifetime, in his own homeland, and within a short span, his influence spread where even the Hindu flag had not reached. That gives a glimpse of his spiritual power that continues to shape the lives of millions all over the world, even after 2500 years of his passing away.

Historians believe that this great prophet of religion and humanity was born on the full moon day of May, in the year 623 B.C. His father, Suddhodana, was the king of Kapilavastu, in the foothills of the Himalayas in Nepal. The customs of India and Nepal being similar, the young prince was ritualistically named Siddhartha with the family name Gautama. The astrologers then predicted that the young prince would become either a monarch or an enlightened saint (Buddha).

Worried at the predictions of the astrologers, the young prince was watched carefully and made to indulge in materialistic pleasures so that his mind could stay tied down to worldliness. At the age of sixteen, Siddhartha was married off to Yasodhara, and for nearly thirteen years he led a luxurious life, blissfully ignorant of life outside the palace gates.

One glorious day, as he went out of the palace to see the world outside, prince Siddhartha came in contact with the stark realities of life. Thereafter, on his way to the park on different days, his eyes met the sights of a decrepit old man, a diseased person, a corpse, and a dignified hermit. The first three sights exhibited to him the sad nature of life, while the fourth revealed the means to overcome the ills of life and to attain calm and peace. These four unexpected sights made him restless. Realising the worthlessness of sensual pleasures, so highly prized by the worldly, he contemplated leaving his secure world in search of 'truth' and 'eternal' peace.

This turning point in the prince's life is not a pointer to 'sudden conversion', as popularised by Saint Paul's life, nor is it an ordinary phenomenon. If there were a cause-effect relationship in this kind of conversion, then several more would have become monks after visiting a hospital run by monks, where one can simultaneously see all the sights mentioned above!

This riddle can be explained in two ways. The first one is that when God incarnates, his powers are of a different kind. His acts cannot be judged by ordinary human standards. There are numerous examples from the lives of the incarnations that defy common understanding. The second explanation is that when a person is inherently ready for a great act, which he does by accumulating power in small amount over the years, he needs only a little stimulus for his supersaturated thoughts to crystallise.

Siddhartha was still deliberating deeply on what he had experienced when the news of his son's birth was conveyed to him, to which he exclaimed, 'An impediment (Rahu) has been born; a fetter has arisen.' The palace now appeared to him like a cage, and so he decided to leave everything behind that very night and go out in search of that which lay beyond sorrow. Indeed, he had a larger duty towards himself and the humanity than playing the dutiful husband or the father.

That night, the prince opened the door of the chamber where his wife slept with the newborn, blissfully ignorant of the storm raging in the mind of her beloved husband. Going by Siddharth's past attitude, his love for his dear ones must have been great at this parting moment, but his yearning for the knowledge, which would liberate the humanity from suffering, was greater. It could not be that he loved his family any less, but he definitely loved humanity much more. So, leaving everything behind, he melted in the dark in search of eternal light.

The prince's renunciation was not that of an old man, who had his fill of worldly life, nor was it the renunciation of a poor man who has nothing to leave behind. It was the renunciation of a prince in the full bloom of youth and in the plenitude of wealth and prosperity—a renunciation unparalleled in history. He was only twenty-nine.

As a seeker of truth, he approached a distinguished ascetic and stayed with him for some time to practise austerities. After mastering the art of concentration, he felt that what he was learning was not enough to take him to the ultimate state of peace. So, he left his teacher and moved on.

Those were the days when there were no major political disturbances in India, particularly around Pataliputra (modern Patna) that was soon going to be the capital of the then India. The political stability helped sages, scholars, and learners focus on study and exposition of knowledge. Seekers and teachers of learning, as also those who left home for spirituality, were well looked after by the society. So, there was no dearth of good teachers, nor a lack of disciples.

When the quest for knowledge burns bright, one gets the right teacher too. It was thus that Siddhartha soon found a new teacher, who was more to his liking than the former. From his new teacher, he mastered the new doctrine and attained the final stages of mental concentration, which is the realm of neither perception nor of non-perception. This is the highest stage in certain branches of Yoga when consciousness (awareness) becomes so subtle and refined that it cannot be said whether it exists or not.

Siddhartha still felt that his quest for the highest truth was not achieved. He had gained complete mastery of his mind, but his ultimate goal still eluded him. He then felt that the highest truth was to be found within oneself, and so he stopped seeking external guidance and decided to practise *sadhana* on his own.

He reached Magadha (modern Gaya) and eventually arrived at Uruvela, where he found a lovely spot, a charming forest grove, a flowing river, with pleasant sandy fords by the side of a village where he could obtain his food. The atmosphere was peaceful and the place was congenial for meditation.

In ancient India, there were two schools of religious practices. The first one laid stress on rites and rituals, while the other one emphasised back-breaking asceticism, without which no deliverance from the cycle of birth and death could be gained. Following the trend, Siddhartha made a super-human struggle to practice all forms of severe austerities. His delicate body was reduced to almost a skeleton, but the more he tormented his body the farther his goal seemed to recede from him. Later he was to recount:

> As I took such small quantity of solid and liquid food, my body became extremely emaciated. Just as are the joints of knot-grasses or bulrushes, even so were the major and minor parts of my body owing to lack of food...the skin of my head got shrivelled and withered due to lack of sustenance. And I, intending to touch my belly's skin, would instead seize my backbone. When I intended to touch my backbone, I would seize my belly's skin. So was I that, owing to lack of sufficient food, my

belly's skin clung to the backbone…Then the following thought occurred to me…by all these bitter and difficult austerities I shall not attain excellence, worthy of supreme knowledge and insight, transcending those of human states. Might there be another path to enlightenment! *(Buddha and His Teachings)*

Siddhartha's severe austerities were commendable but were not enough to enlighten him. The spiritual reality is not an object that can be attained through some effort. Hence, austerities, prayers, meditation, worship, learning, etc. are necessarily preparatory stages for enlightenment, which comes on its own to the mind made pure by these practices. Gautam decided to sit for deep meditation till he could attain enlightenment. It was then that Mara (temptation) appeared before him as the last obstacle to his enlightenment.

Mara is a popular character in Buddhism. He roughly corresponds to the personification of the evil side of Maya of the Hindu scriptures. Maya is the divine ignorance whose one aspect is its bewitching powers of lust, anger, greed, hankering, arrogance, and jealousy. When this divine power wants to ensnare someone, it appears to him in different forms befitting the staying power of that person. In its most gross form, it appears as a common man's desire to possess wealth and women, while at the subtle levels it appears as Mara, Devil, Satan, etc. These are the last barriers of the spiritual mind before it becomes one with the Divine. In the Indic religions, consciousness is not intrinsic to the mind but makes the mind appear conscious, the way one sees light in a fluorescent tube when electricity passes through it. When consciousness wants to be itself, the mind creates all kinds of illusions, so that it may not become subservient to what it had held as its own till then.

Temptations come into the lives of every great spiritual personality during his sadhana. One has to conquer it or else his effort goes waste temporarily. Gautama's long and difficult sadhana had made his resolve too strong to be tempted or terrified. He had conquered all attraction and aversion, which is at the root of all human problems and bondage. He responded to Mara, 'The army of yours, which the world along with the gods cannot conquer, I will destroy it by my wisdom the way I would destroy an unbaked bowl with a stone,' (*Padhana Sutta*). Mara was helpless against this, so he fled.

Later, when Siddhartha had attained wisdom, Mara accosted him again and tried to dissuade him from teaching his new gospel to the people, arguing that it was futile to teach the worthy as well as the unworthy. The worthy do not need it, and the unworthy do not want to take the path, said Mara. It is said that Buddha was nearly convinced, but then he got filled with *karuna* (compassion) for the whole world, and he resolved to preach his new gospel.

By the time Mara had appeared for the first time, Gautama was convinced of the utter futility of asceticism, since it actually weakened one's intellect and also resulted in a weakening of spirit. He abandoned forever this painful extreme torturing of the body, as he also condemned the other extreme of self-indulgence that retards moral progress. He then conceived the idea of adopting the golden mean or the middle path, which later became the salient feature of his teachings. He realised that enlightenment could not be gained with an exhausted body, and that physical fitness was essential for spiritual progress. He decided to nourish his body by taking some simple food.

Regaining his lost strength with milk pudding brought to him by Sujata, a village girl, he sat in deep meditation under the banyan tree with a firm resolve, 'Either I will gain realisation or I will die here.' His resolve bore fruit and he gained the perfect one-pointed state of the mind, which had become like a polished mirror in which everything was reflected the way it truly was. With his thoughts tranquil and free from lust or other impurities, he directed his mind towards the supreme knowledge. It was then that layer after layer of the coverings was torn away from 'truth.' That night was the night of enlightenment for him when ignorance was dispelled from his mind and knowledge arose—the knowledge that is everyone's birthright. His pure mind and the Absolute Consciousness had become one. Darkness now made way for the eternal light. He realised that 'Happy in this world is the non-attached.'

He was now Buddha—the Enlightened One. He was thirty-five.

THE WAY

Buddha got up from his seat under the Bodhi tree that had been the only witness to his transition from Prince Gautama to Gautama, the Buddha. No wonder the tree has become as famous as the master himself, since then.

Buddha, the enlightened, now proceeded towards Varanasi with the intent of preaching unto mankind the truth that he had realised. To him, the world now must have appeared as seething and wriggling under the darkness of ignorance and consequently suffering endlessly despite there being a way out to enlightenment. The ignorant of the world remained oblivious of the path, and so they busied themselves with desires, which made them toil endlessly, perform endless rituals, practise asceticism, and wrangle with words. To end the misery of the world Buddha had to act, which he did by setting up the Dharma Chakra, the virtuous cycle to counter the vicious cycle that this worldly existence was. The followers of Lord Buddha believe that by practising the way of the Lord, one contributes to the continuation of that chakra. To remind this, wheels are placed at every sacred place of the Buddhists and are constantly turned around.

The Master's first stop was at Mrigavana at Sarnath where he came across the five ascetics with whom he had earlier practised sadhana. Seeing him approach, the vain ascetics decided to ignore him when he came near. But when Buddha finally reached them, they could not control themselves and fell down at the master's feet as his first disciples.

This incident, talked about in detail in every biography of Buddha, explains the crucial aspect of spiritual masters. The knowledge of God is known as *svasamvedya* (subjective). So, any charlatan can claim to have that knowledge. However, a true man of God gives a push forward to the spiritual evolution of everyone with whom he comes in contact with. Depending on one's preparedness, a person is bound to move higher after his interaction with such greats. The yogic powers of a master erroneously called miracles, invariably causes a major change in the hearts and personalities of even the crudest, as one can see in the transformation of Angulimala, the robber who became a saint by a word from Buddha. Similarly, when Jesus asked the crowd to cast the first stone at the fallen woman only if one had never sinned, the gathering dissipated. The words of masters do not make everyone a saint, but a shift in one's perception is very much expected.

Buddha had started his 'wheel of goodness' by making his earlier comrades as his first disciples and had continued spreading the message of the great noble path till he attained *parinirvan* (release from this body). To reach the masses directly he used their native language instead of Sanskrit and taught only what was truly needed by a person to lead a healthy life—worldly and spiritual. So, he got rid of theological discussion, polemics, and theories. The direct appeal of spirituality was too great for the masses to ignore. People in thousands became his disciples. The infinite power of the spiritual message that the Brahmins had kept confined to the chosen few, was unleashed by the Saviour. His was an intensely practical religion that continues to be as practical today as it was during his own time.

The essential teaching of Buddha says that the root of all suffering lies in 'craving', a self-created mental state. How and when this craving originates is incomprehensible, but since it is created by oneself, it can be destroyed only by oneself. The goal of human life is to eradicate all cravings from the mind, which leads to *nirvana*, the state of ultimate freedom. His teachings are known as the *Chatvari Arya Satyani* (Four Noble Truths), codified in *Dhammapada*:

> Of paths, the eightfold is best. Of truths, the four sayings.
> Of qualities, dispassion. Of two-footed beings, the one
> with the eyes to see.

The four truths are:

* Dukkha: Life is full of suffering.
* Dukkha samudaya: There is a cause to this suffering.
* Dukkha nirodha: It is possible to stop suffering.
* Dukkha nirodha gamini: There is a path to accomplish this.

In these four truths, Buddha taught that there is suffering because the world is *anitya* (non-eternal). Hence, all things are impermanent here.

Suffering comes due to *trishna*, thirst for material things. Because the world is imperfect, impermanent, and not separate from human beings, a man clings to various objects in the hope that these will give him permanence. Besides trishna, there is *dvesha*, which means aversion or aggression. To add to all this, there is *avidya*, ignorance or the refusal to perceive things correctly.

Nirvana is the overcoming of attachment. It literally means 'blowing out,' but is often thought to refer to either a Buddhist heaven or complete nothingness. Actually, it refers to the letting go of clinging to hatred and ignorance and accepting the imperfection, impermanence, and interconnectedness of the world.

And lastly, the path to liberation is dharma. Buddha called it the middle way, which is elaborated as the eightfold path.

THE EIGHTFOLD PATH

Misery is an unavoidable fact of life, while knowledge of truth is blessedness. A man with spiritual knowledge never again has to walk the path of sorrow: 'By day shines the sun; by night, the moon; in armour, the warrior; in dhyana, the Brahman. But all day and all night, every day and every night, the awakened one shines in splendour.' *(Dhammapada.387)*.

How to overcome suffering, is one question that everyone wants to know from the religious teachers. Lord Buddha placed the option of not getting into the suffering in the first place. It is good to come out of a mess, but it is better not to get into it at all, was his message. He prescribed the famous eightfold path for avoiding suffering, which can also be used to get out of it.

* Samyak dristhi: The right view is the true understanding of the Four Noble Truths.
* Samyak sankalpa: The right aspiration is the true desire to free oneself from the worldly shackles. For this, it is advised to give up worldliness, ill feeling towards others, and to desist from harming others.

These two are referred to as *prajna* or wisdom.

* Samyak vak: Right speech involves abstaining from lying, gossiping, or hurtful talk.
* Samyak karmanta: Right action involves abstaining from hurtful behaviours, such as killing, stealing, and immorality.
* Samyak ajiva: Right livelihood means making one's living in such a way as to avoid dishonesty and hurting others.

These three are referred to as *shila* or morality.

* Samyak vyayama: Right effort is a matter of exerting oneself in regards to the content of one's mind. Bad qualities should be abandoned and prevented from arising again. Good qualities should be enacted and nurtured.
* Samyak smriti: Right mindfulness is the focussing of one's attention on one's body, feelings, thoughts, and consciousness to overcome craving, hatred, and ignorance.
* Samyak samadhi: Right concentration is meditating in such a way as to progressively realise a true understanding of imperfection, impermanence, and non-separateness.

The last three are known as *samadhi* or meditation.

The first seven steps of this path are essentially the ethical aspect of Buddhism, while the eighth, Samyak samadhi, makes it a religion. The goal of every religion is to make a person divine, and not merely moral or ethical. Morality is a mere stepping stone to spirituality.

Buddha's teaching is not about heaven, hell, soul, etc. but focussed on the way out of suffering. Ridiculing theologies, he narrated the parable of the poisoned arrow:

> It's just as if a man were wounded with an arrow, thickly smeared with poison. His friends and companions would provide him with a surgeon, and the man would say, 'I won't have this arrow removed until I know whether the man who wounded me was a noble warrior, a priest, a merchant, or a worker.' He would say, 'I won't have this arrow removed until I know his name, clan name…whether he was tall, medium, or short…until I know whether the feathers of the shaft with which I was wounded were those of a vulture, a stork, a hawk, a peacock, or another bird…' The man would die and those things would still remain unknown to him.

The goal was to come out of suffering, which meant that one should lead a good life, for which he needed values. Buddha called them Panchasheela, the five moral principles, compulsory for every Buddhist.:

* Avoid killing or harming any living thing.
* Avoid stealing or taking what is not ones to take.
* Avoid sexual irresponsibility, which for monks and nuns means celibacy.
* Avoid lying or any hurtful speech.
* Avoid consumption of alcohol and drugs, which diminish the clarity of consciousness.

Dhammapada records these as:

> Whoever kills, lies, steals, goes to someone else's wife and is addicted to intoxicants, digs himself up by the root, right here in this world. So, know, my good man that bad deeds are reckless. Don't let greed and unrighteousness oppress you with long-term pain.' *(246–48)*

In addition to these five, there are also the Paramita—ten virtues that everyone should strive to achieve: *dana*—Generosity; *sila*—moral discipline; *khanti*—patience and tolerance; *panna*—wisdom or full-consciousness; *viriya*—vigour; *nekkhamma*—renunciation; *sacca*—truthfulness; *adhitthana*—determination; *metta*—loving kindness; and *upekkha*—equanimity.

As can be seen, these teachings can be interpreted as some kind of ethical system that one can follow without being religious. This made some scholars call Buddhism the ethical idealism, which it is not. The only goal of Buddhism through all these values and ethics is to go beyond the cycle of birth and death and be established in nirvana.

SACRED TEXTS

There are many similarities between the two great teachers of religion, Jesus and Buddha. They both grew up in the traditions of their mother religion, they both came up with core spiritual teachings that were overlooked by the then priests, they both used parables to convey what they had to say, their teachings were addressed to particular persons or groups, and those teachings were collected to form the sacred texts of the respective paths of enlightenment, after their passing away. Unlike the Vedas, Upanishads, or Quran, there was no tradition of disciples to maintain the absolute certainty of the teachings of Buddha or Christ. However, spiritual teachings do not get contaminated due to the shortcomings of the keepers. So, the sacred texts of Buddhism are as good as having come from the Lord himself, although these were recorded much later.

Tripitaka

Three months after Buddha's passing away (*parinirvana*), five hundred monks met at the first council at Rajagriha to collect the teachings of the master from his various disciples. Upali, a highly respected monk, recited the monastic code (*vinaya*) as he remembered it. Ananda, Buddha's cousin, friend, and favourite disciple recited Buddha's lessons (the Sutras). The monks then debated details and voted on final versions, which were then organised into three books (*pitaka*, lit. basket) and were committed to memory by other monks.

Of these three, the first one is known as the *Suttanta pitaka*. It contains the narrative discourse of Buddha in which ideas like the Four Noble Truths are examined and then explained. These are mostly original teachings of Buddha. The second collection, *Vinaya pitaka*, contains disciplinary rules and regulations for the monks and nuns. The *Abhidharma pitaka*, the third basket, is the collection of works by a number of anonymous followers of the Buddha. These contain philosophical discussions on the nature of reality, which form the basis of Buddhism and also makes it a highly philosophy-centric religion.

Jataka

At some point in time, Buddha was identified with godhood, and also with someone who is perfect but chooses to stay in the world to help the different species in their moments of crisis. This special personality is known as Bodhisattva. The life stories of Bodhisattvas, in different bodies, are collectively called Jataka stories. It is believed that these stories started getting shape pretty early in the history of Buddhism. The stories are highly inspiring and easy to grasp, which make them popular with readers of every age group.

Dhammapada

This small book of 423 verses is as important to Buddhists as Gita is to the Hindus. Unlike Gita, however, it does not get into metaphysical discussions. Its focus is entirely on ethical principles and an exhortation to lead a spiritual life. To give an idea of what Buddhism stands for, and what Buddha taught, here are some quotes from *Dhammapada*.

> As rain seeps into an ill-thatched hut, so passion, the undeveloped mind; as rain does not seep into a well-thatched hut, so passion does not, the well-developed mind. *(13–14)*

> Knowing this body is like foam, realising its nature— a mirage—cutting out the blossoms of Mara, you go where the King of Death cannot see. *(46)*

> The path to material gain goes one way, the way to 'unbinding', another. Realising this, the monk, a disciple to the awakened one, should not relish offerings, should cultivate seclusion instead. *(75)*

> Like a deep lake, clear, unruffled, and calm: so, the wise become clear, calm, on hearing words of the Dhamma. *(82)*

Greater in battle than the man who would conquer a thousand men is he who would conquer just one—himself. Better to conquer yourself than others. When you've trained yourself, living in constant self-control, neither a *deva* (gods of the Hindu pantheon), nor *gandharva* (celestial beings), nor a Mara banded with Brahmas, could turn that triumph back into defeat. *(103–105)*

If a person does evil, he shouldn't do it again and again or develop a penchant for it. To accumulate evil brings pain. If a person makes merit, he should do it again & again, and develop a penchant for it. To accumulate merit brings ease. *(117–8)*

Your own self is your own mainstay, for who else could your mainstay be? With you yourself well-trained you obtain the mainstay hard to obtain. *(160)*

Swans fly the path of the sun. Those with the power fly through space. The enlightened flee from the world, having defeated the armies of Mara. *(175)*

The liar observing no duties, filled with greed and desire: what kind of contemplative is he? But whoever tunes out the dissonance of his evil qualities—large or small—in every way by bringing evil to consonance: he is called a contemplative. *(264–65)*

Dhamma his dwelling, Dhamma his delight, a monk pondering Dhamma, calling Dhamma to mind, does not fall away from true Dhamma. *(364)*

Other than these sacred books, there is a huge storehouse of literature, most of which were destroyed during Islamic invasions in India but were later rediscovered from Tibet and China in the local languages, and then retranslated into Indian languages.

PREACHING THE WAY

India had not seen the kind of preaching Buddha was prescribing. Religion in those days meant rituals and sacrifices, while Vedanta was preached mostly in the confines of hermitage. There were the wandering ascetics, who were like walking spirituality, but they did not interact much with the householders other than seeking alms from them. Buddha changed all that. He was the walking Vedanta, ever ready to preach the highest truths, even to the most unwilling, and was thus making a huge number of converts from different stations and walks of life to the new way of life, Dhamma.

Among his followers and admirers was Bimbisara, the king of Magadha, who is considered to have laid the foundations for the later expansion of the Maurya Empire and is credited to have built Rajgir. The king had met Buddha when he was still in search of knowledge and later became an important disciple. It helped Buddhism that the king joined him since a religion spreads faster under state patronage.

There is a popular story about how Buddha stopped Bimbisara from sacrificing a goat, 'If you think that this goat can take you to heaven then kill me. I make a better offering than these animals.' From that day the king stopped all animal sacrifices.

One thus finds the importance that Buddha laid on non-violence, and also how firm he was in practising what he preached. According to a popular story in the Buddhist tradition, Buddha wanted the dreaded killer, Angulimala, to change his ways. When an angry Angulimala ordered Buddha to stand still, the Tathagata (lit. one who has arrived at the truth; a name for Buddha) replied: 'I am still. Why don't you be still also?...I am still in that I harm no living being. You kill and therefore you are not still.' The power behind these words converted the cruel to the way of peace forever.

One gets a glimpse of how calm Buddha was, and what kind of peace he preached his followers to aspire for, from the incident of the furious Brahmin who one day abused Buddha viciously for no reason. Buddha calmly said, 'All those abuses remain with you since I have not accepted even a single abuse from you! Dear brother, suppose you give some coins to somebody, and if he does not accept them, with whom will those coins remain?'

Established that he was in the virtues of spiritual truths, Buddha could change the hearts of the most infatuated by his mere words. There was his favourite disciple Ananda to whom a village girl, Matang, took a fancy simply because he had been kind to her. When Buddha came to know about it, he had the girl called, and advised her to be a *bikkhuni* (nun) for a year, after which she could have Ananda for a husband. Obsessed as she was, she gladly agreed. But a year's stay at the monastery and the teachings of Buddha made her realise her mistake, and she told him, 'Buddha! I am awake now. I will not behave the way I behaved.' From that day she became a complete convert.

Then there was the famous courtesan Amrapali, who was so vain of her beauty that she invited a monk to live with her during the four rainy months when monks stay in a safe shelter. Buddha, confident that he was made of the virtues of his teachings, allowed the monk to be Amraplai's guest. The monk came up to his expectation, leaving a dismayed courtesan realise her limits. She became Buddha's follower.

There were thousands of such converts everywhere. It is said that Buddha walked literally with more than a thousand monks when he went out with his begging bowl, asking for food. In the process, the highest of spiritual truths spread to the darkest corners of the society.

THE FIRST MONASTIC RELIGION

Buddha had studied under ascetics who stayed in small monasteries or as wandering monks. This influenced his way of life and preaching after his enlightenment, and he started a new monastic organisation, called Sangha, which thousands joined. Soon the way of Buddha became a prime religious way, which was taken up even by the great Brahmins of the period. Shaved heads, in yellow robes, walking in thousands, they must have presented a sight wherever they went!

Wandering like this, Buddha once reached Kapilavastu, his place of birth. Several years had now passed from the day he had left his sleeping wife and son. Yasodhara, his wife, was still smarting under the pique of separation from someone she had loved passionately. She sent their child Rahula to ask for his inheritance of crown and treasure from his father. When asked thus, Buddha asked his disciple, 'Sariputta, ordain him a monk.' Buddha, like any other committed monk, did not see himself belonging to the family in which he was born but drew his inheritance from the ascetics, whose ways he had chosen to tread.

Buddha had been raised by his foster mother, Mahaprajapati. She too wanted to take to the path of Buddha, but the Master refused to admit women into the Sangha. The lady pursued her case relentlessly along with hundreds of others till Buddha agreed to start a women monastery, most unwillingly. He knew well that spirituality or no spirituality, staying together of male and female was sure to bring ill actions within the monastery.

Although the consequences of the women monastery did not prove to be quite healthy in later times, the idea of an organised church for women was revolutionary and first of its kind in the world of religion. Hinduism had female sages, who had contributed to the corpus of vedic hymns, but an organised body of female ascetics was unheard of. In fact, Hinduism saw its first women monastery, inspired by the words of Swami Vivekananda, more than 2500 after Buddha had passed away.

It is customary for a monk joining the order to take triple vows of:

> *Buddham Sharanam Gachhami / Dharmam Sharanam Gacchami / Sangham Sharanam Gacchami*
> I take refuge in the Buddha (wisdom) / I take refuge in the Dharma (virtue) / I take refuge in the Sangha (discipline).

For the last 2500 years, Buddhist monasteries have continued to thrive all over the world through these three exalted vows.

WORLD VIEW

Lord Buddha was born and brought up in Hindu traditions; therefore, he freely referred to the names of Hindu gods like Indra and Brahma, although he denied the supremacy of the Vedas and their rituals. The theory of karma was also accepted by him and was later refined by the philosophers. The inevitability of karma, as believed by the Hindus of present times, has in fact been perfected by the Buddhists. In earlier times, it was a loose concept and acted like a model to explain the universe and its diversity. Buddhists made it a complete cause and effect theory.

THE DOCTRINE OF ANATMAN

In contrast to the then Hindu religious traditions, Buddha avoided any direct reference to technicalities of religion. To him the only thing that mattered was one's own life as perceived here and now. The goal was to attain knowledge and rise above both good and bad, the way Vedanta teaches. But unlike Vedanta, Buddha neither admitted nor refuted the existence of atman. This created complications for his followers. When the great masters teach, they can change the mental outlook of a person by their mere presence, glance, touch, words, or reasoning. Their followers, unfortunately, do not possess similar spiritual prowess. In the absence of the ability for rigorous arguments, premises, theology, and conclusions, they may propagate something that is in contradiction to what the master preached. This leads to confusion. Something similar happened in Buddhism.

Buddhist philosophy of later times had to explain *samsara* (existence) without accepting the presence of all-pervasive atman, and also had to counter the increasing attacks by the traditional schools of Hindu philosophy, particularly Vedanta. These issues brought before them the challenge—why does one perceive a self if none exists? This gave birth to the theory of 'dependent arising', which was to support the theory of *anatman* (non-self). It was explained that what one sees as 'self' is really a collection of aggregates or a complex of notions that seem to indicate a self. These aggregates are matter, sensations, perceptions, mental formations, and consciousness. It was much later that Theravada school of Buddhism perfected this theory of anatman that resolved the issues. They hold the belief that the self gives rise to the idea of the self and the other, and to the ideas of 'me' and 'mine'. This eventually gives rise to clinging to impermanent things to satisfy cravings. The system is explained by the theory of 'dependent arising or origination', whose steps are:

* Avidya: Ignorance—incorrect knowledge of the true nature of existence.
* Samskara: Karma Formations—the burdens of karma become apparent.
* Vijnana: Conditioned consciousness—consciousness forms.
* Nama-rupa: Mental/physical complex—a sense of mind and body develops.
* Sadayatana: Basis of senses—the five senses and the mind come into existence.
* Sparsa: Sensory impressions—these sense organs and mind experience sensations.
* Vedana: Conscious feelings—sensations produce reactions in the consciousness.
* Trishna: Desire—the consciousness develops a desire for these sensations.
* Upadana: Clinging—desire makes one pursue these sensations.
* Bhava: Being born or becoming—the sense of individuality develops in a person.
* Jati: Rebirth—the 'individual' is born into the world.
* Jara-marana: Death—the individual grows old or sick and passes away, only to allow the wheel to begin again.

To a Hindu thinker, these steps would appear familiar as the triad of *avidya–kama–karma*; ignorance leads to desire, which makes one act, and thus goes the cycle. The difference is that Hindus can never think of existence without atman, while Buddhists deny it. When Shankaracharya (8th century AD) came up with a cohesive philosophy of the vedic religions (i.e. Hinduism), he attacked the theory of anatman viciously, which ultimately ended the prominence of Buddhism in India forever.

Unlike any other religion, Buddhism is inherently philosophical and derives its strength from strong premises and cohesive arguments. This makes Buddhist philosophy challenging to understand, but also quite appealing to evolved minds even if it is only for refuting it. The differences arising out of arguments to settle the basics of Buddhist outlook resulted in the formation of two major sects and four major philosophies in it.

SECTS

Mahayana

In the next few centuries, the unity of Buddhism began to fray. The most significant split occurred after the second council, held at Vaishali a hundred years after the first. After debates between the liberals and the traditionalists, the liberals left and labelled themselves the Mahasangha—the great Sangha. Eventually, they evolved into the Mahayana tradition, popular in China, Japan, and other northern countries. It is also known as Northern Buddhism or Sanskrit Buddhism since most of the writings were in Sanskrit. Their more liberal attitudes towards monastic tradition allowed householder devotees to have a greater voice in defining the nature of Buddhism. For better or worse, the simpler needs of the common folk were easier for the mahayanists to meet.

The Mahayana sect of Buddhism introduced three main concepts for its followers:

* The ideal of a Bodhisattva: An individual who has attained enlightenment, but who chooses to remain in this world of samsara in order to bring others to enlightenment, was considered a Bodhisattva.

* Buddha as God: Mahayanists identified Buddha with the transcendental reality, and the historical Gautama Buddha as the incarnation of that reality, the Buddha. This reality is also thought of as manifesting itself in this world as the *dharmakaya*, the regulator of the universe, who is full of compassion for all beings and helps them towards salvation. Jataka stories have come out from this concept only.

* Acceptance of Self: Bhagavan Buddha himself neither admitted nor refuted the existence of the soul. This made the early Buddhist philosophers refuse the existence of self, which in turn resulted in people rejecting the religion. Mahayanists introduced the concept of *mahatman* (the transcendental self), which is self of all beings, as opposed to the individual ego, which is false.

Hinayana

The traditionalists, on the other hand, were derisively called Hinayana (lit., the lesser craft), but they prefer calling themselves as Sthaviravada or 'way of the elders' (or, in Pali, Theravada). It is also known as Southern Buddhism (popular in Sri Lanka, Myanmar, and Thailand), and also as Pali Buddhism since most of its writings were in Pali. Compared to Mahayana Buddhism, it is quite stern in its approach and outlook towards religious life.

It developed a complex set of philosophical ideas beyond those elucidated by Buddha. These were collected into the Abhidharma or 'higher teachings.' But they also encouraged disagreements, so that one splinter group after another left the fold. Ultimately, eighteen schools developed, each with its own interpretations of various issues.

This system, like Jainism, is without God. The place of God is taken up by dharma, the universal moral law; the life and teachings of Buddha provide the ideal and inspiration for liberation, and the organised church (Sangha) adds to spiritual aspirations. It is thus that an aspirant takes the threefold vow (*tisarana*), 'I take refuge in Buddha, I take refuge in Dhamma, I take refuge in Sangha.'

This religious school is very difficult to hold on to since it requires extreme self-descipline. It was due to this that the masses moved towards Mahayana.

SCHOOLS

Hinduism and Buddhism had a symbiotic and also competitive relationship in matters of yoga practices and philosophical outlook. The great teachers and philosophers of both religions chiselled their systems to withstand the onslaught of each other. In the process, they both attained perfection and also created complicated systems of thought, which became incomprehensible to a common devotee.

There are four major schools of thoughts in Buddhism (and sometimes a fifth, Tantra).

* Madhyamika school of Sunyavada: This tradition was systematised by Nagarjuna. According to it, all phenomena are

empty of 'self-nature' or 'essence' (*svabhava*), meaning that they have no intrinsic, independent reality, apart from the causes and conditions from which they arise. Indian philosophers misunderstood the system and named it *sarva vainasika vada*—ruinous. But the philosophy is actually the rejection of two extremes of absolute reality and the absolute unreality of things. *Sunyata* is an aspect of the dependent nature (explained earlier) of things. This philosophy denies the phenomenal world, but not all reality. In the process, it stresses upon the indescribable nature of phenomena.

* Yogachara/*Vijnanavada*: This philosophy is credited to two brothers, Asanga and Vasubandhu. They agreed with the Madhyamikas but added that the mind cannot be treated as unreal, like the phenomenal world. It was thus that the philosophy moved in the direction of idealism or *chitta-matra* (mind). According to them, everything exists is mind or consciousness. What one thinks of as physical things are just projections of one's minds. To get rid of these one must meditate, which for the Yogachara school means the creation of pure consciousness, devoid of all content. Because this philosophy admits of consciousness, it is also known as Vijnananvada.

* Sautrantika: These philosophers attach importance to Sutra Pitaka. They accept the reality of mind and also the reality of the external objects. However, they conclude that the external objects are not perceived directly; they are inferred. The arguments used by this school against the above two subjective idealism schools are quite similar to the later day realist school of philosophers.

* Vaibhasika: This school is based more on Abhidhamma Pitaka, and follows a particular commentary called, Vibhasa. This system is also a realist school of thought, like the Sautrantikas, but they add that external objects are directly known in perception and are not inferred.

* Tantra: This system is far more comprehensive than the earlier ones. Tantra refers to certain writings, which are concerned not with philosophical niceties, but with the basics of enlightenment. In order to accomplish this, dramatic methods are employed. Tantra was the domain of the *siddha* (the adept)—someone who knew the secrets. The system involves the use of various techniques, including the well-known mandalas, mantras, and mudras. Mandalas are paintings or other representations of higher awareness, usually in the form of a circular pattern of images. Mantras are words or phrases that serve the same purpose, such as *Aum mani padme hum*. Mudras are a form of hand and finger movement that symbolise certain qualities of enlightenment. Buddhist Tantra is also known as Vajrayana and has been popular in Tibet and other Himalayan regions.

These philosophical systems are not without criticism. Madhyamika is criticised as wordplay. Yogachara is criticised as reintroducing atman. Tantra has been criticised for its emphasis on secret methods and strong devotion to a guru. However, it is due to these philosophical achievements that Buddhism has managed to survive the decay brought into the system by the insincere insiders, and the vicious outsiders.

Buddhism is essentially a monastic religion, which became popular with the masses because of Lord Buddha's exalted personality and compassion. Being a monastic religion meant that the focus of sadhana was on meditation and ethical values. To help the masses, elements of bhakti were added in later times, and in some areas, the clandestine practices of Tantra thrived. This took away the vitality of the then Buddhism in India, and the resurrected Hindu philosophy of the eighth century cut at the root of its hollow practices and more hollow practitioners. The modern-day Buddhism, popularised by Zen, focuses on meditation (*dhyana-jhana*), and have perfected this in its many forms.

BE A LIGHT UNTO YOURSELF

For forty-five years Buddha went about the country, preaching and persuading men to follow his way of life. It was time to leave behind the human frame that had held the precious being for so long.

One day at Pavanagar, near Kushinagar (in Uttar Pradesh), Buddha was invited for a meal by a devotee. Unfortunately, the food (rumoured to be a type wild mushroom), was not acceptable to his delicate frame, and he suffered the conditions of food poisoning. He knew that his time on this earth was over, so he took his last bath in the nearby river, and lay down. Thinking that people may blame his host for his plight, he told his disciple Ananda to convey his penultimate words, 'two offerings to the Buddha are of an equal gain. The offering of food just before his supreme enlightenment, and the offering of food just before he passes away. This is the final birth of the Buddha.'

Lying between two large sal trees, Buddha saw Ananda shed tears. He then gave his now famous last message '*Appa deepo bhava*'—be a light unto yourself. With this, he attained *parinirvana*, the ultimate liberation at eighty.

Buddha was not a person, nor a personality, nor a phenomenon, but a state of blessedness. He was born a human being, but he became a Buddha, lived as a Buddha, and left this world as a Buddha. This was achieved by honing two of his chief characteristics—self-determination and self-dependence. He laid stress on his human origins and left no room for anyone to believe that he was an immortal being

He proclaimed to the world the latent possibilities and the invincible power of the human mind. Instead of placing an unseen almighty God over man, and giving man a subservient position in relation to such a conception of divine power, he demonstrated how man could attain the highest knowledge and supreme enlightenment through his own efforts. He thus raised the worth of individuals. He taught that man can gain his deliverance from the ills of life and realise the eternal bliss of nirvana without depending on an external God or mediating priests. He taught the egocentric, power-seeking world, the noble ideal of selfless service. He declared that the gates of deliverance were open to all, in every condition of life, high or low, to a saint or a sinner, who would care to turn over a new leaf and aspire to perfection.

His will, wisdom, compassion, service, renunciation, perfect purity, exemplary personal life, non-intrusive nature of propagating the Dharma have inspired almost one-fifth of the population of the world to hail Buddha, as their spiritual ideal.

Lord Buddha compared nirvana to snuffing out of a flame. The notion of an 'I', strengthened over an infinite number of births and passed on like one flame, lit from another, comes to an end once the spiritual aspirant exhausts his karma. This can be achieved through the right knowledge, obtained through the eight steps mentioned earlier. There is no doubt that many such 'snuffing out' must have taken place by following the path of Buddha. It is to his credit that his religion continues to burn bright and will continue doing so till there is even an iota of suffering in the human race.

Jainism
Religion of Asceticism

THE TWENTY-FOUR TEACHERS

In India, the supremacy of the Vedas and the tradition of some ascetics opposing its rituals coexisted forever. Unlike the supporters of the Vedas, these ascetics followed the instructions of their teachers and the diktats of their own purified mind to create their own spiritual path. The *jina*s (the conquerors of the self), belonged to this tradition and were known for their strict codes of life, making renunciation the central issue.

Jain dharma is founded on the sacred teachings of the twenty-four jinas, who are also known as Tirthankaras. Of these 24, the more famous are: Rishabhanatha, Neminatha, Parshvanatha and Mahavira (Vardhamana). Rishabhanatha was the first Tirthankara with whom the tradition starts. Neminatha, believed to be a contemporary of Sri Krishna, was the 22nd Tirthankara and is famous for strongly condemning violence of any kind. Parshvanatha, the 23rd Tirthankara, made the religious movement quite strong against the ritualistic vedic religion. Mahavira was the 24th and the last Tirthankara. He popularised the spiritual tenets of the jina tradition among the masses. Since Jainism existed before Mahavira, his teachings were based on those of his predecessors.

In this way, Mahavira is only a link in the chain of spiritual leaders of an already existing tradition, although he is popularly accepted as the founder of this way of life.

The exact birth year of Vardhamana Mahavira draws conflicting dates. It is generally accepted that he was born 250 years after Parshvanatha, and lived in 6th century BCE. He is also referred to as the Nirgrantha Nathaputta—the naked ascetic of the Jnatr clan. He was born in Vaishali district of Bihar, to King Siddhartha and Queen Trishala.

When Mahavir was still in his mother's womb, she had dreamt of fourteen distinct images—an elephant, a bull, a lion, goddess Lakshmi, a garland of flowers, the sun, the moon, a flag, a pitcher, a lotus pond, an ocean, a heavenly chariot, jewels, and smokeless fire. These are considered auspicious symbols, and if one sees them in their dreams then the progeny is expected to become an exalted emperor or a Tirthankara. Mahavira was, naturally, expected to be a famous king.

Since his childhood, Mahavira was deeply interested in meditation and the religious way of life. Keeping with the social traditions, he married a princess (debated by some) and had a daughter, Priyadarshana. However, he could not be drawn into worldliness. Around the age of thirty, he renounced everything and went out in search of knowledge by getting initiated in the ways of a Tirthankara.

Knowledge, according to Jain traditions, is of five kinds: direct perception through senses and the mind (*mati jnana*), from sacred books (*sruta jnana*), inner/intuitive knowledge (*avadhi jnana*), knowledge of others' thoughts/subjective knowledge (*manahpraya jnana*), and the knowledge of the ultimate truth (*kevala jnana*).

Mahavir was born with the first three, acquired the fourth when he was initiated in the ways of a Tirthankara, and was determined to gain the last kind of knowledge, kevala jnana. For this, he had to leave the comforts of his royal family, which he did. The prince renounced everything to master the knowledge of everything. For the next twelve years, he was engaged in intense *sadhana*, after which he achieved absolute knowledge, finally, becoming a person of infinite harmony, knowledge, and self-control.

The life of an ascetic, even in a religious country like India, is not fraught without difficulties as evident in Mahavira's life. During his early days as a wandering ascetic, one cow-herder took him for a scheming thief, and Mahavira had to leave the village in a hurry. Later, while crossing a river, his garment got caught in the thorns on the banks, and he was left naked. It is said, after that incident Mahavira refused to put on any clothes.

Soon he found a companion—Makkhali Goshala. However, Goshala had the unwelcome habit of teasing and mocking people. This resulted in the duo getting beaten up several times. During one of those travels together, they were suspected to be spies of the enemy state and were thrown into a well. Fortunately, they were recognised by some devotees of the Jain tradition and rescued. It is said, Goshala felt so humiliated after this that he decided to go his way. According to other sources, the parting was due to differences in their philosophical outlooks.

Goshala rejoined Mahavira after a period of six months. However, their fate did not fare any better. They were time and again beaten up, taken for spies, and even tortured. In a place called Ladha, in West Bengal, where tribal culture prevailed, dogs were set upon them. Another time, when Mahavir was lost deep in meditation, in Chammanigama, his ears were pierced by a hostile cowherd.

Jain traditions explain these cruelties inflicted upon Mahavir as ramifications of his past karma, which had to be experienced before attaining supreme knowledge. The idea of cleansing through one's past karma, as a key step to attaining spiritual fulfilment, is a fundamental philosophical tenet in Jainism.

Next, Mahavira travelled to the northern bank of the river Ujjuvaliya (believed to be near Pavapuri in Bihar), to the farm of a devotee, Samaga. There, under a shala tree, Mahavira attained knowledge (*kevala*) on the tenth day of Vaisakha (April), at the age of forty-two.

When Mahavir was finally ready to preach his message to the world, his first religious convention drew a blank. During the second meeting, he got only nine disciples, who came to be known as *gandhara*s (apostles) of Mahavira. Some sects in Jain religion do not subscribe to this but agree that Mahavir was thereafter ready to show light to the humanity.

MAHAVIRA, THE TEACHER

After attaining knowledge, Mahavir started preaching his way through villages and cities, mostly in Bihar and eastern Uttar Pradesh. Among his early visitors was his daughter, Priyadarshana, and her husband, Jamali. They both took the vow of asceticism under the guidance of the blessed one. Jamali was so devoted to the master that he accompanied him everywhere and learned the eleven scriptures. The master made him the head of the mendicants of his order. Unfortunately, this arrangement was short lived. Soon there was a schism between Mahavira and Jamali on a rather trivial issue. Jamali started boasting that he had attained omniscience. He told Mahavir that he had become all-knowing, all-perceiving, an *arhat*, here on earth. His wife Priyadarshana also joined him in his heresy, initially, but soon returned to the original fold. This incident shows how it is one thing to be a prophet, but getting followers to the fold, even if they are close ones, is a different matter altogether.

Lord Mahavir travelled and preached the message of the jinas barefoot and without clothes. It is said that at some point in time, he had over 400,000 followers. His power of attracting people was a cause of some envy to his companion Makkhali Goshala, who soon became a rival.

The similarity between the lives of Mahavir Jain and Buddha, the founders of two great religious traditions, is captivating. They were both born in the same period of history, were princes, got married, had children, and performed spiritual practices in the present-day Bihar, which was the then cultural and spiritual centre of India. As preachers too, they were similar—both of them had a long life, started monastic institutions that continue till date, rebelled against the vedic systems, their children joined them at some point in their lives, and they both taught in local dialects instead of Sanskrit, the language of the elite.

Mahavir preached in Ardha Magadhi, the language that later gave birth to Hindi, Gujarati, and Marathi. His words, coming as they were from one who knew the truth, attracted an immense crowd and also the wrath of the Brahmins, who had no inkling of the realm of knowledge that lay beyond their restrictive world of rituals. The eternal war between the prophet and the priests was raging once again. However, the words of the prophet, which talked of simple ethical practices like non-violence, truth, etc. were easy to understand and practical enough to follow.

SACRED TEXTS

The teachings of Mahavira focus on attaining knowledge that liberates one from the bondage of this world.

> All unenlightened persons produce sufferings. Having become deluded, they produce and reproduce sufferings in this endless world. *(Uttaradhyayana.6.1)*

> All other phases of my existence to which I am attached are external occurrences that are transitory. *(Niyamasara.99)*

> Let me treat all living beings with equanimity and none with enmity. Let me attain samadhi (tranquillity) by becoming free from expectations. *(Mulachara.2.42)*

> One who remains unaffected in the midst of pleasures and pains is a sramana, being in the state of pure consciousness. *(Pravachansara.1.14)*

These teachings point at equanimity of the mind as the goal of life—the state that is beyond the dualities like pleasure and pain, expectations and disappointments, gain and loss. A person who attains this state through rigorous discipline and meditation achieves all that is to be achieved in this world. One need not be a monk to be able to do so; anyone who has a firm resolve can achieve this.

Echoing the words of the masters that only knowledge of the self can liberate a person, Lord Mahavir said:

> The unenlightened takes millions of lives to extirpate the effects of karma, whereas a man possessing spiritual knowledge and discipline obliterates them in a single moment. *(Bhagavati Aradhana.10)*

Writing, as a means of preserving these practices, was not popular in early India. The Vedas, despite their huge corpus of verses, were maintained by an oral tradition, running for thousands of years by the Brahmins. Because of this prevalence of the oral tradition, sacred books were missing in both Buddhism and Jainism. This resulted in a loss of some of the sacred teachings. It also created discrepancies in the available Jaina texts.

Lord Mahavira's teachings, known as the Agamas, are the most sacred works for a Jain. These are compiled into sperate parts, known as the *dwadashangi* (twelve parts) and contain biographies of the Tirthankaras and kings, code of conduct for the Jain followers, description of the cosmos, and metaphysics that describe the nature of reality, life, etc. A Jain follower, particularly a monk (*sramana*) is expected to know the sacred books thoroughly. This stems from the belief that spiritual knowledge comes only from the sacred books, and not through observation or inferences.

> A sramana devoid of the knowledge of Agama neither know himself nor others. *(Pravachansanasara.3.32)*

> Other beings perceive through their senses whereas the sramana perceives through the Agama. *(Pravachansara.3.34)*

After the passing away of Lord Mahavir, his disciples spread his teachings all across the country. The gandharas were responsible for remembering the texts. They made the texts available to other teachers as they had learned them from Lord Mahavira. However, as with any oral tradition, which is not maintained meticulously, some discrepancy developed in these sacred texts. This resulted in the first council of monks to be held at Pataliputra, 160 years after Lord Mahavir's nirvana. The assembled monks could compile only the first eleven Angas by recollection, and so the twelfth Anga was lost. Many monks, particularly from the south, did not agree with this compilation. This resulted in the birth of the two sects, Svetambaras and Digambaras.

The second council was held in Mathura, 825 years after the nirvana of Lord Mahavir. The third council was held 980 years after his nirvana. The texts of Jain scriptures are believed to have been written down systematically only after this third council.

Passage of time corrupted scriptural texts. So, a method for checking their validity was developed. A scripture was considered valid only if it contained the revealed words of a *sarvajna* (omniscient), did not contradict reason, described the four *purusartha* (dharma, artha, kama, moksha), and led a person towards the supreme goal of *mukti*.

WORLD VIEW

Jiva

Jainism accepts soul as permanent but believes that its condition changes according to its karma. Thus, where Hindus believe only in permanence, and the Buddhists believe only in change, Jainism harmonises both.

For Jains, every living being has an eternal soul, called *jiva*. All souls are equal because they possess the potential to be liberated and attain *moksha*, which is the state of perfect knowledge, power, and joy. Consciousness thus lies only with the soul, and the soul alone knows things, performs activities, experiences pleasure and pain, and illuminates itself and the surrounding.

Jiva is eternal, but it also undergoes a change of states. Owing to past karma, jiva takes up various bodies and spreads throughout it. This spreading out of the soul throughout the body is possible because the soul is not material but is more like a living light. Thus, the jiva of an elephant is of elephant shape, and that of an ant is of ant shape. Being non-material, many souls can live in the same place.

Jainism believes in five classes of beings, and six kinds of bodies, with a varying number of senses. The jiva (souls that have not attained liberation) inhabiting in these bodies (five of them) have consciousness of varying degree. At the highest end are the perfect souls, who have overcome all karmas, and are not limited by their senses anymore. They are the ones who have attained moksha —the state in which is the expulsion of matter particles from the soul and thus stopping the play of karma. The goal of Jain religion is to establish one's soul in its pristine purity through self-control, meditation, and the knowledge born of these two.

> Discipline is the means of achieving liberation. *(Shila-pahuda.20)*

> Keep yourself always awake. One who keeps awake increases his wisdom. He who falls asleep is wretched. Blessed is he who keeps awake. *(Brihat Kalpa Bhasya.3387)*

> The yogi, who is indifferent to worldly affairs, remains spiritually alert to his own duty, namely, his duty towards his soul. On the other hand, one who indulges in worldly affairs is not dutiful to his soul. *(Moksha-pahuda.31)*

If one's vision is capable of expelling the darkness, he would not need a lamp. Likewise, the soul itself being blissful, there is no need for an external object for bliss. *(Pravachansara.1.67)*

As the fire quickly consumes dry wood, even so, an adept, whose soul is equipoised and unattached, causes the accumulated karma structure to disintegrate. *(Acaranga.4.3.33)*

A monk engrossed in meditation renounces all evils. Meditation is, therefore, the best way of regression from all transgressions. *(Niyamasara.65)*

Ajiva

*Ajiva tattva*s are the lifeless things and are of five kinds. *Pudgala* (matter), which can be perceived by the senses, and which requires expelling out before one acquires nirvana; *dharma*, the medium of motion throughout the universe; *adharma*, the medium of rest; *akasa*, the space in which all other tattvas reside and lastly, *kala* (lit. time), which brings about modifications in all other objects. Here dharma and adharma should not be confused with the same terms in Hinduism, meaning virtue and vice. In Jainism, these are real particles, with set properties.

The five *ajiva tattva*, along with the *jiva tattva*s are the six *dravya* (substances) that form the universe.

Karma

Mahavir preached that since eternity, every living being (soul) is in a bondage of karmic atoms accumulated by good or bad deeds, born of *kashay* (passions). These could be variations of emotions, such as *krodha* (anger), *mana* (ego), *maya* (deceptions), and *lobha* (greed). Reeling under karma, the jiva seeks temporary and illusory pleasure in materialistic possessions, which is the prime causes of self-centred emotions. These, in turn, give rise to anger, hatred, greed, and other vices, and the further accumulation of karma.

The soul has infinite potentials, but due to karma, it gets associated with matter and its limitations. This causes bondage, which is real and is caused by matter particles, which infect the soul and overpower its infinite nature. The body of any living being is matter (*pudgala*), which can be arranged and organised in a particular fashion only by the guiding force of the soul's own passions. This means that a soul gets the body that it inwardly craves for. The root of all this is karma.

In all, there are *ghatiya* and *aghatiya* karma. The four ghatiya karmas are karmas that obstruct the soul's innate abilities of omniscience (*jnanavaraniya karma*), omniperception (*darsanavaraniya karma*), supreme bliss (*mohaniya karma*), supreme strength or omnipotence (*antaraya karma*).

The four aghatiya karmas are the karmas that cause temporal bondage. *Vedaniya karma* cause happiness and unhappiness. *Nama karma* determines the type of body the soul will take birth in. *Ayu karma* determines lifespan. *Gotra karma* determines birth in a high status or a low-status family.

Universe

The universe in Jainism is believed to be like a gigantic cosmic human body. Above the body is a canopy, which contains *siddha*s, the liberated beings. The chest region is the celestial world where gods reside. The waist is taken up by human beings, where they live in concentric rings of land and ocean. Below this disc of concentric rings lies (a variation of) hell, where sinners land up in heat, thirst, pain, etc.

However, neither the land of gods nor the hells are permanent. By doing good karma, and working out the accumulated ones, one can rise higher in life to attain mukti, which is the ultimate goal of Jainism.

Mukti

Death being a certainty, one must try to get one's soul liberated from the bondage of matter (*pudgala*) at the quickest. For spiritual advancement, Mahavir stated that both men and women are equal, and so females too can renounce the world in search of moksha or ultimate happiness.

Jainism does not believe in an omnipotent supreme being, creator or supervisor (*karta*). However, it accepts an eternal universe governed by natural laws. Jainism views God as the unchanging traits of the pure soul of each living being. This can also be described as infinite knowledge (*ananta jnana*), perception (*ananta darshana*), consciousness (*ananta caritra*), and happiness (*ananta sukha*). Instead of God, it believes in godlike Tirthankaras.

Jainism is similar to Purva Mimamsa of the vedic school in the sense that they both accept karma as the basic principle of samsara. It is similar to Vedanta in the sense that they both accept that every individual jiva is potentially the *paramatman* (the universal soul). In matters of spiritual practices, Jain philosophy has similarities with Yoga philosophy.

PHILOSOPHY

Astik and Nastik Darshan

Indian philosophy is usually classified into two—*astik darshan* (orthodox) and *nastik darshan* (unorthodox). The former comprises the six systems of Hindu philosophy based on the Vedas, while the latter comprises Charvaka (materialists), Jain, and Buddha philosophies (four of them) since they do not consider the Vedas as the ultimate source of knowledge.

The six systems of Hindu philosophy and also the four systems of Buddhist philosophy can be quite confusing to a beginner due to the verbosity, wordplay, intellectual gymnastics, and misplaced analogies in the text. Contrastingly, Jain philosophy is much more cohesive, and the differences that its various schools have are minor.

As with every religious philosophy, the world view of the Jains is based on the words of the masters, and on the logical conclusions of those truths. The most fundamental principle of this is that the living and the non-living somehow come into contact with each other, and forge certain energies, which cause various transformations like birth, death, disease and other experiences. This process can be stopped, and the energies already forged can be destroyed by a set of disciplines, which can lead a person to mukti.

The principle and process of mukti in Jainism has seven propositions, known as seven *tattva*s: *jiva*, the living; *ajiva*, the non-living; *asrava*, the influx of karma; *bandha*, the bondage of karma; *samvara*, the stoppage of influx of karma; *nirjara*, shedding of karma; and moksha, liberation. Sometimes *punya* (virtues) and *papa* (vices) are added to this list of seven.

These seven tattvas form the foundation of Jain philosophy and can be understood by the metaphor of a man going across a river in a leaky boat. The person can be likened to jiva, the boat to ajiva, the water entering the boat through the hole is asrava and it accumulates there as bandha. If the person makes efforts to save the boat by blocking the hole, then it can be likened to samvara, and throwing the accumulated water outside the boat is nirjara. Moksha is like getting across the river in that boat. The goal is to go across the river of life and death, and so one should focus on getting rid of karma, both good and bad. According to Jainism, as with every other religion of India, the cause of bondage is an attachment to sense pleasures. Just as an elephant sunk in the marsh can see the bank but cannot reach it, a man attached to sense pleasures knows about liberation but cannot attain it.

Because of the concept of asrava, Jainism stresses a lot on the law of karma, and have evolved elaborate propositions and consequences of it. To work out the endless karma accumulated over countless births, one requires many bodies and, consequently, many rebirths. Mukti is not possible until even a little of the residual karma remains. This argument leads to the theory of cyclic creation, and so the goal of life for everyone is to come out of the unending cycle of life and death.

Anekantavada and Syadvada

Anekantavada is the foundation stone of Jain philosophy. It literally means, 'the multiplicity of reality'. This principle actually consists of tools for overcoming inherent biases in any one perspective on any topic or in reality in general. The logical conclusion of this outlook is the doctrine of postulation, *Syadavada*, which is considered to be the great Jain contribution in the Indian logic system.

Jainism believes that the great spiritual vows cannot be fully implemented without accepting the philosophy of non-absolutism, Anekantavada, and the theory of qualified prediction, Syadavada.

According to Anekantavada, different systems of philosophy represent a different partial aspect of reality, as the observation by the blind of an elephant suggests. This implies that every judgement should be qualified by the expression 'somehow/probably' (*syad*). Thus, one should say, 'somehow the pot exists.' This view makes Jain philosophy extensive and tolerant.

According to Syadvada (also called, Saptabhangi), there are a possible of seven standpoints that can be taken regarding any object: 1. It is (*syad asti*), 2. It is not (*syad nasti*), 3. It is and is not (*syad asti ca, nasti ca*), 4. It is indescribable (*syad avayaktam*), 5. It is and is indescribable (*syad asti ca avyaktam ca*), 6. It is not and is indescribable (*syad nasti ca avyaktam ca*), 7. It is, is not, and is indescribable (*syad asti ca nasti ca avyaktam ca*).

Essentially, these seven principles imply that one cannot say with certainty about an object. Every object has innumerable characters (*ananta dharmakam vastu*), both positive and negative. It is impossible to know all these traits, and without it, one can never know an object completely. For example, a man has two eyes, two ears, etc., and lacks a tail, wings, feathers, etc. To know a man fully, one must know all his positive and negative characters, which will be in a large number. Moreover, any object keeps acquiring and losing characters continuously over time. So, any object can have infinite characteristics, which is impossible to be known by a common man. Hence the philosophy of Syadvada.

It is only the omniscient person (*kevali*) who can have a complete knowledge of things and objects. Such a person, who has this kind of knowledge, is the highest being, though not God.

WAY OF LIFE

As discussed, Jain religion accepts bondage as real and suggests realistic means to get out of this bondage. To liberate oneself from the cycle of birth and death, Mahavira taught the three gems (Triratna)—the necessity of right faith (*samyak-darshana*), right knowledge (*samyak-jnana*), and right conduct (*samyak-charitra*).

> There's no knowledge without right faith. No conduct is possible without knowledge. Without conduct, there's no liberation, and without liberation, no deliverance. *(Uttaradhyayana.27.30)*

> That with the help of which we can know the truth, control the restless mind, and purify the soul is called knowledge. *(Mulachara.5.70)*

> Righteousness consists in complete self-absorption and in giving up all kinds of passions including attachment. It is the only means of transcending the mundane existence. The jinas have said so. *(Bhava-pahuda.83)*

> The right conduct has the five great vows: *ahimsa* (non-violence), *satya* (truthfulness), *asteya* (non-stealing), *brahmacharya* (continence), and *aparigraha* (non-acceptance of gifts). O, Self! Practice truth, and nothing but the truth. Enlightened by the light of truth, the wise transcends death. *(Acaranga.3.3.66)*

> The ascetic who never thinks of telling a lie out of attachment, aversion, or delusion is indeed the practitioner of the second *vrata* of truthfulness. *(Niyamasara.57)*

> Truthfulness indeed is *tapa* (penance). In truthfulness do reside self-restraint and all other virtues. Just as the fish can live only in the sea, so can all other virtues reside in truthfulness alone. *(Bhagavati Aradhana.842)*

> One may have a tuft or matted hair on the head or a shaven head, remain naked or wear a rag. However, if he tells a lie, all this is futile or fruitless. *(Bhagavat Aradhana.843)*

An aspirant speaks words that are measured and beneficial
to all living beings. *(Kartikeyanupreksa.334)*

The king of all virtues in Jainism is *ahimsa*—non-violence. *Ahimsa
paramo dharmah* or non-violence is the highest virtue. Compassion
for all life, human and non-human, is central to this philosophy and
is practised to the extreme. It is the only religion in which complete
vegetarianism is preached and practised. Jains do not even take
up agricultural work for the fear of killing the worms and insects
that live in the earth. Most Jains do not eat after the sunset for the
same reason.

Later Jain preachers have shown how ahimsa alone is the
value that manifests as truthfulness, continence, etc. For example,
being untruthful is same as being violent towards truth, stealing is
being violent towards the property of others, and anger is violence
towards peace.

> Don't kill any living beings. Don't try to rule them.
> *(Acaranga.4.23)*

> The essence of all knowledge consists in not committing
> violence. The doctrine of ahimsa is nothing but the
> observance of equality. It is the realisation that just
> as I do not like misery, others also do not like it.
> *(Sutrakrtanga.1.4.10)*

> To kill any living being amounts to killing oneself.
> Compassion for others is compassion to one's own self.
> Therefore, one should avoid violence like poison and
> thorn (that cause pain). *(Bhagavati Aradhana.797)*

> The *bhikshu* (ascetic) should not be angry with one who
> abuses him. Otherwise, he would be like the ignoramus.
> *(Uttaradhyayana.2.24)*

If somebody were to beat a disciplined and restrained ascetic, the latter should not think of avenging himself considering the soul to be imperishable. *(Uttaradhyayana.2.27)*

By practising celibacy, one can fulfil all other vows, chastity, *tapa*s (penance), *vinaya* (humility), *sayyama* (self-restraint), forgiveness, self-protection, and detachment. *(Prasnavyakarana.9.3)*

The soul is the Brahman. Brahmacharya is, therefore, nothing but the spiritual conduct of the ascetic concerning the soul, who has snapped out of a relationship with the alien body. *(Bhagavati Aradhana.877)*

An amorous person, failing to achieve his desired objects, becomes frantic and even ready to commit suicide by any means. *(Bhagavati Aradhana.889)*

Living beings have desires. Desires consist of pleasure and pain. *(Kartikeyanupreksa.18.14)*

CODE OF CONDUCT

To treat religion and philosophy as extensions of ethics is wrong. The goal of every religion is divine oneness alone, while ethics is a mere benchmark of nobility. However, in an interesting observation, Buddhism has been termed ethical idealism while Jainism received the tag of ethical realism. This distinction, if not anything else, throws some light on the ethical aspect, and the realistic approach of Jain dharma.

The code of conduct in Jainism is simply too huge to recount here and is impossible for someone not born in this tradition to follow them. The emphasis on the ethical way of life is so much that the struggle to be good seems to overpower the goal of spirituality, which is to rise above good and bad. Also, the codes of a householder and those of a *muni* (ascetics) are not essentially different in Jain dharma. A muni is merely expected to adhere to the vows and *tapa*s (austerities) much more strictly than a householder.

The codes prescribed for householders have the observance of twelve *vrata*s or vows; eleven *pratima*s or stages in a householder's religious life; six *avasyaka*s or daily duties; and general principles of conduct.

The vratas are five *anu-vrata*s, essential vows, three *guna-vrata*s, multiplicative vows, and four s*iksa-vratasy*, disciplinary vows. These vows form the core of Jain code of conduct, by practising which a devotee is expected to attain final liberation.

It is also enjoined that the five faults, resulting from the non-observance of the vrata, should be avoided in three ways—*krta* (not commit by himself), *karita* (not incite others), and *anumodita* (not approve). If these vows are very strictly observed they are known as *mahavrata*s and can be practised only by the ascetics.

To fix these five vows in the mind, five kinds of meditations are advised. Further, every person must meditate upon the five faults resulting out of neglecting these five vows, since those faults are like pain personified, dangerous, and of censurable character in this world as well as in the next.

There are six obligatory duties, which Jain followers practise every day:

Chaturvishnati-stava: prayers in the praise of Tirthankaras; *kayotsarga*: meditation; *pratikramana*: the cleansing of past sins twice, daily; *pratyakhyana*: giving up of things; *samyika*: practising serenity; *vandan*: respecting teachers and ascetics.

A householder, desirous of attaining greater heights in ethical and spiritual progress, can do so by regulating his way of life. The word *pratima* means stages of growth by a householder in his practices. These are perfect faith in the ways of Jain dharma— perform twelve vows, be like an ascetic, at least temporarily, regulate fasting, abstain from eating uncooked food, refrain from eating at night, maintain celibacy, refrain from activities that may cause some kind of *himsa* (violence), give up of all attachments, increase vigour towards asceticism, and live the life of a hermit.

The asceticism and the ethical code prescribed in Jain dharma is unparalleled in its details. The idea of being good and doing good to others is ingrained in every Jain follower, who having grown up with the forces of goodness, accumulated over twenty-five hundred years, considers it his sacred duty to be true to his religious duties. The idea of purity is so deep with the Jains that they do not proselytise, and they keep their own practices quite private. The aspects of non-violence and truth, as preached in this religion, have practically become the national ideal of India, particularly after Gandhiji practised these two to the extreme.

A religion that focuses more on spirituality and less on observations acquires vitality of a high order. Lord Mahavira acquired *kevala jnana*—absolute knowledge that is beyond good and bad and is the ultimate test of spirituality.

> Those who are ignorant of the supreme purpose of life will never be able to attain *nirvana* (liberation) in spite of their observance of the *vrata*s and *niyma*s (rules) of religious conduct and practice of *shila* and *tapa*s (penance). *(Samayasara.153)*

PRAYERS AND RITUALS

Most religions take care of the devout, who need prayers to offer and rituals to practice. After all, prayers are the verbal expression of the supreme reality, and rituals are concretised philosophy.

A few centuries after Lord Mahavir's passing away, the Jain Sangha (religious order) grew more and more complex. There were splits on minor points, although they did not affect his original doctrines. Later generations saw the introduction of rituals and complexities and some criticised the idea of placing Mahavir and other Tirthankaras on the throne, similar to Hindu deities against whom Lord Mahavira had rebelled.

Elaborate forms of rituals are usually performed in the temples where the statues of liberated souls such as Tirthankaras, Siddhas or Arihants are kept. The worship can be offered as *dravya puja* (physical worship) or *bhava puja* (mental worship)

The Jaina prayer has five lines:

Namo Arihantanam—I bow to the Arihant.
Namo siddhanam—I bow to the Siddha.
Namo ayriyanam—I bow to the Acharya.
Namo uvajhyanam—I bow to the Upadhyaya.
Namo loye savva sahunam— I bow to all the Sadhus.

As is evident, this prayer is not towards any God, nor towards any creative principle, but towards the great spiritual achievers. Of these, arihants are the highest pure and noble souls (including the twenty-four Tirthankaras), and the other four are lower on the scale of spiritual evolution. They all help ordinary people move towards liberation.

In addition, a practising Jain is supposed to perform eleven annual obligations:

* Deva dravya: fundraising for temples
* Mahapuja: worship and recitation of sacred texts at a grand scale
* Ratri jagarana: singing religious hymns through the night
* Sadharmik bhakti: deep respect to fellow follower of Jainism
* Sangha puja: service to Sangha (the holy order of monks and nun)
* Shuddhi: confession of faults
* Snatra puja: a ritual related to the praise of the conception and the birth of the last Tirthankara
* Sutra puja: veneration of scriptures
* Tirth prabhavana: celebrating important occasions of Jain dharma
* Udyapana: displaying objects of worship and participant at end of religious activities
* Yatratrik: participation in religious festivals and pilgrimage.

There are also duties that should be performed at least once in one's lifetime which include building a temple and celebrating renunciation of a family member.

SECTS

It is generally believed that about 200 years after Mahavira's nirvana, the Jain Sangha (monastic organisation) was divided into Digambaras and Svetambaras. In Sanskrit, *ambar* refers to a covering like a garment and *dig* refers to the cardinal directions. So, Digambara means 'those whose garment is only the four directions' or 'sky-clad'. The ascetics of this sect go about without clothes. Sveta means white and Svetambaras are those who put on white coverings.

Some historians believe that there was no clear division between the two till the 5th century AD. Their differences are anyway quite minor. Digambara monks do not wear clothes because they believe clothes are like other possessions that increase dependence and desire. Svetambara monks wear white, seamless clothes for practical reasons and believe there is nothing in Jain scripture that condemns wearing clothes. However, *sadhvi*s (nuns) of both sects wear white. Digambara followers believe that women cannot attain moksha in the same birth, while Svetambaras believe that women may attain liberation and that Mallinath, a Tirthankar, was a female. Digambaras believe that Mahavira was not married, whereas Svetambaras believe that Mahavira was married and had a daughter. In the first Jain prayer, the Digambara believe that only the first five lines form the Namokara Mantra, whereas Svetambaras add four more lines to it.

As with every other religion, these sects too got divided into further sub-sects mainly based on topography and minor differences in rituals.

THE ANNUAL LIGHTING OF LAMP

Thirty years had passed since Mahavira began his ministration. Nature's eternal power of disintegrating every material thing finally came to take away the mortal frame of the great ascetic. Unlike an ordinary person, Mahavira knew in advance his time of departure from this world, and also knew that once he departs from here he would guide the humanity from a different plane of existence.

When the time to depart came, he was at Pavapuri, near Rajagriha, an important pilgrim centre in Bihar. By then nine out of the eleven gandharas had passed away. A day before his passing away, Lord Mahavir sent away his trusted gandhara, Gautam, thinking that he may be demonstrative about the master's passing away. Mahavira had always been a serious person, who did not like demonstrative emotions. According to Svetambara traditions, Lord Mahavira, the great teacher of humanity, gave up his mortal coil in 527 BCE.

Lord Mahavira was the light of his age and the eternal light for his followers. To mark the passing away of this light, the followers of Lord Mahavira started lighting lamps to symbolise this. Seen alternatively, it is the day that Lord Mahavira attained *mahanirvana* (final liberation). Over the period, this gesture gave rise to the ceremony of Deepavali, the festival of lights, to mark the master's passing away. Today, the light of Deepavali (Diwali), and the light of ethics lighted by the great Lord continues to burn brightly.

Sikhism
Religion of the Gurus

BEFORE THE STORY BEGINS

For almost two thousand years, after the passing away of Buddha and Mahavira, nothing much happened on the Indian spiritual stage. This led to a spiritual ennui. There was, of course, Acharya Shankara (c. 8th century CE), who wove the unwieldy spiritual and philosophical thoughts of the Hindu scriptures into a cohesive whole and established Vedanta as a prime moving force behind Hinduism. There were also Ramanuja (11th century CE) and Madhava (13th century CE), who adopted the methodology of Acharya Shankara and established their philosophies, which emphasised on the practice of devotion more than anything else.

Apart from being great saints, these three were great scholars as well. They used every branch (like grammar, logic, etc.) of the then-existing knowledge to establish their systems. The subtle nature of these works made it difficult for a common man to understand them completely. The scholars made things worse by indulging in wordplay and intellectual wrangling while explaining these texts, making it difficult for even the learned to make sense of what they said.

The other two religions, Buddhism and Jainism, had lost popular appeal after a few centuries of existence. By then, they were practised by a handful of people located all over the country. The absence of great spiritual ideals made the Indian mass adopt their own brand of religion, consisting of rituals, prayers, pilgrimage, and practices, which they learned from the, mostly, semi-literate local Brahmins. The spiritual vacuum created due to these factors left people wanting for something more.

In the meanwhile, by the beginning of the 8th century, Islam had started making inroads into the physical, cultural, and spiritual boundaries of India. By 11th CE it had penetrated deep with its twin forces of Sufi saints and royal power. This let loose a frightening trail of conversion, fear, and apprehension. India, accustomed to the sage-like behaviour of Buddha, Mahavira, and their followers, was suddenly facing persecution in the name of religion. The simple folks did not know how to react to this and how to protect themselves.

It was in those days of turmoil that a series of great saints—Kabir (c. 1440 CE), Guru Nanak (c. 1469), Surdas (c. 1478), Chaitanya Mahaprabhu (c. 1486), Mirabai (c. 1498), Tulasidas (c. 1497), Dadu Dayal (c. 1544) and many others—appeared on the Indian spiritual stage. It is in the nature of things that when the time is ripe for change, be that in whatever field, a large number of people are born to take that idea forward. Thus, a great many saints, mostly from the Bhakti school of religion, were born within a hundred years, after a parching spiritual drought for thousands of years. It was only after the advent of these greats that Indians could breathe more freely despite the presence of proselytising forces.

As discussed earlier, Hinduism accepts God as personal and also as impersonal. Of the followers of impersonal God, there are two types—the *jnana margi* (those who contemplate), and *bhakti margi* (those who practise devotion). Saints like Chaitanya, Tulsidas, Mirabai, and Surdas were devoted to the personal aspect of God, while Dadu and Kabir followed the jnana marg of the impersonal aspect of God.

Guru Nanak, the founder of the Sikh religion, belonged to the unique class of personalities who worshipped the impersonal like a personal God. Sikh dharma is unique because of this very trait. Guru Nanak in his enraptured state of devotion could reach a state where the sense of separateness and even the idea of being one with God melted away. What remained, remained.

It was difficult for a common man to achieve this state. Thus, worshipping the guru or the spiritual master was the best alternative. Since, the guru and God become one in divine communion, worshipping one was as good as worshipping the other. Sikhism grew around this idea of worshipping the guru as God.

This idea of *guru-shishy parampara* (tradition of teacher-disciple) has been very old in India. The conservatives believe that the divine spark and understanding can come to an aspirant only by the grace of a guru. There are many stories in the Upanishads and the Mahabharata that highlight this approach. Acharya Shankara was so emphatic about the importance of spiritual tradition handed down from the teacher to the disciple that he wrote, 'even if a person knows all the Vedas and other scriptures, he should be treated as a fool if he has not learned wisdom through an unbroken tradition of the enlightened'. The Sufis too believe in *silsila*, the tradition of gaining spiritual wisdom from the unbroken tradition starting with the Prophet. It was left for Sikh dharma to institutionalise the concept of guru worship—a tradition that began with Guru Nanak, who had attained the divine oneness with Wahe Guru, God.

EARLY LIFE OF GURU NANAK

Guru Nanak was born on 15 April 1469 in Talwandi, in a simple Hindu family. From an early age, Nanak made friends with both Hindu and Muslim children and was very inquisitive about the meaning of life. He learned both Sanskrit and Persian from competent teachers. Having come from a pious Hindu family of Bedis (one who knows the Vedas), he was well versed in the vedic tradition. His teachings in the later life clearly point to a rich cultural and spiritual inheritance of both the Hindus and the Muslims. It was this exposure to both the cultures that made Nanak establish this new religion that imbibed the good elements of both.

Nanak proved to be an unusually gifted child with an uncommon wisdom and piercing insights. When it was time for him to be invested with the sacred thread, as per traditional Hindu custom, he refused, and instead sang out:

> Let mercy be the cotton, contentment the thread, continence the knot, and truth the twist. O, Priest! If you have such a thread, do give it to me. It'll not wear out, nor get soiled, nor burnt, nor lost. Says Nanak, blessed are those who go about wearing such a thread.

This couplet reflects the budding spirituality, poetic talent, insight, and the mindset of the great master, who was to give a new kind of religion to the world. With this same indifferent attitude, he approached everything he considered worldly.

Thinking that marriage may help improve the situation, a suitable match was found for him, and at the age of sixteen, he was married to Sulakhni. She later gave birth to two of his sons. However, as time passed, Nanak grew more detached from his family and its affairs. He now focussed more on *naam, daan, isnaan,* and *gyan* (prayer, charity, ablution, and seeking after knowledge—now important rituals for Sikhs). There are many stories of how he gave up all he had to the sadhus and the poor.

His sister made arrangements for him to take up a job with the Muslim governor of Sultanpur, Daulat Khan Lodi. Guru Nanak was joined there by an old Muslim childhood friend Mardana, a gifted musician who served the Guru throughout his life. At Sultanpur, the Guru worked during the daytime and spent his mornings and evenings in meditation and in singing, accompanied by Mardana on the rabab (a string instrument).

REALISATION

Early one morning, when Nanak went to the river for his bath, after plunging into the river, he did not surface. It was feared that he must have drowned. The villagers searched everywhere, but there was no trace of him, and so everyone gave him up for dead.

Nanak, however, appeared after three days at the same spot from where he had gone missing (some say it was 40 days). But as one could see, he was no longer the same person who had earlier entered the river. Now there was a divine light in his eyes, and his face was shining with the light of spiritual wisdom. It was through this learning that the Guru uttered the praise of the Lord:

Ik aumkaar sat naam kartaa poorakh, nirbhau, nirvair,
Akaal moorat, ajoonee, saibham gur parsaad;
Jap aad sach jugaad sach hai bhee sach naanak hosee bhee sach

(There is but one God, His name is Aum, He is the creator, He fears none, He is without hate, He never dies, He is beyond the cycle of births and death, He is self-existent,

> He is realised by the kindness of the true guru. Recite:
> He was true in the beginning, He was true when the ages
> commenced and has ever been true, He is also true now)

This mantra is recorded at the beginning of the Sikh holy scriptures, the Guru Granth Sahib, and is the *mool mantra* (the chief chant) of the Sikhs, the way Gaytri mantra is for the Hindus.

Anyone familiar with the Upanishads will realise that this mantra praises God in the same way as the vedic sages have done. For example, the very first word, *ik* (one) and the third word, *sat* (existence) are common expressions for God in the Vedas. God is unknowable (*asat*) by the senses and the mind, which makes many conclude that He is non-existent. To counter this possible misconception, it is said that He is *sat*, although He is not existent the way an object is. Similarly, God cannot be said to be one, two, or many, for He is infinite, and there is no way to describe the infinite. This may again make people conclude, wrongly, that He is non-existent. To remove that confusion, it is said that He is one (ik). When taken literally, these two words convey the idea of monotheism as practised by most religions and as understood by most people.

Aum (second word in the mantra) is the most popular expression to denote God in the Upanishads, and in Hinduism. Later, this symbol was adopted by every Indic religion to denote God, both personal and impersonal, as explained in the section on Hinduism.

The other words, of the mantra above, represent the nature of God, as described in the Vedas. This brings out the stark similarity between Hinduism and Sikhism, although there are some minor differences.

After he had come out of the river, Nanak remained in a state of trance and said nothing. He also gave up his job and distributed all his belongings to the poor. When he finally broke his silence, he uttered, 'There is no Hindu, no Muslim'. This was to convey the idea that a spiritual person never sees the external, but always perceives the underlying unity of godhood behind everything. This idea was later repeated often in the sacred books as:

> Following the path of intuitive awareness, one turns away from the world, and one's vision is enlightened. *(Sri Guru Granth Sahib.1329)*

Daulat Khan, the governor of the province, was not convinced by the words of Nanak, so he asked what he meant by saying that there was no Muslim. To this, the Guru replied,

> Let God's grace be the mosque, and devotion the prayer mat. Let the Quran be the good conduct. Let modesty be compassion, good manners, fasting, you should be a Muslim the like of this. Let good deeds be your Kaaba and truth be your mentor. Your Kalma be your creed and prayer; God would then vindicate your honour.

As can be seen from this verse, Guru Nanak, now one with godhood, stripped away pretentious rituals from the core truth and encouraged his followers to stay on this path. It was this power, born of direct experience of the spiritual truth that gave him the authority to speak the way he spoke, and it was this that got him innumerable followers. It is this same power, resonating through the sacred books of the Sikhs, which make his name reverberate in the world.

SPREADING THE MESSAGE

Guru Nanak was thirty-six years old when he had his divine realisation. He spent two years in and around his former workplace before he took to the forests and solitude. After that, he started travelling. Mardana, his old companion, and Bhai Bala ji were with him all along. Bhai Bala ji is also credited with writing the life journey of Guru Nanak. During his extensive travels, Guru Nanak wore outlandish clothes, a combination of styles worn by Hindu and Muslim holy men, and was always asked whether he was a Hindu or a Muslim. He said he was a clown, amusing his master.

Although Guru Nanak knew Sanskrit very well, he used the local language, as did many other spiritual teachers of this period, to convey the spiritual message to the masses. Being a yogi, and in communion with God, he had miraculous powers, which he used judiciously to drive a point home. Added to that were his wit, sense of humour, and an exceptional gift for poetry. These qualities helped him drive his point more easily, even to the unwilling. A few incidents are mentioned here to give an idea of the Guru's personality as a teacher.

Once the Guru chose to stay in a small town with Lalo, a low-caste carpenter. This annoyed Malik Bhago, the local chief, who wanted the Guru as his guest. When asked to explain, the Guru sent for the meal served by Malik Bhago and also some of the simple meal served by Lalo. Holding these in two hands he squeezed them. Blood spurted out of the rich food of Malik Bhago, while milk streamed out of Lalo's simple bread. Malik Bhago was put to shame, and he realised that his riches had been amassed by exploiting the poor, while what Lalo offered was the milk of honest work.

When Guru Nanak visited Hardwar, he saw a large gathering of devotees taking ritual baths in Ganga and offering water to the sun. The Guru asked, 'Why do you throw water like that?' The pilgrims replied that they were offering it to their ancestors. Hearing that, Guru Nanak started throwing water in the opposite direction. When the pilgrims asked him the reason for doing so, he replied 'I am sending water to my farm, which is dry.' The pilgrims realised their folly and fell at the Guru's feet. There are innumerable such incidents recorded in Guru Nanak's life.

After twelve long years, Guru Nanak returned home. His second journey took him as far south as Sri Lanka. When he took up his journey to the West, he dressed in the blue garb of a Muslim pilgrim and visited Mecca, Medina, and Baghdad. One night, arriving at Mecca, Guru Nanak fell asleep with his feet pointing towards the Holy Kaaba. When the watchman on his night rounds noticed this, he kicked the Guru, saying, 'How dare you turn your feet towards the house of God'. At this Guru Nanak woke up and said, 'Kindly turn my feet in the direction where God is not.'

On his return journey home, he faced the invasion of the first Mughal Emperor Babar. Unfortunately, he and Mardana were both taken prisoner by the Mughals. While in jail, Guru Nanak sang a divine hymn about the senseless slaughter of the innocents by the Mughal invaders. The jailer reported this to the king. Babar sent for the Guru, and upon hearing him realised that Guru Nanak was a great saint. Babar asked for the Guru's forgiveness and set him free, offering him a pouch of hashish. Guru Nanak refused it saying he was already intoxicated with the love and name of God.

After having spent a lifetime of travelling abroad and setting up missions, an aged Guru Nanak returned home to Punjab and settled down at Kartarpur with his wife and sons. Pilgrims came from far and near to hear the hymns and preaching of the Master.

Guru Nanak believed in a casteless society that had no distinction based on birth, religion, or sex. It was due to this that he institutionalised the common kitchen called *langar*, where all could sit together and share a common meal.

While working the fields, one day in 1532, Guru Nanak was approached by a new devotee. He said, 'I am Lehna,' Guru Nanak looked at him and replied, 'So you have arrived Lehna—the creditor. I have been waiting for you all these days. I must pay your debt.' *Lehna* in Punjabi means debt or creditor. Lehna became an ardent disciple of the Guru, and his devotion to the Guru was absolute.

Once, while accompanied by Lehna and his two sons, Guru Nanak came across what looked like a corpse covered with a sheet. The Guru asked his companions, 'Who would eat it?' His sons refused to eat the corpse, but Lehna agreed. As he removed the cover, he found that it was a tray of sacred food. Guru Nanak said:

> Lehna, you were blessed with the sacred food because you could share it with others. If the people use the wealth bestowed on them by God for themselves alone or for treasuring it, it is like a corpse. But if they decide to share it with others, it becomes sacred food. You have known the secret. You are my image.

Guru Nanak then blessed Lehna with his *ang* (hand) and gave him a new name, Angad. 'You are a part of my body,' he said and placed five coins and a coconut in front him and bowed before him. He had Angad anointed with a saffron mark on his forehead. When Guru Nanak gathered his followers together for prayers, he invited Angad to occupy the seat of the Guru. It was thus that Guru Angad was ordained the successor to Guru Nanak.

When the end of Guru Nanak came, his Hindu and Muslim devotees started quarrelling over the last rites, but when the sheet covering his dead body was removed, it was seen that there was only a heap of flowers left behind! His devotees could now share it equally and do what they considered fit.

It was this unalloyed oneness in the heart of Guru Nanak for the Hindus and Muslims that he is praised in the couplet:

Baba Nanak Shah Fakeer/ Hindu ka guru, Mussalman ka peer
(Guru Nanak, the royal mendicant; guru for the Hindus, and a peer (saint) for the Muslims)

THE TEN GURUS

From the day Guru Nanak anointed Angad as his successor, the tradition of gurus started in Sikh religion and continued till the tenth guru. The ten gurus are Nanak, Angad Dev, Amar Das, Ram Das, Arjan Dev, Har Gobind, Har Rai, Har Krishan, Teg Bahadur, and Gobind Singh. Since every follower of this religion is like a disciple (*sishya*), the name Sikh (from *sishya* or *siksha*) became its popular name.

The contribution of each of the ten gurus was immense in the spread and consolidation of the religion. Guru Angad invented Gurumukhi, the sacred alphabet of the Sikhs; Amar Das instituted the langar to get rid of the caste system; Ramdas (son-in-law of Amar Das) founded Ramdaspur, which later came to be known as Amritsar; Arjan Dev (youngest son of Ram Das) compiled the

Adi Granth. It was during this period that Sikhs started acquiring wealth and power, so much so that Jahangir, the Emperor of Delhi, grew envious of him and started harassing the Sikhs.

Har Govind (the only son of Arjan Dev), the sixth guru, had the first Sikh stronghold constructed for the protection of the Sikhs and the Hindus.

From the time of Har Rai (grandson of Guru Har Govind), the seventh guru, the Sikh history becomes quite painful to read, in which one sees Aurangzeb letting loose his forces to snuff out Sikhism. Har Kishan (the second son of Har Rai) became the guru when he was only five years old and died of smallpox at the age of eight when summoned to Delhi by the Moghuls.

Guru Teg Bahadur was the youngest son of the sixth guru, Har Govind. His name meant 'the mighty sword', and his valour in the battlefields against the Moghuls indeed brought honour to his name. When he was finally arrested by the forces of Aurangzeb, he was brought to Delhi and was asked to accept Islam. On his refusal to do so, he was beheaded publicly. His courage and firmness got him the name 'Hind Di Chadar'—the Shield of India—to refer to his great sacrifice in protecting the Hindus.

Guru Gobind Singh (son of Guru Teg Bahadur) was the tenth and the last Guru of the Sikhs. Born near Patna, he lost his parents early due to Aurangzeb's cruelty in enforcing Islam in India, and he was anointed guru at the age of nine. During his time, Guru Gobind Singh founded the Khalsa, the powerful Sikh community to fight the intolerant Moghuls. He also introduced the concept of taking *amrita* (sacred water in which a two-forked knife is immersed) and to always put on the five K: *kaccha* (tight underwear for fighting), *kripan* (knife), *kesha* (long hair, the mark of the holy), *kada* (steel bangle), and *kangha* (comb to keep hair in shape).

After Guru Nanak, Guru Gobind Singh is the most famous and popular guru who gave a defining culture to the Sikhs and made Sri Guru Granth Sahib the all-time guru for the future generations. There were not to be any more human gurus after him. A great religious leader and a great military commander, his inspiring life and spiritual compositions, exhorting his men to have strength, gave Sikhs a clear roadmap for leading an exalted life.

SACRED TEXT

Sri Guru Granth Sahib ji, also known as Adi Granth is the most sacred book of the Sikhs. It was first compiled by the fifth Sikh guru, Guru Arjan Dev (1563–1606), from hymns of the first five Sikh gurus and other great saints, including those of the Hindu and Muslim faith like Kabir, Namdev, Saina, Pipa, Shekh Farid, Trilochan, and others. This gives Sri Guru Granth Saheb a universal outlook, not confined only to its gurus.

Guru Gobind Singh, the tenth guru, had proclaimed the sacred text Adi Granth as his successor, and thus stopped the line of human gurus forever. Since then the text has continued to be the holiest scripture of the Sikhs and is revered as the living embodiment of the Ten Gurus. So much so, the damaged copies of the sacred text are cremated with a similar ceremony as cremating a holy person.

Adi Granth contains 1430 *ang*s (pages), compiled and composed during the period of Sikh gurus. It is a collection of hymns or *shabad*, which describe the qualities of God and the reason why one should meditate on God's name. Its hymns and teachings are called Gurbani (word of the Guru).

The historical writings, unauthentic writings, or apocryphal compositions in name of Sikh gurus and other writings by Sikhs are not considered as Gurbani and are referred to as *kachhi bani* (secondary teachings). Some select verses from Adi Granth have been compiled in *Nitnem* (book of daily prayer) which is used for the daily recital by the devotees.

The recital of *Japji* every morning after a bath is an important daily ritual for every practising Sikh. This small prayer book consisting of thirty-eight hymns of prayers, including the mool mantra, is the essence of the whole Guru Granth Sahib and contains the basic teachings of Guru Nanak. This book is a treasure of spiritual wisdom and is written in the sutra or mantra form. Its theme covers a suggested course of training for an ordinary man that would enable him to attain spiritual perfection. It favours man's participation in the affairs of the world, combined with an integration of wisdom and selfless activity.

Japji begins with the statement on the nature of God and concludes with the statement that the knowledge of God is obtained only through the grace of the guru. In between, it describes the basic concepts of Sikhism.

The essence of these works can be summed up as:

- Bhakti or *simran* (devotional prayer) is considered the best way to God-realisation.
- *Hukam*, the Divine Will, explains the need to surrender oneself to the Lord's will. A complete self-surrender leads a person to receive His grace.

The creation is explained as the result of God's command or word. No one knows the expanse of the Lord's creation. There are millions of lower and upper worlds. The infinity of the creation and manifestation is beyond count or measure. There is the description of five stages of spiritual progress by which one can attain the eternal:

* Realm of Duty (Dharam khand)—The world is regarded as an inn, where man has a temporary stay. As the world is only one stage in man's spiritual journey, he should react to it dispassionately. Human birth provides the opportunity to fulfil one's social, moral and spiritual duties. The world is governed by the law of karma, where every action produces an equal reaction or consequence.

* Realm of Knowledge (Gyan khand)—God has not only created the world in which one lives but has also created numerous other solar systems and beings. Apart from a basic knowledge of the arts and sciences of this world, there is also the higher spiritual knowledge, para vidya, which is obtained through reflection and intuition.

* Realm of Effort (Saram khand)—After gaining knowledge of the second stage, the seeker becomes inspired to take further steps to make the life richer and nobler. This stage requires sustained endeavour on the part of all seekers to probe within themselves, to cast away their egocentricity and replace it with God-consciousness.

* Realm of Grace (Karam khand)—Man's spiritual efforts without God's grace cannot come to fruition. He is always a seeker and a devotee whose hope is to receive the grace of the Lord. It is only then that one becomes a true devotee.

* Realm of Truth (Saach khand)—It is the state when one finds God everywhere, and where the seeker and God are linked.

> In the Realm of Truth, abides the formless one.
> He watches over all he has created with bounteous eyes!
> (*Japji.37*)

WORLD VIEW

Unlike Buddhism and Jainism, Sikhism did not work out a systematic philosophy to differentiate itself from Hinduism or any other system of thought. Sikhism is a way of life, in which speculations and conclusions concerning creation, soul, God, epistemology, and other trappings of philosophy are discarded altogether. There is a mention of all this in the sacred books, but they are reflections of a heart full of spiritual light, instead of intellectual corollaries.

> The cosmos sprang from a single act of *hukam* (command of God) generating innumerable currents of creation. From the union of the mother's egg and the father's sperm, the form of infinite beauty has been created. The blessings of light all come from You; You are the Creator Lord, pervading everywhere.

The main tenets of Sikh philosophy have come from the realisation and the words of Guru Nanak, who was influenced by the traditional Hinduism, the orthodox Islam, the Bhakti movement of the Hindus, Sufism, and by the works of Kabir, the great poet-saint who preceded him by some years. The spiritual and the philosophical outlook of Kabir and Nanak are quite similar, but while Kabir left only a spiritual sect behind him, Guru Nanak's path came to be accepted as a religion. The general outlook of

Sikh religion and philosophy come from the Hindu scriptures, but because they emphasise certain aspects more than others, a situation of difference and non-difference with Hinduism is created. Most importantly, Sikhism accepts the Vedas as a sacred scripture, but it does not see it as the ultimate authority in any matter.

> O, Human Being, search your own heart every day and do not wander around in confusion. This world is just a magic show; no one will be holding your hand. The Vedas and the scriptures are only make-believe, O, Siblings of Destiny, they do not relieve the anxiety of the heart. If you will only centre yourself on the Lord, even for just a breath, then you shall see the Lord face to face, present before you. *(Sri Guru Granth Sahib.727)*

To consider the Vedas as 'make-believe' is a major departure from the orthodox Hindu thinking. Although one finds such mention in Hindu spiritual works, it is there to take one beyond the realm of words to the realm of realisation. Sikhism is thus fundamentally different from the Hindus on this point. Also, Sikhism does not pay importance to the caste system, as Hindus do.

On the other hand, the major thrust of Sikh followers has been to protect the hapless Hindus, and they respect the divinities like Rama, Krishna, and others in the same way as the Hindus do.

In matters of the soul, Guru Nanak has the same approach as Hindu religion, according to which it is neither born nor does it die:

> Who has died? O, who has died? Says Nanak. The Guru has revealed God to me, and now I see that there is no such thing as birth or death…No one dies; no one comes or goes.

This outlook towards the true nature of a man is absolutely same as the nature of atman, the true individuality of a person, as described in the Upanishads and Gita. This is popularly known as Advaita, according to which man is eternally free, but he considers himself in bondage. The goal for everyone is to come out of this bondage and be free. This is mukti.

However, the thrust in Sikhism is not on mukti or to go to heaven, but to bring out the divine that is within everyone. This can be best done by having faith in His name, worshipping His name, and repeating His name:

> By thinking, He cannot be reduced to thought, even by thinking hundreds of thousands of times. By remaining silent, inner silence is not obtained; even by remaining lovingly absorbed deep within. The hunger of the hungry is not appeased, even by piling up loads of worldly goods. Hundreds of thousands of clever tricks, but not even one of them will go along with you in the end. So how can you become truthful? And how can the veil of illusion be torn away? O, Nanak, it is written that you shall obey the hukam of His command, and walk in the way of His will.
> *(Sri Guru Granth Sahib.1)*

God, according to Sikhism, is both *nirguna* (absolute, without attributes) and *saguna* (personal, with qualities), although the stress is more on the formless aspect. Before the creation, God alone existed in His glory, but when he thought of making Himself manifest, He entered into the realm of the relative. It is in this aspect that He became His name, and in order to realise Himself, He made nature, in which He has His seat, and from where He diffuses Himself in the form of love. Aum is the name of God.

In each and every heart, the Lord, the Lord of the forest, is permeating and pervading. In the water, on the land, and in the sky, He is pervading but hidden; through the Word of the Guru's Shabad, He is revealed. In this world, in the nether regions of the underworld, and in the Ethers, the Guru, the true Guru, has shown me the Lord; He has showered me with His Mercy. He is the unborn Lord God; He is, and shall ever be. Deep within your heart, behold Him, the destroyer of ego.
(Gurbani Sorath Mehalaa.2)

God is not an abstract idea or a moral force but a personal being who should be loved, and yet, His presence is everywhere in the creation. In this way He is not like a mechanic, designing something new from some pre-existent material. He does not exclude matter but includes and also transcends it. He is the father of all, who fashions the world and supports it from inside (not from outside, as the dualists believe). He is unborn, and He Himself stands for the creative agencies like maya, the word, and Brahma. He is truth, beauty, and eternal yearning of the heart after goodness (*satyam, shivam, sunadaram*).

The ultimate source of all that is, is God alone. Even an evil person cannot act independently without Him. Like a fish that can run with or against the current of the river but not outside it, one can do good or bad things but can never escape His will.

Guru Nanak did not stress on Trinity of Hindu Gods (Brahma, Vishnu, Shiva), nor did he believe that God can incarnate as a human or any other being. This is an important departure from the traditional dualistic Hindu view. Interestingly, the advaitins of Hinduism also have the same beliefs, only that they do not accept the reality of the creation too. Guru Nanak is midway between the advaitins and dualists in this regard; He accepts the supreme reality of the advaitins, and also the reality of the world as taught by the dualists.

Advaita does not accept the idea of incarnation, nor does Islam accept it. So initially Guru Nanak was worshipped as the Guru of gurus, as in the Yoga philosophy. But with time, he came to be worshipped as God by the devout.

Sikhism treats the universe and the creation as real since it is rooted in God. However, this reality is not final and permanent but is more like a resting place than a permanent home.

> Even the gods long for this human body, so make use of this human body and think of serving the Lord. *(SGGS.1159)*

> Says Nanak, it is like a wall of sand; it shall not endure. Raam Chand passed away, as did Ravana, even though he had lots of relatives. Says Nanak, nothing lasts forever; the world is like a dream. *(SGGS.1429)*

> We are human beings of the briefest moment; we do not know the appointed time of our departure. Pray Nanak, serve the One, to whom our soul and breath of life belong. *(SGGS. 660)*

Sikhism lays stress on God-realisation as the goal of life. This can be achieved through only one path—devotion. There are not many paths to realisation, but only one, and that is to sing His praise and to meditate on His name. The path to bhakti is not through idle mysticism, but through intense activity, while living in the world. So, the householder's life is the primary focus of religious activity. The Guru's system involved morning and evening prayers for the devotees, and also occasional gatherings for them.

The infinite is within everyone like the covered light. It is ignorance and selfishness that covers it and creates the sense of ego. Sin is born of one's identification with this false self. The spiritual journey begins when there is the call of grace. It is then that one comes out of one's sense of will, and surrender to the will of God.

> You, God, are the giver of gifts, the Lord of perfect understanding; I am a mere beggar at your door. What should I beg for? Nothing remains permanent; O Lord, please, bless me with your beloved name.
> *(Gurbani Sorath Mehalaa.1)*

This call of grace or the power to fight evil cannot come into a person's heart of its own; there is a need for an external support, a need for an external agent from where can come the external thrust. This force is the guru. Without the guru, there is no way that a person can escape from his narrow existence. As mentioned, the place of the guru is now permanently taken by Sri Guru Granth Sahib.

Sikhism accepts the law of karma, rebirth, and samsara. However, the way out of samsara is not through renunciation or by any other means, but by the grace of God, which can be attained through a virtuous life and the practise of humility.

In general, there is not much difference in the philosophy and the world view between Sikhism and Hinduism, only the emphasis on certain aspects is different.

RITUALS AND PRACTICES

A lot of importance is attached to one's character for one's spiritual well-being. Virtues should be practised to such extent that character may become a habit since the source of evil is not external but one's own mind. The individual ego, placed by God within all, separates a man from God. The goal is to get rid of this false 'I' ness through a complete surrender at the feet of God by practising the words (*seekh*) of the sacred book.

Some quotes from the great sacred book, Sri Guru Granth Sahib gives an idea of how to achieve the state of blessedness:

I have totally forgotten my jealousy of others since I found the Saadh Sangat, the Company of the Holy. No one is my enemy, and no one is a stranger. I get along with everyone. Whatever God does, I accept that as good. This is the sublime wisdom I have obtained from the Holy. The one God is pervading in all. Gazing upon Him, beholding Him, Nanak blossoms forth in happiness. *(p.1299)*

Do not blame anyone else; blame instead your actions. *(p.433)*

When selfish and conceit are eradicated from within, then there is no attachment to Maya. *(p.121)*

The body within which love of the Lord does not well up—look upon that body as a cremation ground. *(p.1379)*

Fruitful are the lives of those who, have conquered their minds—they have won the game of life. *(p.78)*

Where there is spiritual wisdom, there is righteousness and dharma. Where there is falsehood, there is sin. Where there is greed, there is death. Where there is forgiveness, there is God Himself. *(p.1372)*

To attain this state of purity one needs to practice certain rituals rigorously. These are:

* Naam japana: Guru Nanak himself led his followers to practise *simran* and *naam japa* (prayer and contemplation). As mentioned earlier, surrender to God being the most important spiritual outlook, it is imperative that every practising Sikh follows this rigorously.

* Kirat Karni: To earn honestly by one's efforts while accepting pain and pleasure as God's blessings. The world is God's creation, and so there is no need for *sannyasa* (monasticism) in Sikhism. Of all the Indic religions and sects, Sikhism alone does not approve of sannyasa.

* Vand Chakna: From the time of Guru Nanak, it had become customary to share and consume together within the community what the Sikhs earned. Later, this gave birth to community kitchens, langar, where everyone ate together. This also resulted in the abolition of the caste system or, rather, the abolition of the privileges and limitations associated with various castes.

These practices gave birth to the concept of community life and community service in Sikhism as the most potent force. It is usual to see people from all walks of life serving at gurudwaras, the place of worship of the Sikhs. The idea of religious community as a family, living peacefully with others, is the most distinctive characteristics of the Sikhs.

THE STORY CONTINUES

Guru Nanak infused a new vision in the socio-religious life of his people by founding a religion that had the softness of the Hindus, and the strength of the Muslims without its aggressiveness. It combined the spiritual elements of the Hindus with the practicality of the Muslims and transcends both of them in the equality of treatment of all.

The equality factor and emphasis on a community life, as far as practicable, became the stronghold of Sikhism. A total commitment towards the gurus, along with the sense of surrender to the will of God, made Sikh followers an extremely brave race that could look in the face of death calmly, without being brutal. And that, in fact, is the ultimate test of religiosity.

Zoroastrianism
Religion of Goodness

BEFORE THE BEGINNING

Zoroastrianism is the religion preached and propagated by Zoroaster, i.e. Zarathushtra, the great Prophet of Persia (Iran), centuries before Jesus and millennia before the advent of Islam —the religion that eventually wiped away Zoroastrianism from its own land. At present, only a handful Parsis in India, and fewer still in Iran, are left to hold high the banner of this great religion, which is like a cousin of Hinduism, and which has influenced the ideals, theology, philosophy, outlook, and practices of Judaism, Christianity, and Islam deeply. Hinduism and Zoroastrianism are thus the two parents (or foster parents) of every living religion of the world. But while Hinduism could weather external assaults, and also absorb the minor religions that it encountered, Zoroastrianism was not that so resilient. That, of course, does not tarnish its exalted stature in the world of religion, nor does that diminish its contribution to religious thoughts of the world.

Even before the advent of Zarathushtra, Iran had a religion that was similar to that of the early Hindus (i.e. vedic religion). The names of their gods, evil forces, rituals, hymns, priest craft, practices, language, etc., bear testimony to this fact. Even the name that they give to their race, Aryan (noble), is same. The sketchy tradition suggests that these two, Hindus and Parsis, had a common existence at a place called Airyana Vaeja (the cradle land of the Aryans) during the long forgotten historical past. Earlier, it was thought that this place was somewhere in Central Asia, but it is now guessed that it could be somewhere in Punjab or Kashmir. Wherever that place might be, the fact remains that these two races have a common ancestry.

The Vedas talk about *deva*s (lit. the shining ones, gods) and *asura*s (lit. those with intelligence), born of the same father, Sage Kashyap, but of different mothers, who were sisters. These two clans of divine beings (or tribes) were at continuous war with each other, in which the asuras usually won. Indra, the leader of gods, often got beaten by the asuras, which would make him get into stratagems to win back his privileges.

The followers of the Vedas worship Indra and his tribe of gods and treat asuras as evil. The Zoroastrians do the reverse. To them, the asuras (*ahura*s) are godly, while devas are devilish. And yet both these religions have similar rituals like worshipping the fire and making offerings of the Soma juice.

There is a possibility that in the remote past some kind of differences cropped up between two closely related tribes, prompting one to move away from their original home. This kind of clannish war has been usual in India, of which the war of Mahabharata, fought between two cousins, is most famous.

ZARATHUSHTRA—
THE PROPHET OF GOOD DEEDS

Before the advent of Zarathushtra, the religious tradition of Iran dwelled on practices like exposing the dead, fighting evil forces through magic and charms, interpreting dreams, offering prayers to deities of nature to propitiate them, etc. These were carried out by the local wise persons known as Magi, made famous in the Christian traditions because of the gift that they brought for the newborn Jesus. These people were worshippers of Mazda, meaning wisdom. At some point of time, the supremacy of this tradition was challenged by the Daeva-yasni creed, which probably means 'performers of *yajna* (sacrifices) to *daeva*s (Sansk. *deva*)'— a practice that was common with vedic people. But like any other non-spiritual religious tradition, these daevas were more like godlings, presiding over natural objects and, at times, were the masters of evil qualities. The fact that vedic gods were worshipped in West Asia, is also corroborated by a treaty concluded about 1380 BCE between the Hittite emperor and the king of Mitanni (north of Egypt).

Zarathushtra changed all that. He stopped his people from worshipping daevas and instead persuaded them to worship Ahura Mazda. Ahura was the asura of vedic people, and Mazda (wisdom) was the local God. The term means 'the Light/God of wisdom'.

This legend has faint echoes in the Itihasa–Purana traditions of the Hindus. Mahabharata mentions how Kach, son of Brihaspati, the spiritual teacher of deva clan went to learn the secret of immortality from Shukracharya, the teacher of asuras. Although this story makes asuras appear superior to vedic gods, the Hindu tradition differs on who got the secret of immortality or the supreme knowledge of God, first. The Upanishads narrate how Indra, the King of gods attained it through *tapasya* (austerities) and contemplation, while the story of Kach hints differently.

In another story, Vrishparva, the asura king of that period had to give away his daughter Sharmistha as a slave girl to Devyani, his teacher, Shukracharya's daughter. Later both of them got married to Yayati, who was a descendant of the deva clan. Much later, Sri Krishna was born in that particular lineage. There is also the famous story of Prahlad, who although born in asura clan, was a great devotee of Vishnu. Prahalad's father tried everything to stop him from worshipping someone who belonged to the rival camp, but in the process, he himself got killed. These unverifiable stories hint at how great spiritual personalities belonged to both lineages, and how they vied for supremacy despite the matrimonial alliances. In later literature, such exchanges fade away, probably due to the non-proximity of the two clans.

The idea that there was a spiritually enlightened person in one's clan fills a person, and also a society, with the conviction and hope that there would be divine intervention during its days of despair and hopelessness. The spiritual leader born during such a period is often called the Saviour, Prophet, Buddha, or Avatar. Zoroastrians call it Saoshyant (lit. one who will bring benefit) and accept Zarathushtra as one. They also believe that future Saoshyants would come from the Prophet's own seed, miraculously preserved in the depths of a lake, in which a virgin will come to take a bath and be the mother of Zarathushtra's three children at the interval of a thousand years each. However, this belief is not shared by all.

This great prophet of the Parsis was born Zarathushtra Spitama anytime between 6000 BCE and 600 BCE, depending on whether one takes side with Indian traditions or Christians traditions, who lay claim to its genesis. Spitama was Zarathushtra's family name, and his own name probably meant 'possessor of old or yellow coloured camels'. Of course, such meanings have no bearing on the nature or personality of a person, particularly in Indo-Iranian traditions.

As with every spiritual master, myths have built around Zarathushtra that may or may not be true. It is said that even while in his mother's womb he glowed with lustre, and this increased to brilliance as the time of his birth neared. At the time of his birth, instead of crying, he smiled and, in turn, nature sighed with satisfaction, 'In whose birth and in whose growth/Rejoiced waters and plants'.

Since his early days, Zarathushtra was filled with a sense of the imminent end of the world, which made him more and more withdrawn in the worship and love of his creator. He longed to see Him, to converse with Him, to reach, and to serve Him by establishing goodness on this earth. At the age of fifteen, he withdrew from the world and spent several years in seclusion, lost in divine contemplation on the nature of God, universe, and moral order.

At last, when the longing to see Ahura Mazda and the thirst for the vision divine consumed every other desire, Vohu Manah, the embodiment of the good mind, appeared unto him in a vision and led him into the presence of the Lord. The fulfilment of this prayer is recorded as,

And I recognised Thee as the Beneficent, O Wise Lord, when I saw Thee first at the creation of Life, that Thou will make the deeds and words to be recompensed evil for the evil and good for the good through Thy generosity at the last turning point of the Creation.

Ahura Mazda revealed to Zarathushtra that He had an opponent, Ahirman, the spirit and promoter of evil. He then gave Zarathushtra the responsibility of inviting all human beings to choose between Him (good) and Ahirman (evil). It was the call of God that filled Zarathushtra with the urge to persuade his fellow beings to be good and bring goodness to this beautiful earth.

The wisdom of Zarathushtra unnerved the evil spirit Ahirman, who approached him saying,

> Do not destroy my creatures, O holy Zarathushtra! Renounce the good religion of the worship of Mazda and thou shall gain such a boon as was gained by the son of Vadhaghna (Zohak), who eventually became the ruler of nations.

As mentioned in earlier sections, this kind of temptation comes during the spiritual journey of every spiritual aspirant, great or ordinary. The prophet rejected the offer.

Zarathushtra was now the master of the spiritual wisdom with which he could bring light to his people. Yet, for the next ten years, no one cared to listen to his words. Instead, he was denounced as a heretic and a sorcerer, which made him wander from place to place before he could make his cousin, Maidhyomah, the first convert to his faith. He then travelled eastwards and went to Bactria (near modern Afghanistan), where the King Vishtaspa became impressed with his message and got converted. This made his work easy, and his message spread rapidly throughout Iran.

The success of Zarathushtra got him powerful enemies too. The chiefs and priests entrenched in the old tradition, felt threatened by the new gospel. They started spreading rumours that the Prophet was a sorcerer and had him imprisoned. He had to stay there for a time, and after his release, he continued to spread his message of goodness for around fifty years.

SACRED TEXTS

The sacred books of the Parsis are Avesta, sometimes also called Zend Avesta, which is a misnomer. Zend or Zand means 'interpretation' and refers to a much later Middle Persian (Pazend and Pahlavi) commentaries on the Avestan books. These commentaries are not sacred like the main text, Avesta, but the name has stuck because of the misunderstanding caused by Western scholars.

In the Avesta, Zarathushtra's teachings are recorded in the hymns called *gatha*, which form the oldest part of these scriptures. According to tradition, Ahura Mazda created twenty-one *masks* (books) which the Prophet brought to his king-disciple, Vishtaspa. These hymns were in the old Avestan language, which only had an oral tradition. So, by the time these were compiled and written down many centuries later, its major portions were already lost. The little that remained was due to the priests, who all knew the prayer portions used during worship. The modern Avesta contains only those parts of the text that are used during worship and is more of a prayer book than a complete scripture.

The portion that contains gatha and also some more sacred texts are collectively called Yasna, which has seventy-two sections. This section is recited by the priests during the ceremony of the same name, *yasna* (Sansk. *yajna*, sacrifice).

Next in importance is *Khurda Avesta*, which is the book of community prayers. It contains the most famous mantra of the Parsis, which translated into English reads,

> The will of the Lord is the law of righteousness/The gifts of Vohu Manah to the deeds done in this world for Mazda/He who relieves the poor makes Ahura king.

Videvdat or *Vendidad* contains myths, prayers, and religious observances, meant to defend against sources of infection and evil. It also discusses ways of disposal of corpses and other dead matter (*nasu*) to avoid polluting the earth, water, etc.

The Siroza enumerates the deities presiding over the thirty days of the month. The *yasht*s (hymns) are each addressed to various deities such as Mithra, Anahita, or Verethraghna (Indra, the vedic God). The *Hadhokt Nask* (section containing sayings) describes the fate of the soul after death.

Other than these, there are translations, commentaries, and other related books on the Avesta. *Bundahishn* (primal creation), discusses cosmology, *Menok-i Khrat* (Spirit of Wisdom) is a summary of a doctrine based on reason, and *Book of Artay Viraf* describes Viraf's descent into the netherworld as well as heaven and hell, and the pleasures and pains awaiting the virtuous and the wicked.

The striking feature of these scriptures is the sweetness, instead of sternness typical of many other religions, with which they implore people to take the right path of goodness. It is like the persuasion by a mother to his child to be good and not to be naughty.

GOD

God—the Almighty, eternal heavenly Father—is greeted in gatha with the words:

Ahura Mazda, by Thy spirit, which is ever the same!

The Prophet used these words and the inherent message to get rid of all the false gods that had entered his land and establish the supremacy of one God. The natural corollary to the belief in one supreme God was the repudiation of the army of false gods (in this case, the daevas) that had invaded the old faith. The dominating feature of the creed was, therefore, a strong attack against these gods, which meant a complete break with the earlier traditions, including the animal sacrifices to daeva. The twelfth Ha of the yasna prays,

> I curse the daevas. I declare myself a Mazda worshipper, a supporter of Zarathushtra, hostile to the daevas, fond of Ahura's teaching...I pledge myself to the well-thought thought, I pledge myself to the well-spoken word, I pledge myself to the well-done action.

It is interesting to note that the Hindu sages realised Vishnu, a 'daeva', as the supreme God, while Zarathushtra realised His antithesis, 'Ahura' as the same God, the Lord. On the face of it this sounds strange, but in fact, it is not so. As discussed in the first chapter, a spiritual aspirant perceives the supreme reality as God only through the intervening medium of his own mind, which is coloured by the choice of his ideal, whom he loves and adores. This form can be anything—Jehovah, Allah, Vishnu, Kali, Ahura Mazda—simply anything. God is not like a person limited by a particular form. Hence, search for God is not like the search for a person, who will appear only in a fixed form. So, whatever may be the form or name of God these prophets preached, they are all non-contradictory.

One wonders why is then so much of bloodbath, intolerance, and zeal to be acknowledged as 'the best'. Surprisingly, this idea of intolerance begins with Zoroastrianism only. Their first cousin, the Hindus, had a strong tradition of sages, who realised the fact that God is a mere mask of the infinite, and that both the personal and the impersonal aspects of God are true. This made them learn the art of acceptance, and not mere tolerance, of every religion and religious idea. They could thus accept and absorb every idea, great or small, by giving them proper place and respect. But Zoroastrianism, and consequently every other West Asian religion, failed to incorporate this idea of religious freedom and acceptance in its system. Freedom blooms only where there is a cross-current of ideas related to an ideal. For example, democracy and science flourished in Europe due to the checks and balances by many great minds dedicated to these fields of knowledge. So, a lack of powerful minds in any religion is bound to make it dogmatic. Zoroastrianism, however, was never an aggressive religion.

The rejection of false gods is common to every religion excepting Hinduism. A great sage or a prophet realises the true nature of God as all-powerful, merciful, non-material, adorable existence. The gods, on the other hand, represent a finite dimension of worldly existence. In many cases, such gods also personify evil, demanding worship and sacrifices, without which they would let loose their vengeance in the form of death, disease, and destruction. A prophet, compassionate that he is towards his people, knows better, and so persuades them, sometimes sternly, to come out of their narrow existence. Hinduism treats this differently. It keeps the persona of these gods but modifies the ideas that they represent. Throughout India, one comes across local deities, metamorphosed as personifications of the Divine, instead of being a mere force of nature.

God in Zoroastrianism is the living-active-existence, the eternal being, who can be perceived only in the depths of meditation, but whose governance of the universe is apparent to all. He should be served and adored all the time; He is the creator from whom everything comes into life and existence. Brighter than the brightest of creation, older than the oldest in the universe, better than the best, first and foremost, He sits at the apex among the divine in the highest heaven. Time and Space cannot limit Him. Hence, He is unchanging and perfect. The mover of everything but moved by none, He has destined the benefits of His kingdom for all who led a life of truth and goodness. It is He who decides victory between the rival hosts of good and evil, and everything comes from Him and through Him—the Lord of all.

God has unparalleled qualities that He Himself enumerates in the form of His names:

> God (Ahura Mazda) replied unto him (Zarathushtra): My first name is, 'I am,' Oh holy Zarathushtra. My second name is the Giver of Herds. My third name is the Strong One …

God then continues with the list of His names, as Holiness, Possessor of understanding and knowledge, Repository of blessing, Most beneficent, A harmless, loving being, Unconquerable, All-seeing, healing, creator, etc., and finally, the twentieth name, Mazda, the omniscient one.

He is thus the great noble Lord, who presides over all that is good. This is a dualistic approach in which one sees only the good but does not go to the level of abstraction that is beyond good and bad.

WORLD VIEW

It is difficult, if not impossible, to know God without attributes and qualities. One may talk of the formless God, but the very act of praying by the devout makes Him merciful and just, thus taking away His formlessness. Keeping that in mind, instead of maintaining an abstract nature, Zarathushtra attributed six divine qualities called the Amesha Spenta to God. These qualities are— *Asa Vahista* (truth/righteousness), *Vohu Manah* (good mind), *Vairya* (desirable dominion), *Armaiti* (devotion), *Haurvatat* (wholeness), *Ameretat* (immortality).

It was hard for the layman to contemplate on the formless or live in mere abstractions. So, they instinctively, deified good qualities, turning them into divine beings. The defects became evil beings. It was thus that the six attributes of Ahura Mazda soon came to be revered as male and female divine beings, next in rank to Him. The importance of laying stress at developing these qualities within was soon lost sight of and, instead, the personalities became central in the myths that followed.

The creation is the playing field of the good and the bad, represented by the terms *asha* and *druj* respectively. Ahura Mazda, the Lord of all that is good, and Ahriman, the Master of all that is wrong, have existed since eternity, and they made their respective choice of asha and druj as their way of life. They kept the cosmos in balance through their powers until Ahriman wanted more for himself. This resulted in a prolonged war. In order to vanquish his foe, Ahura Mazda created the world as a battlefield, knowing well that the war would last 9,000 years, after which goodness will prevail permanently.

To win the war, Ahura Mazda created the six divine beings, Amesha Spenta, of which three were male and three female. They cluster around Ahura Mazda on golden thrones attended by angels and are the makers, modellers, guardians, protectors, preservers, and rulers of the creation of Mazda. Each of them has a special month, festival, and flower dedicated to them, and each one presides over an element in the world order. These six hold their councils on the heights of the heavens, from where they descend into the seven zones, into which the world is divided, which they rule. They also come down to the homes of the devout by the path of light and accept their sacrifices—an idea that is prevalent in the Vedas for the gods. In the final battle against Ahirman, each one of these six will smite his or her adversary at the time of the resurrection.

Of the six, Asha Vahishta and Vohu Manah are on the highest rung of importance. Asha Vahishta is the lawful order of the universe. He presides over fire as the essence of truth and thus holds out the path of justice and spiritual knowledge for the devotees. Vohu Manah is the spirit of divine wisdom, illumination, and love. It was he who had led Zarathushtra in the presence of Ahura Mazda. In this world, he presides over domestic animals, and in Paradise, he welcomes the noble souls. The devout are enjoined to bring Vohu Manah into their lives through fidelity in marriage and love towards one's fellow man. Khshathra Vairya lords over metal and is the power of Ahura Mazda's kingdom. His power can be realised in action guided by Asha Vahishta and Vohu Manah.

Of the female divinities, Spenta Armaiti is the spirit of devotion and faith, who guides and protects the believer and also presides over the earth. Haurvatat and Ameretat are mentioned as sisters, like the dual divinities in the Vedas. They preside over water and plants and come to the devout as a reward for a good life.

The importance accorded to Vohu Manah and Asa Vahista in Zoroastrianism, both as abstraction and as a deity, reflects the spiritual aspect of the religion. In the final stage of the spiritual journey, one is taken forward by one's noble mind alone, propelled by truth and righteousness. When a mind is established in goodness, it is known to have attained *sattva*, according to Vedanta. This state is the penultimate towards spiritual realisation. In spirituality, goodness is not the end, but the last rung before the end, which is a direct realisation of God. It is the good mind in which realisation takes place as per His will. The struggle of an aspirant ends when he attains the purity of mind; the remaining is done by the Divine. To illustrate this fact, Zarathushtra is described as having been taken by the noble mind to God.

With the divine beings having been created, it did not take long for the followers of Zarathushtra to create the devilish beings, who opposed each of them. This tendency to create the opposite of good reached its crescendo when later scriptures came to describe Ahura Mazda and Ahirman oppose each other, by creating the good and the bad personalities. This implied that Ahura Mazda was not the father of the twin spirits. He was more like the equal of his foe, Ahirman. This seems to limit the power of the supreme being, but more ideas were incorporated to get around this. In the final take, the scriptures have left these two as equal, but with the final outcome as the victory of Ahura Mazda.

Zoroastrian has a distinct division between good and bad. A constant war between their forces has been raging since the creation of the universe, and it is going on all the time everywhere, including within oneself. The moral plane of the dual forces of good and bad is known as *asha-druj*. Asha means rightness, correctness, and moral, and its concept is similar to that of *rta* (right order) in the Vedas. However, the Vedas do not pay attention to *anrta*, but in Zoroastrianism *druj*, the bad, plays an equal role in theology. This idea of equal power, but not the ultimate, of the evil against good, has shaped its philosophy, ethics, and its way of life.

After the creation of their respective armies, Ahriman's first attack was defeated by Ahura Mazda with the help of the Ahuna Vairya prayer (the most sacred Zoroastrian prayer), which made the aggressor lie prostrate for 3,000 years. Ahirman was then brought to life by the primal woman, adept at black magic. Once revived, Ahirman went to war with a vengeance, killing the important creatures responsible for life and prosperity on this earth.

The war went on, but finally, Ahura Mazda succeeded in vanquishing Ahriman, trapping him into the magical Tree of Life. After seeing the destruction the war caused, He ascended into the stars, guiding and leaving the Ahura, to guard and protect the Tree of Life. Now the goal of every human being and also that of the human race is to join the righteous war, which is being fought out at the moral plane of asha-druj.

In making their choice between asha-druj, the daevas took sides with Ahirman. Since then, they have been out to corrupt human beings in their choice of the right path. The first human couple got influenced by Ahriman, and it was only with the advent of the Prophet after 3,000 years, that his power came to an end.

Due to the aggression of Ahirman, man is mortal, although he does not die altogether. There are five immortal parts within a person: *ahu* (life), *daena* (religion), *baodah* (knowledge), *urvan* (soul), and *fravashi* (pre-existent souls). The idea of *farvashi* is similar to the idea of *pitrah* of the vedic people, who are the ancestors living in the high heavens, and who help those born in their lineage. This idea of something immortal behind the mortal is the common thread that runs through every religion and is the cardinal principle that distinguishes religion from humanism or science.

After death, the soul meets his own religion (*daena*) in the form of a beautiful damsel, if he has lived justly; otherwise, he meets a hideous hag. The soul has also to undergo a judgement; it appears before Mithra and his two companions, Sraosha and Rashnu. Finally, it ascends through successive stages representing, respectively, his good thoughts (the stars), good words (the moon), and good deeds (the sun) to the paradise (of infinite lights).

Asha Vahishta, the Lord of fire, burns and detects truth through fire. Ahura Mazda dispenses justice through the radiance of His fire and the strength of *asha*. An individual who has passed the fiery test has attained physical and spiritual strength, wisdom, truth, and love. Altogether there are some thirty kinds of fiery tests in which the wicked get scorched. The hell has four levels where the souls with bad deeds go. There is also an intermediate place for those whose good actions exactly balance their evil ones.

In later literature, it is said that at the end of everything the universe will return to the primaeval state of things when everything was good and pure. In the last great struggle, the host of good and the host of evil will vie with each other, and each soldier of Mazda will defeat and kill his own special adversary. This will restore the state of peace that had prevailed initially. The entire mankind, resurrected after the final battle, will have to traverse the fire of molten lead in which the wicked will be burnt down, but which will feel merely warm to the good ones. This suffering of the wicked will, however, last only three days, after which everyone will enjoy happiness. Men and women will become shadowless and sinless and will taste the joy of family life forever. With Ahirman either destroyed or made powerless, the hell will be sealed forever. Existence will now be simply good and pure.

In his time, Zarathushtra had got rid of the daevas. Later literature reinvented some of them. One finds the names of Mithra, Airyaman, Apam Napat, Verethraghna (Indra), and Vayu in these books. On the other hand, his ideas of heaven, hell, and the resurrection of the body are well reflected in various forms in the Semitic religions.

PHILOSOPHY AND ETHICS

The dualistic ideas of Zoroastrianism make it high on ethics, but easy on philosophy. Human beings as individuals, and more importantly as the race, are free to choose between the dualities like right and wrong, truth and falsehood, etc. This choice and its consequences that get reflected in intent and action would affect one's life after death. Zoroastrianism promotes the idea of two judgements—the first one of the individual soul right after death, and the second one of the entire human race after a general resurrection. Surprisingly, the religion is silent on the idea of rebirth, which is central to Hinduism. In that respect, it is closer to Semitic religions than the Indic.

The idea of one God ruling supreme over other gods (monotheism) was tried by the vedic people but was given up by them as inadequate. Zoroastrianism, on the other hand, came up with this idea and continued with it, although it was never aggressive about it.

Similarly, its ideas of dualism in the form of good and bad, right and wrong is important but not absolute. Good and evil fight an unequal battle in which the victory of the former is assured. Ahura Mazda, the omnipotent, faces only a temporary limitation in this battle, which makes the evil not an absolute entity.

For human beings too, this duality is not absolute. Humans must enlist because of their capacity of free choice, but this enlistment is with his soul and body and not against his body, as the other dualistic religions preach. This fight between good and evil of the Zoroastrians is not same as the fight between the spirit and matter of, say, Christians. And since the body is not to be negated, Zoroastrianism does not accept fasting and celibacy as important, except as part of purificatory rituals. For the same reason, monasticism finds no place in it.

Future life is determined by the balance of the good and evil deeds, words, and thoughts of the whole life, but Zoroastrianism also allows simple human follies and weakness. One can get out of the idea of the sin of such weaknesses through confession, prayers, and rituals.

The focus on goodness as the goal and end of life requires purity at every level. Defilement is not merely a taboo; in its extreme, it results in endogamy, and in its milder form it does not permit any kind of pollution of earth, water, or fire. Due to this, the dead of the Parsis is neither buried nor cremated. They are left ritually to be eaten away by the carnivore birds.

Even though human beings do have a free choice between the good and the evil, their actions are dictated by destiny. As mentioned, the outcome of the battle between Ahura Mazda and Ahirman is already decided. This predestined truth at the macro-level filters down to the micro level. This makes every action of an individual predetermined. The scriptures say that 'though one be armed with the valour and strength of wisdom and knowledge, yet it is not possible to strive against fate.' Although this attitude borders fatalism, a common man does not surrender himself to helplessness but struggles hard to fulfil his freedom of choice.

Destiny, or the will of God, finds special mention in every religion. They all accept that the all-knowing God has to be in the know of things, past and future. This leads to serious consequences in the philosophy of religions and also in the lives of the devout. Can God do something original? Such questions are logical traps, ignored by the learned but held strongly by the ignorant. So many theories and models have been offered to get around the dichotomy of free choice and God's will, but none can explain it satisfactorily. Seen from the spiritual standpoint, reality exists at two planes—absolute and relative. The reach to absolute reality is the prerogative of only the greats; the rest have to remain satisfied with the relative. Those who have spiritual realisation, see the absoluteness of God (call it by any name), which means that to them it is all His will. Due to this most sages refuse to preach, since they see everything as His will. But at the relative plane, governed by the mind and matter, only free choice, randomness, karma, etc., seem to work, as experienced by everyone. This makes the job of the prophets singularly difficult since they see both the realities as true, but working at different planes. The idea of God's will, used by the ignorant, is bound to lead to fatalism. So, the prophets preach as if there is a free choice, and yet talk about the divine will as the supreme. Indeed, ideas like God's will can be meaningfully uttered only by someone who has realised God. For the rest, use of such expressions is a sham that can lead only to fatalism.

Zoroastrians accept that their religion is based on the principles of *Humata, Hukta*, and *Harvasta*—good thoughts, good words, and good deeds, which of course, is true.

PRACTICES

The devout Zoroastrians worship facing a flame or a source of light five times daily at home, in the open, or in a temple. The concept of the temple was not there in early Zoroastrianism, but it is now usual for them to worship there, called fire temples. The temple contains an inner sanctum where a fire is maintained or placed, which represents the eternal flame, and also asha, the moral order. The holy fire is fed pure fuels so that it too may burn with vigour and brightness. The eternal flame implies passing of Zoroastrian ideas and values from one person to the next, and from one generation to another without interruption.

The sacred fire must be kept burning continually and has to be fed at least five times a day. The founding of a new fire involves a very elaborate ceremony. There are also rites for purification and for regeneration of a fire.

Yasna

Yasna is the chief ritual in Zoroastrianism which requires the daily preparation of the sacred drink *haoma* (Soma in the Vedas) and sacrifices. The goal of the yasna is the maintenance of the cosmic integrity of the good creation of Ahura Mazda. The ritual is carried out by reciting prayers from the book with the same name, Yasna, which has seventy-two sections. To mark these sections, Parsis put on *kushti*, a sacred girdle of seventy-two threads, round their waist. This practice of putting a girdle round one's waist has been a central practice for boys and girls during the vedic times and is even now practised in many Hindu homes.

There are three types of purification in order of increasing importance—ablution, bath, and a complicated ritual performed at special places with the participation of a dog whose left ear is touched by the person and whose gaze puts the evil spirits to flight.

Penance is performed by reciting the firm resolve not to sin again, and the confession of sins to a *dastur* (high priest) or to an ordinary priest if a dastur is not available.

Their most defining ritual, of course, is leaving their dead in the towers of silence to avoid polluting the sacred earth, fire, or water.

Festivals, in which worship is an essential part, are characteristic aspects of Zoroastrianism, a faith that enjoins on man to be happy. The principal festivals in the Parsi year are the six seasonal festivals, *Gahanbar*s, and the days in memory of the dead at year's end. Also, each day of the month and each of the twelve months of the year is dedicated to a deity. The day named after the month is the great feast day of that particular deity. The New Year festival, Noruz, is the most joyous and beautiful of Zoroastrian feasts.

A TOUCHING CONTINUATION

A touching Parsi legend relates the meeting between Jadi Rana, the local king in Gujarat, and the newly landed emigrants from Iran. When the Zoroastrians requested asylum, Jadi Rana motioned to a vessel of milk filled to the brim to signify that his kingdom was already full and so he could not take in more people. In response, one of the Zoroastrian priests put some sugar in that bowl of milk, indicating that they would not bring the vessel to overflowing and indeed make the lives of the citizens sweeter. The king felt happy at the response and gave shelter to them, with the permission to practice their religion and traditions freely. Centuries have passed since this happened. During the period Zoroastrians have only brought peace and prosperity in India through their goodness and hard work.

It is sad to see how much this religion has passed through, and what reversal of fortune its adherents had to face. As a race, it gave Persian language and culture to the world, unparalleled in their refinement. Its king, the mighty Darius, is still remembered for valour. And yet, both the religion and the race of Zarathushtra had to suffer extreme humiliations and deprivations. Even its sacred books underwent distortions.

In spite of all this, the good religion survives, exhorting the mankind to be good, and to do good unto others.

Judaism
Religion of Obedience

In the beginning, God created the heaven and the earth. Now the earth was unformed and void. Darkness was upon the face of the deep, and the spirit of God hovered over the face of the waters. And God said: 'Let there be light.' And there was light. And God saw the light that it was good. God divided the light from the darkness. And God called the light, Day, and the darkness, He called Night. And there was evening, and there was morning...

Torah, the sacred books of the Jews, begins thus, whose contents are revered by the Christians, and its imprints are abundantly evident in Islam as well. More than this, the outlook towards life and the world presented in the Jewish scriptures have shaped the entire Western civilisation—its religion, myths, philosophy, ethics, science, art, literature—everything. No aspect of the Western life has remained untouched by the basic tenets of these scriptures. The great minds of the West have either tried to conform to those views or have struggled to rebel against them, which has ultimately resulted in the evolution of the human mind. Indeed, to understand the mindset of the West, one has to have at least some knowledge of Judaism—the grand old religion of the Middle East, younger only to Hinduism in its antiquity.

Judaism, an old word derived from Judea, is an adaptation of 'Judah', the land that originally encompassed the territory of the Israelite tribe of that name and, later, the kingdom of Judah, near modern-day Israel. It is mostly a desert land, mountainous and arid, making life difficult for its inhabitants and affecting the outlook of its religion.

Judaism is not merely a religion; it is also the history, culture, and aspirations of its people. The various aspects of this religion—its philosophy, rituals, social conduct, and mythologies, along with the family history, social laws, etc.—are inextricably mixed in its sacred books making it difficult for a student to differentiate its core spirituality from the lesser important aspects of religion. Jews, however, treat everything in their book as sacred, its huge corpus of religious literature requiring a rabbi, a Jewish scholar, to maintain and interpret them.

After initiating the process of creation, as described in the first chapters of the Bible, God created the world, heaven, Garden of Eden, Adam and Eve, and then instructed Adam, 'You may freely eat of every tree of the garden; but of the tree of the knowledge of good and evil you shall not eat, for in the day that you eat of it you shall die.' But tricked by the Serpent, Adam and Eve ate that fruit surreptitiously, and so were expelled from the heaven to work out their destiny. This story of the great fall from heaven or the divine grace is accepted in Judaism, Christianity, and Islam as the defining moment of creation. According to them, the story of human civilisation begins from that point. Christians term this fall as 'original sin', which makes every Christian a born sinner, while Islam refers to it as 'gaflah', a mistake. The Jewish tradition, however, does not pay any special importance to this event other than accepting it as the beginning of creation.

Why someone should be punished for eating from the 'tree of knowledge of good and evil', is a big question for the Hindus, who believe knowledge must comprise both right and wrong, good and evil. It is all the more intriguing for Hindus, who perceive God as omniscient and, consequently, the repository of all knowledge. Many explanations have been offered by the learned commentators to explain this, and the devout accept those explanations reverentially.

In Judaism, knowledge of self or God is not important. Life is important, and life with God is the goal. So, disobedience of God's will is perceived as a sin, which violates the fundamental code of life—obedience to His sacred commands. Seen from the Hindu perspective, the fall of Adam and Eve appear quite logical, since the dichotomy between the absolute and the relative gets explained through this fall. God is absolute. He is beyond good and bad, virtue and vice, birth and death. He does not belong to the world of relative existence.

Creation begins with duality, as described in the opening lines of this chapter, and so wherever there is duality, there is a fall from the divine. The term 'knowledge', as understood in this world, is indeed the knowledge of the duality. However, spiritual knowledge is not about good but is about being beyond good and bad. In this sense, spiritual knowledge cannot be termed as 'knowledge'. However, it is often used interchangeably for easy understanding. The goal of every spiritual life is to go back to the Garden of Eden where there is no good or evil. Vedanta terms this fall as 'maya', which causes the idea of duality in the mind. The destruction of maya is caused by knowing one's true essence as divine, the way Adam and Eve were before the fall—in divine oneness. The story of Adam and Eve's fall, thus, symbolises the great truth about God and the existence in Him.

Religious rationalists, however, take the story of Adam and Eve literally. Centuries ago, James Ussher, an Archbishop of Ireland proposed 4004 BCE as the year of creation, based on the Bible. This date is even today accepted in the Christian world as the year when creation began. Later, the great astronomer Kepler calculated this date to be 3992 BCE, and then Newton worked out this to be 4000 BCE.

There is also a possibility that the story of Adam and Eve symbolises the fact that they left their homeland during that period out of some compulsion to start a new way of life. Like the religious rationalists, Jews believe this date to be 3760 BCE and count the beginning of their calendar from that date.

PROPHETS AND FOUNDING FATHERS

Around a thousand years after Adam and Eve, Noah was born. By then people had degraded so much that God wanted to destroy his creation and start afresh. Seeds were collected in pairs, of male and female of every species, by Noah and kept in the ark when the great flood took place. After the floods, Noah offered burnt offerings to God, who promised not to hurt the humanity in future, even though they were evil by nature *(8.20–21)*.

The sacred name for God in Hebrew, the language of the Jews, is YHVH, the unutterable name. It is composed of the four Hebrew letters Yod, Hey, Vav, and Hey and is also referred to as 'the four letters.' This unutterability of the name of God is a common feature in religions, as discussed in the earlier sections while describing Aum as the name of God. The sacred name

YHVH was later transliterated as Yahweh and is now commonly pronounced as Jehovah.

Jehovah promised certain blessings to His folks in return for certain acts of commission and prohibition on their part. This is known as *b'rit*, an integral aspect of Judaism, according to which an individual or a group of people enter into a contract with God. It involves rights and obligations on both sides, usually ratified by shedding of blood or some other sacrifice.

This concept is unique and central to the understanding of Judaism. Unlike a devotee offering prayers in anticipation of some result, b'rit involves a prior covenant that God establishes with His people. The sacred books of Judaism are full of these covenants, of which the more important ones are those that He had with Adam and Eve; with Noah after the great floods; and with Abraham, Issac, and Jacob. He also had b'rit with deliverance from Egypt, and then there was this pact with David that one of his descendants would sit upon the throne of Israel forever.

Roughly a thousand years after Noah, Abraham (c. 1880 BCE) has been credited to have given shape to the destiny of his folks in more ways than one. Judaism, Christianity, and Islam find in Abraham their common ancestor. Hence, these are collectively known as Abrahamic religions. These three religions are also known as Semitic religions. Semite implies the group of people with a common culture and language, who had descended from Shem, son of Noah.

Abraham's original name was Abram. He belonged to a time when people of his land were idol worshippers. His father was an idol merchant and his idols represented different destinies. This kind of practice was prevalent in the early years of most religions, particularly among the Greeks, Romans, and Arabs. It is still practised by the aborigines all over the world. Abram questioned the faith of his father and sought to know the truth behind the mystery of creation. Through deeper contemplations, he came to realise that the universe was the work of a single creator, and the innumerable idols worshipped by his folks were created by people themselves. There was only one God, whose words were the law for all. Convinced with the prophetic truth, Abraham began teaching the idea of one God to everyone.

There is a popular story of Abraham once taking a hammer and smashing all the idols in his father's shop, except one. He then placed the hammer in the hands of the last idol and waited for his father to return. When asked to explain his conduct, Abraham said, 'The idols got into a fight, and the big one smashed all the other ones.' His father said, 'Don't be ridiculous. These idols have no life or power. They can't do anything.' To which Abraham replied, 'Then why do you worship them?'

Much later, Prophet Mohammed was to break three hundred and sixty idols that were worshipped in Mecca. He too, like his predecessor Abraham, was to exhort his people to worship one and only one God, Allah. This practice of worshipping one God, exclusive of everyone else, is known as monotheism and is the hallmark of Middle East religions.

One day, the God, whom Abraham worshipped, called him and made him an offer as He had done with Noah earlier. He told Abraham,

> Leave your country, your people and your father's household and go to the land I will show you. I will make

you into a great nation and I will bless you; I will make your name great, and you will be a blessing. I will bless those who bless you, and whoever curses you I will curse, and all peoples on earth will be blessed through you.' Abraham accepted this offer, and the b'rit (covenant or contract) with the Jewish people was established. *(Gen.12)*

From this point of time, the Jews started believing that they were the chosen people of God. Throughout the centuries of suffering, in the hands of tyrannical powers, this faith of their being the chosen ones of God, sustained them.

Instructed thus, by the Lord, Abraham took up a nomadic life, travelling through the land of present-day Israel. He had two sons, Isaac from his wife, and Ishmael from a slave girl. Isaac headed the Jewish people, while Ishmael became the ancestor of the Arabs.

Abraham, Isaac, and his son Jacob are considered the true patriarchs of Judaism, physically and spiritually. It was from their period that their descendants came to be known as Jews, and the spiritual path worked out by them was Judaism.

Jacob, the grandson of Abraham, was a particularly spiritually gifted person. One night, while contemplating on God, he was made to wrestle with a man until daybreak. At the end of it when Jacob demanded a blessing from the man, he revealed himself to be an angel and blessed Jacob. He also gave him the name 'Israel' (Yisrael), meaning 'the one who wrestled with God'. So, the Jewish people came to be referred as the Children of Israel, signifying their descent from Jacob.

Jacob had twelve sons, who became the heads of the twelve tribes of Israel, who form the origin of all Jews. Being the chosen people of God, they avoided intermingling with others and did not allow conversion. One had to be born from a Jewish woman to be the chosen one.

As centuries passed, the Jewish people became slaves in Egypt under the Pharaohs, and like any other slave race of that period suffered untold miseries. As per the covenant made by God to make the children of Abraham great, He finally brought them out of slavery under the leadership of Moses—whose life strung with miracles, makes it believable that he was the chosen one of God.

During one of his hiding periods from the king of Egypt, Moses took shelter at Mount Horeb. There God appeared to him in the form of a bush on fire but not consumed by it; it was the divine light that only the spiritually gifted could see within their hearts, in a super-sensuous experience of the consciousness. It is only through this kind of experience that the first intuitive wisdom of spiritual truths starts appearing within a person. This kind of experience may appear as a miracle to the uninitiated, but it is a common phenomenon with the trained.

In the form of that burning bush, God commanded Moses to lead his people out of slavery. The overwhelming experience left Moses struck, but he was not sure if others would believe him. When he expressed this, the Lord told him to go tell his people, 'I am is who I am. This is what you are to say to the Israelites: 'I Am has sent me to you.''

God is beyond name and form, so one can refer to Him only indirectly. The names like Krishna, Kali, etc., which one uses so often, are merely indicative of a trait of the Divine to convey and refer to. This understanding can come only to those who have experienced the Divine. For example, if one says 'ocean' to someone who has never seen an ocean, the word will not convey the idea that it intends to convey; the listener will form an image of it depending on his past experiences, without coming anywhere near the reality. People fight over the details related to the names of God, the forms represented by them, and the superiority of the one over the other, without realising the truth.

The Lord, whose vision Moses had, did not reveal His name as Jehovah to him. However, since God was being referred to by that name for a long time, that name stuck.

Moses did as he had been instructed by the Lord and led his people to freedom. But it did not come easy for the ruler or for the ruled. There were deaths and suffering on both sides, and there were miracles, time and again, to show everyone the power of God and to create faith in the believers.

The journey to freedom is known as the Exodus, in which they were led through the wilderness to Mount Sinai. Here God appeared to them as smoke covering the mountain and ordered them with the sound of the thunder that if they obey Him and observe His covenant, they would be the most beloved of nations, a kingdom of priests, and a holy nation. (*Ex.19*)

This was God's covenant with the Children of Israel. According to the tradition, every Jewish soul that would ever be born was present at that moment and agreed to be bound by this covenant. This makes the people of Israel particularly 'chosen' since no other people of the world have this kind of agreement with God.

In passing, it may be mentioned that the followers of every religion and every sect consider themselves 'chosen' due to one reason or the other. The sense of superiority ingrained within a person due to his religion tends to become a powerful driving force, which at times can also be the cause of one's ruin.

The deliverance of the Israelites from the Egyptian rule is celebrated as Passover. It is when God revealed the Torah to his people, both in written and oral form. Torah is a technical term in Hebrew to mean 'to shoot the arrow to hit the mark'. Torah is thus the instructions that teach the truth about God, although it is loosely translated as 'law'. By following Torah, a believer is expected to grow morally and spiritually and become the beloved of God.

In his final act at Sinai, God gave Moses instructions for the tabernacle, the mobile shrine by which he would travel with Israelites to the Promised Land. Tabernacle means 'a place of dwelling'. In Jewish tradition, it meant a sacred place where God chose to meet His people, and where He would be worshipped and offered sacrifices during the forty years of wandering in the desert that was to follow. It was a mobile tent with portable furniture where the elders of the tribe would congregate. God dwelled among His people in the tabernacle in the wilderness and appeared as a pillar of cloud over the tabernacle by day and a pillar of fire by night in the sight of all Israel. The people would not set out on their journey unless the cloud lifted. It was an unmistakably powerful visual statement, indicating God's presence among them.

The promised land of 'milk and honey' did not come to Moses and his people immediately. There were disbelievers among the Israelites, who were not willing to accept the words of Moses. This angered Him and He cursed that for forty years they will have to wander, till the generation of the disbelievers was gone. It was after this suffering of forty years that the Jewish people could finally settle down in the present-day Palestine area. Moses then instituted priesthood under his nephews.

The Jews believed that real power was with God. Their reverence and faith were reserved for Him, and not for any mortal king. But the fighting all around forced them to make David their first king, who brought the Jews around Jerusalem together into a unified kingdom. There was then the covenant which stated that David's descendants will always occupy the throne of Israel.

After David, Solomon took over. During this time the Jewish kingdom split into two—that of Judah and Israel. Judah came under foreign dominion, with Babylonian and Egyptian influences on its religion, myths, and practices.

In brief, this is the history and core religious experiences that shaped the mainstream Judaism. The later priestly religion tied it down to legalism, taboos, observances, ritualism, and obsession with the purity of blood through which a Jew was expected to go back to the pristine state of Garden of Eden. Law entered every domain of Jewish life and continues to do so.

> Now, therefore, give not your daughters to their sons, and take not their daughters for your sons, and seek not their peace, nor their prosperity for ever: that you may be strengthened, and may eat the good things of the land, and may have our children your heirs forever.' *(Ezra.9.12)*

The purity of blood demanded that there be no free mingling or interfaith marriage. In the process, spirituality, the force that sustains a religion, was somewhere compromised. There were voices that opposed the concept that God exacts a stern penalty for man's transgressions. They believed that God was greater than a mere intervener in man's destiny. But not many were willing to listen to these voices. There was also the influence of Persian culture and religion on it, like that of Ahriman, who was like Satan. Over and all, man was now considered insignificant before God, his divine nature being questioned.

SACRED TEXTS

The basis of Jewish law and tradition is the Torah, which contains the Ten Commandments that God gave to Moses, written on stone tablets, for the people of Israel. These are:

* I am the Lord your God, who brought you out of the land of Egypt, out of the house of bondage. You shall have no other gods before Me.
* You shall not make for yourself a carved image—any likeness of anything that is in heaven above, or that is in the earth beneath, or that is in the water under the earth; you shall not bow down to them nor serve them. For I, the Lord your God, am a jealous God...
* You shall not take the name of the Lord your God in vain, for the Lord will not hold him guiltless who takes His name in vain.
* Remember the Sabbath day, to keep it holy. Six days you shall labour and do all your work, but the seventh day is the Sabbath of the Lord your God...
* Honour your father and your mother, that your days may be long upon the land which the Lord your God is giving you.
* You shall not murder.
* You shall not commit adultery.
* You shall not steal.
* You shall not bear false witness against your neighbour.
* You shall not covet your neighbour's house; you shall not covet your neighbour's wife, nor his male servant, nor his female servant, nor his ox, nor his donkey. You shall not covet anything that is your neighbour's.

As one can see in these commandments, which is central to Jewish practices, these are more of moral obligations than spiritual outlook. Jewish traditions became more and more dependent on laws that regulated every aspect of their life, and soon the number of commandments grew to a whopping six hundred and thirty-one. Those who know Indian religious traditions would realise how similar Jewish religious tradition is to the religion of the Smritis (law books like *Manusmriti*).

In the second commandment, God declared that 'He is a jealous God'. Seen spiritually, it means that no worldliness can be permitted in the minds of spiritual aspirants; there cannot be 'two swords in one scabbard'. Jewish people, however, treat this commandment literally. They believe that a person will be punished for his lack of faith 'in God', which is a sin. This tradition of sinning 'against God' continued with Christianity and Islam.

In Hinduism and other Indic religions, the idea that God can be 'jealous', as understood by Abrahamic religions, is an alien concept. God for the Indians is neither a jealous God nor a demanding one. The divine being infinite, He can appear in any of the myriads of forms, and so, there is no room for jealousy. Similarly, the idea of sinning due to a lack of faith 'in Him' does not make sense to them. They rather believe in forgetting God in their daily life as a sin or, more correctly, a mistake that can cause a delay in one's journey to freedom. To belong to the world or to take up the path of divinity is anyone's choice with consequences. The world being God's, getting entangled here cannot be a sin.

These commandments also bring in the idea of God's will and free will. Why should one accept the values as instructed in the commandments? The answer is that these are from God and that

He will smite the non-believer. But exactly this is what one hears from the Christians and the Muslims! Also, why should God allow evil ways, since He is all-powerful and can thus change the mind of a non-believer by His mere will? There are many more questions that come up due to the Cartesian divide between God and His creation. Scholars and philosophers have come up with great answers, but they have not been able to remove doubts altogether.

Tanakh, also known as the Hebrew Bible, is the sacred scripture of the Jews. Tanakh is an acronym formed from the three primary divisions of the Hebrew Bible: Torah (law), Nevai'im (prophets), Kethuvim (writings). These three have a total of twenty-four books, of which Torah has five that contain the sacred laws, Nevi'im has eight that contain books on prophets, and Ketuvim has eleven books known as writings.

Torah, the written and oral laws by the Divine, was revealed directly by God to Moses. Being words of God, these are non-different from Him. Just like the Vedas, Torah too is treated as the source of all knowledge in the world, both spiritual and secular.

People often confuse the Old Testament (of the Christians) with the Hebrew Bible (of the Jews). These are nearly the same; although there are some differences in the order of arrangement of the books and their contents. The Old Testament is spread over thirty-nine books by splitting some of the twenty-four books of the Tanakh into more than two. These thirty-nine books are grouped under sections known as Torah, History, Wisdom, Major Prophets, Minor Prophets, and are available in translations, while Tanakh is still maintained only in Hebrew. Also, the Old Testament has two versions, the Protestant and Catholic, of which Protestant version is closer to the Hebrew Bible.

Mishnah are the oral laws that were compiled and written around 200 CE. Judaism had a very strong tradition of maintaining oral laws starting from the days of Moses. These helped the elders run their system efficiently, although these were not written down till quite late. These books are, however, secondary in importance to Torah.

Then there are Talmud, the rabbinic teachings and opinions on the Tanakh and the Mishnah, believed to be compiled around 500 CE. The rabbis are Jewish scholars, dedicated to the study and interpretation of the scriptures. The subjects covered in Talmud are quite varied, like history, law, ethics, philosophy, customs, etc. These became the basis for the later Jewish law that governs the social and religious life of the devout even today.

A close look at Tanakh reveals the lateral shifts that have taken place in the Jewish religious traditions over the last four thousand years or so. Genesis, the first books of Tanakh, describes God as the centre of existence and the creator of the universe. Then came the free spirit and rebellious nature of the humankind that made them arrogant and disobedient towards God. Adam and Eve were expelled because of this nature, and later God wanted to destroy His own creation during Noah's time. There are many more examples of the rebellious nature of the humankind.

This fault line between the sacred and the secular is central to every Middle East religion, particularly in Judaism. God wants His creation to conform to the cosmic order that He set into motion, but humans repeatedly transgress it. God thus appears as a divine monarch demanding obedience from an unruly subject. In Hinduism and Buddhism too, one comes across the impersonal cosmic order, dharma, but its God does not directly punish those who transgress dharma; one's karma delays one's salvation.

The next phase in the scriptures is when God chooses a family to maintain the order, the way a king uses regents. But men being men, they always find ways to disobey the Almighty, who then uses His powers through His chosen ones, known as prophets, to bring the erring members back to the fold. If needed, He gets miracles performed by His prophets. Thus, miracles verging on magic are treated as quite important in Judeo-Christian tradition. Even Jesus is made to perform miracles before he gets accepted as a prophet.

The last phase in the scriptures starts with Moses, in which laws take precedence over everything else and bind people down, so that they do what is right for them to go back to the Eden. The struggle between the divine and the mundane that results in obedience and rebellion, become the core of this last phase. Jewish sages, philosophers, thinkers, and writers took up the various concepts underlying these two primary moving forces within a man to give shape to philosophy, ethics, myths, rituals, injunctions, prohibitions, etc. of Jewish religious traditions so that people can become good, pure, and fit for heaven. Centuries of dedicated work in these fields by the greatest of minds helped the tree of their religion grow to a monumental size, but like any other overgrown system, its core, spirituality, which leads a devout directly to the divine, became inaccessible.

GOD

There are two kinds of religions, exclusive and inclusive. In the exclusive type, the religion stems from the intuitive experience of one single person; the idea of God is fixed in them. In the inclusive type, God is perceived as what many have experienced or described. This results in more than one idea about God. Seen in this format,

Hinduism and early Judaism are the inclusive types, while every other religion of the world belongs to the exclusive type. Later, Judaism became an accumulative religion that kept adding to its corpus what its own prophets said while refusing to take in the spiritual truths of those not belonging to their own fold.

In the early phases of Judaism, there were many gods, as has been described earlier in the story of Abraham. After Abraham, the idea of God slowly changed to Henotheism, which means to accept one God as superior to others, without disbelieving the existence of other gods. This happens when one family or a tribe becomes powerful enough to impose its own beliefs on others without hurting them much. In the case of Jews, Jehovah was that God, although gods like Elohim were accepted in the pantheon along with Jehovah.

With the passage of time, only Jehovah remained as the one single God, who ruled over the destiny of His people. Thus, a cohesive system of monotheism was born that had no place for inclusiveness in any aspect of their religion, and Jehovah came to be viewed as exclusively as one can imagine the God to be.

Since the ancient times, there had been YHVH (unutterable name of God) in the pantheon of the gods accepted by the descendants of Adam and Eve. He was not personalised, as He became during the time of Moses. What Abraham had worshipped as Henotheistic God, became Jehovah the God, after Moses. It was at this time that the Lord also got attributes like omniscience, omnipotence, permanence, righteousness, justice, lovingness, and above all nationalism.

Hindus also had a similar evolution. Vishnu means one who resides in everyone and everything, i.e., God. But in later times,

Vishnu was regarded as the name of a God who had noble traits like compassion, knowledge, power, etc.

The most interesting attribute of Jehovah, the God of Jews, is nationalism. God, religion, and nationalism are so inseparably mixed in Judaism that when David was banished from his country, he treated himself as banished from God. This oneness of God with the Israel nation is fundamental to Judaism, and hence, unchangeable. Islam furthered this idea to create a religious state.

In later literature, God is no more confined to the tribes of the Jews or to their lands; He is the one God whose chosen people are the Jews. The nationalistic God thus becomes the universal God but favouring only one nation, Israel. He then appears to a common mind like a great teacher who has favourite pupils, and whose favours are permanently limited to them. Despite His impersonal divine qualities, salvation remains reserved only for the Israelites. Thus, according to these scriptures, no spiritually enlightened person of any other nationality, religion, or creed can ever hope to enter the heaven. The universe, other than the Israelites, is thus the lesser children of a compassionate God.

This idea of extreme exclusiveness was later taken up by the Christians and the Muslims too, in their own religions, but unlike these proselytising ones, Judaism did not permit conversion, since all those souls who would be saved, were present at Mount Sinai, when God revealed Himself through Moses. So, there is no question of those souls being born in any other religion or any other country. One must be born a Jew, and then be a good Jew to enter the gates of the Eden when the time comes.

Jehovah is a loving God, but He can be ruthless towards the disobedient and is jealous if someone worships some other God. The anthropomorphic features are absent in Him, but the emotions that torment a human being is abundantly present in Him, which He uses to herd his sheep together. Since God made men in His image, the emotions that we have, God too has, although these emotions do Him no harm. He is too powerful for that.

One can thus see how the sages and the prophets of Judaism had the glimpse of the divine the way it is, and yet for the common mind He was presented as someone who could rule the destiny of the humankind, and also intervene on their behalf whenever there was a need. This intervention was always through the prophets (who are essentially human beings), so the possibility of the future prophets always remained open.

The idea of a messiah changed in Christianity and Islam. Jesus called himself the Son of God, so there was to be no prophet of his stature. On the other hand, Prophet Muhammad declared himself to be the last prophet, thus ending any future possibility of a prophet. Surprisingly, there have been sects in both religions that believe in the coming of a messiah, which shows their faith in God's intervention in the future too.

As mentioned earlier, God is in a relationship with His people through covenants. God being all-powerful, He will never transgress His part of the pact. It is left for His people to maintain the agreement by being good and obedient to His will. Thus, there is no possibility of attaining Him here and now. There is no possibility of attaining Him through love, as Jesus did, or through self-surrender, as Prophet Muhammad taught. The only way to salvation is through abidance of laws.

PHILOSOPHY

Jews believed that their scriptures were divine and, therefore, needed no further explanation. Judaism and even the rabbinic

Judaism did not deliberate on the philosophy of the religion until it was challenged by Islam and Christianity. The coming of new religions and the challenges posed by their theologians triggered an exchange of ideas and detailing among the learned of these religions.

This love for learning extended to legal studies, logic, philosophy, mathematics, and astronomy. The early Islamic converts thirsted for knowledge; they tried to get it from wherever they could. In the process, they were influenced by the Jewish scholars. In turn, Islamic scholars influenced the outlook of the rabbis too. All this added to a love for learning among the Jewish scholars, but it did not help much in evolving a transcendent philosophy. It should be mentioned here again that Judaism does not accept the transcendental aspect of religion, spirituality, and philosophy as of real importance.

To give an example, theologians and scholars have been debating for centuries to find out if Judaism permits the idea of predestination. In recent times, a balance between predestination and free will has been accepted to be the Jewish standpoint. However, the idea of an omniscient God, along with the free will of human mind does raise serious philosophical issues.

In the time of Jesus, and much earlier than that, there were Sadducees and the Pharisees, made famous in later times by their united demand for the crucifixion of Jesus. These two groups of scholarly people dictated the philosophical life of the Jews. Sadducees were highly conservative and accepted only the written words of Torah as law. They held important positions, including the post of the high priest, but they were not popular with the masses. The Pharisees accepted the oral Torah as equally valid and were quite popular with the masses. Later, they were to become the intellectual predecessors of the rabbinical traditions. These two groups contradicted each other on the issues concerning Jewish laws and customs. This resulted in some fine discussions on theological issues. However, they too limited their arguments to conform to the scriptures. Ironically, Judaism produced one of the greatest philosophers of the world, Spinoza (17th century), whom the then rabbis excommunicated because of his rationalism.

CREATION

According to *Genesis*, the first book of the Bible, God created the world (universe) in six days by His mere will, and then took rest on the seventh, after seeing that everything was perfect and in order. The first three days were devoted to division, in which He divided the light from darkness, then the waters above from waters below, and finally the sea from the land. The next three days were dedicated to populating these three by creating sun, moon, stars, fish, birds, creatures, and mankind.

Judaism had two models of the process of creation; the 'logos' (speech) model, and the 'agon' (struggle) models. In the logos model, God speaks and shapes unresisting dormant matter into effective existence and order. In the agon model God is prayed as the one who 'smashed sea with your might, who battered the heads of the monsters in the waters; You, it was, who crushed the heads of the Leviathans and left them for food for the denizens of the desert...' (*Psalm.74*). In this model, the seas are interpreted as primordial forces of disorder, and the work of creation is preceded by a divine combat. The later Judaism and Christianity stuck to the logos model.

A lot of discussion by the learned has gone into the dynamics and correctness of this description of creation. However, the learned miss out the fact that no spiritual work is meant to describe the details of the world. They are meant to make people understand that whatever is there is from God. Creation and the created are divine, and must be treated with respect, is what they wish to teach.

The followers of Judaism, of course, go strictly by the words and get entangled in them. The learned of Judaism have worked out from the scriptures that the universes being the creation of God, is static, predetermined; there can be no scope for chance, uncertainty, evolution, or expansion. Interestingly, the same argument can be used to explain evolution. Since God created the universe, it has a purpose, since the Divine cannot get into a meaningless act. If God has a purpose, then life must have a purpose, and nature too must have the same. This leads to arguments, counterarguments, and correctness of this or that standpoint.

Coming back to creation, on the sixth day the Almighty formed man of dust from the earth, and He blew into his nostrils the soul of life. This creation was a special one.

> God created man in His image, in the image of God created He him; male and female created He them. And God blessed them, and God said unto them, 'Be fruitful, and multiply, and replenish the earth, and subdue it: and have dominion over the fish of the sea, and over the fowl of the air, and over every living thing that moveth upon the earth.'

Thus, the superiority of mankind was established over all other creatures created by him.

The interesting thing about this is that human beings alone have a physical body and a 'soul' since He infused the soul of life only in him. This belief permeates Christian thoughts too. Christians believe that animals have no souls; hence, no 'consciousness'. The discussions in modern times on consciousness that one hears from Western scientists, is essentially a Judeo-Christian problem, defined in a way that is unique to human beings.

After God had created man (Adam), He fashioned woman (Eve) from a bone of his rib, and thus man did not come from woman, as happens in the world, rather, the woman came from man. Later, they were taken to the heaven, from where they were expelled back to the earth since they had disobeyed His instructions. The goal of human life is to strive to reach that pristine state once again; however, this does not make the concept of afterlife more important in the early Jewish scriptures. Just like Zoroastrianism, Judaism stresses on the importance of this life, while mentioning the afterlife in passing. It was left for the Christians and the Muslims to work out the details of heaven and hell, based on the prevailing Roman, Greek, and Iranian concepts.

The spiritual afterlife mentioned in the Bible can also mean the messianic age or a higher state of being. The Pharisees accepted the idea of an afterlife, where there are proper prizes and punishments, but the Sadducees rejected the concept since these are not mentioned explicitly in the Torah. The Pharisees, on the other hand, found the concept implied in certain verses.

The place of spiritual reward for the righteous is often referred to in the Tanakh as the Garden of Eden, but it is not the same place where Adam and Eve were. It is a place of spiritual perfection, where one experiences the kind of peace that cannot be described in the worldly parameters. It must be experienced. But it was natural for lesser spiritual minds to conclude that it must be a place of immense pleasure—an idea expanded much in the *jannat* of Islam, with beautiful *houri*s in attendance. Indeed, the Garden of Eden is a spiritual state for the soul, as described by the mystics of every religion.

The very righteous are privileged to go directly to Eden, while the average person descends to a place of punishment (rather purification), referred to as *she'ol*. It is a dark and deep region where 'forgetfulness' causes human beings to descend after death, where he can see his life and actions objectively. This period does not exceed twelve months, after which the soul ascends to the Eden. It is not very clear as to what happens to the very wicked after this period. But a common man becomes fit to see God after this purificatory period according to the Lord's promise, 'I (God) will refine them as silver is refined' (*Zechariah.13:9*).

ETHICS

Judaism is described as ethical monotheism, a religion based on the acceptance of one powerful God whose commandments constitute the moral law. As described earlier, this divine moral law is recorded in the first five books of the Bible, Torah, and in the later literature that recorded the oral commandments of God. Originally, there were Ten Commandments that later grew to be six hundred thirteen. These laws regulate the Jewish life through morality, justice, righteousness, and a desire for political freedom. To this are added ideas like peace and kindness, which sound more like reserved for their own.

As in every other religion, morality is one of the central features of the ethics of Judaism. One comes across statements like: 'The world stands on three things: Torah, divine service, and acts of loving-kindness' (*Avot.1.2*), and, 'What is hateful to yourself do not do to your fellow man. This is the entire Torah; the rest is commentary.' (*Babylonian Talmud. Shabbat.31a*). However, ethics is not founded on some logical outcome of spiritual truth, as in Vedanta, but through the involvement of God. This also adds an urgency towards being good, 'For I know their sorrows,' (*Exodus.3.7*) and '…it shall come to pass that when he cries out unto Me that I shall hear' (*Exodus.22.26*).

Some Jewish philosophers accepted that there are people who can be good without accepting a formal code, or without believing in God's commandment. The highest respect, however, is to be reserved for those who imitate God in behaviour, and thus goes beyond the letter of law when it comes to selflessness in every matter. Thus, the basis of ethics, as believed by the greater Jewish minds, was spirituality through which one must strive to be divine.

Repentance has always been God's preferred and primary means of obtaining forgiveness. Sacrifices were to be offered for certain 'unintentional' sins (*Leviticus.4.2*). If a sacrifice was presented without remorse and repentance the sin was not atoned for, and so, sacrifice served as a tool to motivate the sinner to repent. This was necessary because a person might rationalise that he did not need to repent because it was only an accident. Sins performed intentionally never require a sacrifice, only repentance.

RITUALS

As a religion grows old, it slowly starts getting burdened with rituals, which are in a way concretised philosophy. Judaism is based less on philosophy and more on covenants with God. The scriptures reveal how God made these pacts with an individual or with a group that was binding on both. This can be easily interpreted by a common man that the goal of religion is to appease the powerful God to be saved from His wrath, and if possible, to gain His favours. Crude as it may sound to a rational mind, this is how religion and God are viewed by the most practitioners of every religion.

Judaism thrives on the idea of one powerful God favouring Israelites, and so their rituals too are woven around those very ideas. Jewish prayers, recited twice daily have *Shema* as the centrepiece prayer that contains the essence of Judaism,

Hear, O Israel, the Lord our God, the Lord is one.

Practising Jews consider the Shema to be the most important part of the prayer service, and its recitation, twice daily, as a part of holy duty. Children recite it before they go to bed, and the elders recite it as their last words.

Boys are circumcised when they are eight days old, an important ritual for the Jews. The Lord said:

This is My covenant which you shall keep, between Me and you and thy descendants after thee, every male among you shall be circumcised

Later, Christians gave up this practice to distinguish themselves from the Jews, and much later it was taken up by Islam to distinguish themselves from the Christians.

Burial takes place within twenty-four hours of death. The family is in full mourning for seven days and, while special prayer,

Kadish, is recited for eleven months. It may be recalled that the soul, according to Judaism, remains in a state of animated suspension for that period roughly.

Passover, a very important festival for the Jews, is observed to mark the exodus of the Israelites from Egypt, Hanukkah is observed to mark the survival of the Jews, while Shavuot is celebrated to mark the giving of the Law to Moses.

Since Judaism is founded on the idea of staying straight in the eyes of the Lord, repentance forms an important ritual for them, for which Yom Kippur is observed. And then there is Sabbath, Friday sundown to sundown on Saturday, when the devout set aside their concerns for spiritual pursuits. This being the only ritual instituted in Ten Commandments itself, it is considered the most important ritual.

The place of prayers and worship are known as a synagogue. This practice is quite old, although not from the very beginning.

Judaism forbids the making of images of God, but despite this prohibition, images have been used on items of religious importance such as the Torah, and decorations hung on the eastern wall to indicate the direction of prayers, a practice that was taken up by Islam. Also, to mark some religious work, images of doves are often used, since a dove is treated as a symbol of peace, purity, and love. Its faithfulness to its mate makes it an ideal symbol of devotion. In *Song of Songs*, a dove is used to depict the relationship between God and His nation.

> Just like a dove once she meets her mate never leaves him for another...so are the Jewish people faithful to God

IN RETROSPECT

A look at the historical forces that shaped this religion reveals the compulsions that it had to face and consequently the adjustments that it had to make to survive. The persecution and exodus that the 'chosen of God' had to face throughout its history, makes one feel sad. It also makes one marvel at the inner strength that sustained it.

Mother Nature does not let an unsubstantial thing remain intact for long. When chaff and seed are put together in the soil, the chaff rots while the seed sprouts. The survival of Judaism, against all odds, shows the substance that it carries within it.

Christianity
Religion of the Saviour

BEFORE IT BEGAN

It is one of the great mysteries of the human race as to why or how a spiritual stalwart is born; who while living on this earth stays in divine communion and in time leads his people towards godliness. Unlike the popularity of a mass leader, philosopher, or a sage, the fame of such personalities, based on spiritual power, does not diminish with time, rather it keeps spreading with time over distance like a bell curve. This is the one great test that distinguishes a spiritual personality from every other kind of achievers, including the intellectuals. If one looks at the spiritual leaders, without putting on the spectacles of negativity, one wonders whether they were godlike human beings or God Himself who behaved like a human.

Once the masters depart from this earth, their words are left behind as divine gospel that acts as the foundation stone on which the devout shape their personalities to attain perfection. The devout also believe that by emulating the life of their master and by adhering to their instructions they too would achieve some degree of illumination. In many cases, they also believe that the prophet, whom they revere, will intercede on their behalf to get them divine life after death.

With the passage of time, the core spirituality of the path shown by the master gets covered with the ordinariness of human mind that results in a proliferation of myths around the prophet, rituals to attain divine communion, and codes of conduct to make one fit for the divine life. The importance of spirituality urged by the teacher then degenerates in gloating over one's heritage, creating fantasies about heaven and hell, and thus binding the followers with asphyxiating laws. There is no exception to this degenerative phenomenon. Like any closed system losing its vitality, be it a society, or a water body, a religion too moves helplessly towards more and more entropy unless freshness is infused in its system.

Jews, the 'chosen of God', suffered from this kind of spiritual sloth by the time Jesus Christ was born. Moses, the prophet, had struggled to take his men towards God, through the divine laws, but with time these became so iron clad that these hardly helped a person in his spiritual life. The religious texts too had become complicated for a common man to understand and practise. This resulted in the growth of ample influence of Pharisees and Sadducees, while a firm belief in the covenant (explained in the previous chapter) gave rise to over-dependence on rituals. Worse, the tyranny of foreign dominion, a problem that never seemed to leave the Israelites, made people hopeful of a divine intervention in the form of a messiah, who had been promised in the books of the Jews.

So, when the refreshing words of Jesus touched the hearts of the simple folks of his land and transformed their lives, they knew that he was that messiah. This was also corroborated by the three Magi of the East, who came to pay their ovation to the newborn Jesus, who was to be the King of the Jews.

JESUS, THE PROPHET

Not much is known about the early life of Jesus. The tradition has it that he was born through divine conception to Mary and Joseph in Bethlehem, Judea (modern Israel) on 25 December, 4th century BCE, and was known as Jesus of Nazareth. Joseph and Mary were originally from Nazareth but had to go to Bethlehem for the census when Jesus was born.

At the time of Jesus' birth, Judea, a client state of the Romans, was ruled by Herod. He came to know about the prophecy of the three Magi (wise men) that 'the King of the Jews' was to be born in his kingdom. Fearing his own usurpation, he ordered the killing of all children below two years of age. Coming to know about this, the parents of Jesus fled to Egypt to save the newborn. The family returned to their homeland only after the fearsome tyrant had died.

The Passover is an important festival for the Jews. Joseph and Mary went to Jerusalem every year to observe it. When Jesus was twelve years old, he was found missing after the family had attended the festival. The parents searched for him for three days everywhere in Jerusalem and finally found him in the temple courts with the teachers, discussing scriptures with them. Everyone present there was impressed by his understanding of the scriptures and the answers that he gave. When the distraught parents asked Jesus why he had gone missing like that, he replied, 'Didn't you know I had to be in my Father's house?' This made his already confused parents more confused.

This incident reveals how insightful a god-man can be even in his childhood. This kind of intuitive power to understand the mysteries of God, and thus the power to understand the meaning of scriptures, never comes through bookish knowledge, discussions, argumentation, or other means. One either has it or does not have it; there is just no way to acquire the super intuitive power that differentiates a seeker from the chosen one. This power is inherent in a divine being since childhood, while a sage acquires that only to some measure through sadhana.

Jesus was in the habit of spending hours in solitude, and at times would go to mountains for a good length of time. It was during this period that he was baptised by John the Baptist, a great spiritual personality of his time who went about the land baptising (purifying) people. Jews followed the practice of cleansing oneself from impurities, particularly while entering a place of worship. This kind of ritual purity was one of the 'legal' requirements from the Jews by God. With time, the priests broadened its meaning to perform a baptism on those gentiles (Israelites who were not Jews) who wished to be converted to Judaism as a sign of the covenant given to Abraham. By the 1st century, the reformists in Judaism used this practice of baptism (purifying a person by sprinkling holy water on him) to initiate a spiritual seeker into the ways of God through repentance—a practice that was to become central to Christianity in the form of baptism and 'repentance as a born sinner'.

John the Baptist was one of the reformists who baptised people to bring them on the path to God. Fiercely religious and immaculately pure himself, he used to speak about Jesus without naming him: 'As for me, I baptise you with water for repentance, but He who is coming after me is mightier than I, and I am not fit to remove His sandals; He will baptise you with the Holy Spirit and fire.'

So, when Jesus approached him for baptism on the banks of Jordan, John was initially hesitant to comply with his request, stating that it was Jesus who should baptise him. Jesus persisted, 'Suffer it to be so now: for thus it becometh us to fulfil all righteousness (It is proper for us to do this to fulfil all righteousness).'

The Bible describes what happened after the baptism of Jesus—

> After being baptised, Jesus came up immediately from the water; and behold, the heavens were opened, and he saw the spirit of God, descending as a dove and lighting on Him, and behold, a voice out of the heavens said: This is My beloved Son, in whom I am well pleased.

After this, Jesus was lost from the eyes of the world. The occasional sparks of divinity, visible in him, became a fully blazing conflagration of spirituality. Nothing of the world now mattered to him. Like Buddha, or any monk who gives up all for God, Jesus left everything behind for God, who in turn led him into the desert, where he fasted and prayed for forty days and forty nights.

When he was about to complete his sadhana, the Devil appeared to him and tried to tempt him from the path of attaining divine oneness. This is a common phenomenon among spiritual seekers, ordinary or great, and has been explained in the chapter on Buddhism. Jesus was offered the power to make bread out of stones to relieve his own hunger, jump from a pinnacle and rely on angels to break his fall, and finally, to worship the Devil in return for all the kingdoms of the world. Jesus was no ordinary aspirant who could be tempted with the worldly glamour; he stayed firm on his path.

When he returned from the desert, he was a changed person. The little 'I'ness that he might have had, was now replaced by the universality of the Divine.

> And it was reported to Him, 'Your mother and Your brothers are standing outside, wishing to see You.' But He answered and said to them, 'My mother and My brothers are these who hear the word of God and do it.' *(Luke.8.21)*

It is impossible for a man of the world to appreciate the intensity of divine love behind these words. Those who judge Jesus by the standards of the world can only be termed 'spiritual naive'. Jesus now belonged to God and God alone, and that too as the chosen one.

> I and the Father are one...that they may all be one; even as You, Father, are in Me and I in You, that they also may be in Us, so that the world may believe that You sent Me.

Jesus was now the Prophet and the Saviour of the world, who went around inspiring people for the remaining three years of his life. During the period, he too relied, like other prophets, more on his chosen disciples than on the masses to continue with the divine work after his departure. For this, he handpicked twelve disciples (apostles) who had been ordinary but were made great due to their joining hands in spreading the words of God.

At the height of his ministry, Jesus attracted huge crowds, numbering in thousands, who were dumbstruck with the power of his words.

> When Jesus had ended these sayings, the people were astonished at his doctrine: For he taught them as one having authority, and not as the scribes. *(Matthew.7.28–29)*

The words of Jesus had an urgency and intensity to make people spiritual at any cost. If needed, he would lay down his life to make people walk the path of godliness. To do what he had to do, he started preaching and healing people.

> I am the good shepherd; the good shepherd lays down His life for the sheep. He who is a hired hand, and not a shepherd, who is not the owner of the sheep, sees the wolf coming, and leaves the sheep and flees, and the wolf snatches them and scatters them. *(John.10.11–12)*

It was the practice of men of religion in those days to preach, interpret the scriptures, and also heal the sick through prayers, touch, etc. Jesus did all these so as not to disappoint the believers, although his goal was to spread the spiritual message. He went around the land, teaching in the synagogues and proclaiming the gospel of the kingdom of heaven. During one of these travels, he was enraged to see the outcome of the ritualistic aspect of religion.

> And Jesus entered the temple and drove out all those who were buying and selling in the temple, and overturned the tables of the money changers and the seats of those who were selling doves. *(Matthew.21.12)*

This kind of behaviour was sure to attract enmity. Unconcerned with how many enemies he was making, Jesus went on preaching. Some aspects of his teachings were traditional, but most were unorthodox. For example, he stated, 'Do not think that I came to destroy the law or the prophets. I did not come to destroy but to fulfil', and so he even expounded on Mosaic Law, but he also taught a 'new command' that had never been heard before. His words did not always fit in the accepted understanding, but they were fresh and appealing. It was beyond the power of the illiterate country folk to appreciate the higher elements of religion and spirituality contained in those words, but they had no difficulty opening their heart and soul to the love and compassion of Jesus, who talked in parables and gave examples that people could easily relate with.

The preaching of Jesus reached a crescendo when he delivered, what is now famously known, the Sermon, on the Mount, to his disciples, and a large crowd followed him there. This is where Jesus completely broke free of the calcified religious traditions of the Jews, and yet what he preached seems like a commentary on the Ten Commandments given by God to Moses. This sermon is at the core of Christianity, in which Jesus taught the Lord's Prayer, 'Our Father, who art in heaven/Hallowed be Thy Name/Thy kingdom come/Thy will be done...,' and also the famous injunctions like 'Resist not evil', 'Turn the other cheek', 'Judge not, lest ye be judged.' In this sermon he also commanded people to be chaste, to remain faithful to one's word, to forgive all, to love even one's enemies and to strive for perfection in this world itself.

What Jesus preached was not a thought-out axiom, but the eternal truths that stay one with God, and are revealed only to the chosen ones. To assert the eternity of his words, he said: 'Heaven and earth shall pass away: but My words shall not pass away' (*Mark.13.31*). By 'his' words he meant the words that he was speaking on behalf of his 'Father in Heaven'.

CRUCIFIXION AND RESURRECTION

The 1st century Judaism faced various problems that were viewed differently by the different groups then current in the land. Each of these groups had a different solution for their perceived problems: the Essenes were a small group that considered their society corrupt and hence dedicated themselves to austerities to attain spirituality; the Pharisees were religiously liberal, who accepted the oral traditions of their religion also to be true and were popular with the masses; the Sadducees were conservative elites, who aligned with the Romans in the hope of getting more power for their people; the Zealots favoured the use of brute force to overthrow the Romans. All these four groups had their roots in religious traditions, but they interpreted them differently.

It was at this peak point of social and cultural turmoil of the Jews that Jesus went about preaching that 'kingdom of heaven is at hand'. Like any spiritual prophet, the world did not matter for Jesus. The four groups mentioned above, therefore, had no significance for him. His teachings seemed tantalisingly close to each of them, but it did not endorse anyone in particular. For example, although he favoured change (essentially internal), he stayed in the world (unlike Essenes), longed for peace with the Romans (unlike Zealots), and focussed more on compassion than holiness (unlike Pharisees).

So, when the orthodox forces of the society felt that Jesus was sacralising against their sacred traditions, these groups too sided with them in the demand for his crucifixion. The crowd sided with its vocal leaders.

Jesus knew in advance of the events that were to come in the next few days before his crucifixion. Keeping in sync with it, he made a triumphal entry into Jerusalem during the festival of the Passover, and then shared a meal with his apostles, known as the last supper. During the meal he took bread, broke it, and gave to his disciples, 'This is my body which is given for you'. He also washed the feet of the apostles, giving the new commandment 'to love one another as I have loved you', and then he gave a long farewell talk in which he addressed them as 'friends and not servants'. This episode served the dual purpose of venerating Passover festival of the Jews, and also the establishment of Christianity. The Christians today feel connected to the Saviour and the last supper by taking the sacrament, known as Eucharist (detailed later).

Jesus was arrested next morning and was made to stand trial before the Jewish judicial body, who in the presence of Pilate, the Roman regent, handed him the sentence of crucifixion. Pilate was not happy with the verdict and so he wanted to save Jesus somehow. But Jesus had made too many enemies by then, who all wanted to see him gone.

As ordered, Jesus was flogged and then was mocked with the writing set up over his head, 'This is Jesus the king of the Jews'. He was clothed in a purple robe and was crowned with thorns as a final act of ridicule. Finally, he was crucified and hung between two convicted thieves. He is believed to have endured the torment of crucifixion for some six hours. During this time his mother came weeping to see him. He gave charge of his mother to a close disciple with, 'Behold thy Mother!' This gesture was to play an important role in later Christianity that came to worship Mary as Mother of God.

Two important utterances at this time were when he said 'I thirst', and a little later 'My God, my God, why have thou forsaken me?' Just after crying this out loud, he 'gave up his spirit'. These statements show how even a man of God has to suffer bodily pains when in this world. The learned commentators of Christianity explain these uttering variously, keeping in tune with their tradition, but the Hindu scriptures that deal with incarnations, tell us that even when God takes up a physical body, He has to undergo the pains associated with it, although the emotions linked with the pain do not bind Him, the way they bind an ordinary mortal.

The most famous saying of Jesus during the ordeal was 'Father, forgive them, for they know not what they do.' Established that he was in the inclusiveness born of divine love, he forgave all.

Jesus, as the Son of God and one who was one with God, could not be expected to have such an undignified death through crucifixion, and that too along with two criminals. So, God is believed to have raised Jesus bodily from the dead after three days of his burial. This phenomenon of rising from the dead is known as the resurrection and is accepted to be in accordance with the prophecies made in the Old Testament. Jesus appeared in his physical form to many of his disciples and admirers for the next forty days, after his resurrection, and then he ascended into the heaven to sit at the right of God.

The resurrection of Christ is so central to Christian belief that according to it salvation of the world depends entirely on the sacraments that the believers take on different occasions. These sacraments derive their power from the crucifixion and resurrection of Christ.

Questions are raised whether there was indeed any resurrection? More importantly, is rising from the dead even possible? if one tries to see things from a worldly standpoint, this is, indeed, not possible. However, spirituality neither runs by the laws of the physical world nor depends on faith. It is an entirely different state of reality that cannot be perceived or understood by gross minds. For a Hindu, resurrection is an essential fact of the spiritual world. Saints, sages, and God do appear before a devout physically or otherwise, popularly known as visions.

SACRED TEXTS

The sacred text of Christianity, the Bible, is made of two parts: the Old Testament, and the New Testament. The Old Testament is nearly the same as the Jewish Bible, while the New Testament is about Jesus and his spiritual movement.

What Jesus spoke after his return from the mountains, was a fresh gospel, which meant that these be treated as separate from the existing scriptures. So, his teachings, along with his biographical events were collected in four books by Matthew, Mark, Luke, and John that form the gospels (meaning, good news) of the New Testament. Of these four chroniclers, Matthew and John were the original disciples of Jesus, while the other two are believed to have joined the movement later. The four books taken together are also popularly known as the Bible by the public not well versed in the Christian traditions.

Life and teachings of Jesus were God-centric. He talked about the love of God as the prime concern in life, and his persistence of 'kingdom of heaven is at hand' reveals his pain at the plight of those mired in worldliness. He wanted people to come out of their narrow existence by giving up all that they had and experience the light of spiritual truth. Bible is decidedly in favour of sacrificing everything for God,

> And he said unto another, 'Follow me.' But he said, 'Lord, suffer me first to go and bury my father.' Jesus said unto him, 'Let the dead bury their dead: but go thou and preach the Kingdom of God.' And another also said, 'Lord, I will follow thee; but let me first go bid them farewell, who are at my house.' And Jesus said unto him, 'No man having put his hand to the plough and looking back is fit for the Kingdom of God.' *(Luke.9.59–62)*

There is a licence for those who cannot be so committed:

> But I say to the unmarried and to widows that it is good for them if they remain even as I. But if they do not have self-control, let them marry; for it is better to marry than to burn with passion. *(Corinthians)*

And, talking about the ways to live in the world he favoured goodness that had not been seen in the land of Israel till then:

> Let your statement be, Yea, yea; Nay, nay: for whatsoever is more than these cometh of evil...Resist not evil...let him have thy coat also...love your enemies. *(Matthew.5.37-40)*

New Testament consists of twenty-seven books in total. Other than the four gospels, it also has a narrative of the ministries in the early church, called the 'Acts of the Apostles', epistles consisting of doctrine, counsel, instruction, and conflict resolution, etc., and the 'Book of Revelation', which is a book of prophecy. The New Testament forms the basis of the Christian religion in practice—its way of life, morality, ethics, and philosophy, while some other minor aspects, including mythologies, come from the Old Testament.

One important difference between Bible and every other scripture is that Bible in any language is accepted as valid; one does not have to go to the original language of the composition to be a true believer. This makes Bible more accessible to the masses. However, it also takes away the gravity associated with the original words of the master.

Christianity has a very strong tradition of saints and sages, who have left a huge mass of religious literature that continues to inspire the practising Christians. These are, however, secondary in importance to the Bible.

FATHER IN HEAVEN

Semitic religions are monotheists, meaning, they believe in one exclusive God, in their respective religions, who favours only them and punishes others with damnation. Interestingly, if one were to replace God of one of the Semitic religions with God of the other, it would be difficult for a common man to differentiate between them. The theologians will, of course, find out the subtle differences, but these differences will have no significance for a common man.

God of Jesus was same as God of his religion of birth, but he called Him 'Father in Heaven' to express his oneness and involvement with Him. His God was not someone far removed from the affairs of people as commonly believed, nor was He stern and 'jealous'. On the contrary, He was the kind Father who was ever caring, forgiving and concerned. But the followers of Christ distanced themselves from Judaism and its God, as time passed, because of their existential differences. To this was added the intuitive spiritual experiences, apparently alien to the religious beliefs of the Judaism, by Christian saints, and at the top of all this were the arguments and concepts forwarded by the scholars and theologians, who shaped the religious ideas through intellectual serendipity and localised arguments. All this contributed in formulating a distinctive idea of God in Christianity, which was different, although not radically, from that of Jewish God.

Holy Trinity is the defining principle of Christianity, according to which God appears as three—God the Father, the Son, and the Holy Spirit (or, Holy Ghost). These three are distinct aspects of God. Though they are not one and same, God is one and the same as the Father, the Son, and the Holy Spirit.

Although it is difficult to comprehend this profound spiritual truth, it is easy to understand this through the basic principles of Hinduism. In Hinduism, Brahman (an impersonal aspect of God) alone exists, who through His *maya* (divine power) appears as God (a personal aspect of God), as an *avatar* (incarnations), and also as *jiva* (individuals). These three are one and the same as Brahman, even when they are distinctly different from each other. The difference between God–avatar–jiva ceases in the ultimate state of realisation of 'God alone exists'. God is the eternal being who creates and preserves the universe. His name, God, represents the entire system of truth, revealed only to the faithful as 'enlightenment'.

Jesus prays to God for his apostles:

> All I have is yours, and all you have is mine. And glory has come to me through them. I will remain in the world no longer, but they are still in the world, and I am coming to you. Holy Father, protect them by the power of your name, the name you gave me, so that they may be one as we are one. While I was with them, I protected them and kept them safe by that name you gave me. (*St. John.17. 11–13*)

God is both transcendent and immanent and came on this earth in the form of Jesus to save the sinners. Transcendence implies that He is independent of the material universe and is removed from it, as in Judaism, while immanence implies that He is present everywhere. This idea of the immanence of God is very near to the Hindu view that 'God alone exists', but the fact that everyone and everything are non-different from God, is simply abhorrent in all Semitic religions, although there have been many saints in Christianity and in Islam who talked about being one with God. These voices were, however, either ignored or suppressed.

In spite of the immanence of God, as preached by the enlightened saints, He is popularly treated in Christianity as transcendent, but involved in the affairs of the world. To save the people of the world, particularly the sinners, God's compassion flowed down through the body of Jesus, who is the second of the Holy Trinity as God the Son. This belief in Jesus being the Saviour has its roots in the Bible itself where Jesus says,

> I am the light of the world: he that followeth me shall not walk in darkness, but shall have the light of life.

And also,

Come unto me, all ye that labour and are heavy laden, and
I will give you rest. Take my yoke upon you, and learn of
me; for I am meek and lowly in heart: and ye shall find
rest unto your souls.

The Bible of St. John begins with 'In the beginning was the Word,
and the Word was with God, and the Word was God.' Creation
from logos in Judaism is one of its two theories of creation. In
Hinduism, creation from Word (*Sphota*) is the most accepted theory
of creation, according to which all ideas, words, and forms evolved
from this undifferentiated Word. A word or a name is the verbal
representation, and form is the physical representation of the same
idea. The totality of all the ideas, name and form is known as *Aum*,
which is the Word.

The Bible then narrates how creation flowed from that
'Word', and then, 'The Word became flesh and made his dwelling
among us,' meaning, Jesus is that Word, and his oneness with God
is established even before the universe was created. Thus, there can
never be another Son of God. Jesus is sufficient for the salvation
of every good Christian by vouchsafing for them and damnation of
everyone else by refusing to intercede on their behalf.

This divine process of God becoming a man is known as
incarnation. Christianity differs from other Semitic religions mainly
on this point. Others accept Jesus as a Prophet or a Messenger of
God, but not as God; but for a good Christian, Jesus is God, who
came on this earth to take upon himself the sins of the humanity.

The idea that God can come as man, is a commonplace
acceptance for the Hindus. The very foundation of Hinduism is
based on the idea that God can come amidst any species, in any
form, and any number of times. Who can limit the limitless? If

God wills so, He can appear in any form, anywhere. So, while Christianity accepts only Jesus as non-different from God, who came amidst the humanity, Hinduism accepts an unlimited number of incarnations, both past and future.

Holy Spirit is the third member of the Trinity. In the first sections of the Old Testament, it is said that after God created the universe, the spirit of God moved over the face of the deep. Later, Jesus was to say:

> If you love Me, keep My commandments. And I will pray to the Father, and He will give you another Helper, so that He may abide with you forever—the Spirit of truth, whom the world cannot receive because it neither sees Him nor knows Him; but you know Him, for He dwells with you and will be in you. *(John.14.15)*

Jesus himself was 'conceived by the Holy Spirit, born of the Virgin Mary', known as Immaculate Conception. The Holy Spirit later descended on Jesus as a dove during his baptism. Holy Spirit leads people to faith in Jesus and also gives them the ability to lead a religious life. Believers receive the blessings of the gospel, and a conviction in the Heavenly Father and Jesus Christ through the Holy Spirit, who also helps a believer from becoming immoral. So, to be immoral means to be shut out from God. The non-believers of the gospel are hence headed for hell since lack of morality or faith proves the absence of the Holy Spirit in that person.

WORLD VIEW

Jesus repeatedly talked about 'Kingdom of God', which became another core belief of the Christians. The scholars are not unanimous about what exactly this represents. Jesus himself said:

> God's kingdom isn't something you can see. There is no
> use saying, 'Look! Here it is,' or 'Look! There it is.' God's
> kingdom is here with you. *(Luke.17.21)*

The great saints too describe it as one's own enlightenment through spiritual practices, while cruder minds believe in the existence of a heaven where they will go after the Judgement Day, as the Jews believed. But while Jews believed in going to the heaven within a year, Christians extended this waiting period.

Christianity inherited a lot of its outlook, including its world view, from Judaism. With time the theologians and scholars chiselled these thoughts to suit the rational minds of the period, which unfortunately caused much heartburn for the later rationalists. For example, Christianity depended a lot on the Greek philosophers for their philosophy, reasoning, and the world view, without realising that science and revealed truths belong to different realms of knowledge. So, when scientists like Galileo pointed out the fallacies of Christian beliefs from a scientific perspective, the Church cried foul.

Christianity accepts what the first passages of the Bible (Old Testament) describe as the process of creation by God. But Christians associate Christ with creation, as mentioned earlier in the quote 'In the beginning was Word...' This marks a major departure for Christianity from Judaism and Islam.

How did created matter come into existence? The earlier Greek belief regarding God and matter was that matter was always there but in a chaotic state that became patterned by God's will, while later Judaism and Christianity came to believe that God created matter from *nihilo* (void). This gave rise to cross-current of ideas. At the crude end was the belief that God created the universe, separate from Him, out of the void by His mere will; while on the higher end was the conclusion that everything owed its existence to God, and that God and His creation are non-different. However, the popular belief rests on the simpler explanation of God creating everything from the void.

Creation by God is not a one-time affair but continuous, since if He withdrew his creative presence from something, it would cease to exist. It means that creation and preservation are same, and God is responsible for both. This makes God responsible for all the good or bad that one faces in the world, implying that God's will reigns supreme. But again, Jesus being central to creation and also since he is the Saviour of the souls, the end and purpose of creation lies in Christ. The only thing that truly matters in this earthly existence is to work out one's relationship with God. This brings the idea of free will. As a result, the never-ending conflict between God's will and free will occupies a dignified space in Christian discussions.

HEAVEN AND HELL

In Judaism, two models of creation were mentioned—the 'logos' and the 'agon', of which 'logos' model has been accepted more popularly in Christianity, although 'agon' model has not been given up altogether. Creation in the 'agon' model has a great similarity with Zoroastrianism, which flourished in Iran, not far from Israel. According to this model, God is the divine warrior, who battles the monsters of chaos in which the world of nature joins to defeat the chaos-monsters. God then appears sitting on a throne on a divine mountain, surrounded by lesser deities. His mere words make nature bring forth the created world.

Instead of merely taking up this model for creation, the later Jewish and Christian literature projected it into the future too, to come up with the apocalyptic ideas. Thus, the cosmic battle became the decisive act at the end of the world's history when after God's final victory over the sea monsters, new heavens and a new earths shall be inaugurated in a cosmos in which there will be 'no more sea' (*Revelation.21.1*). When these beliefs and myths were mixed with the words of Jesus on the Kingdom of God, a heady cocktail came up that contained a mix of ideas from Greek, Roman, Persian, and Jewish traditions, along with a strong desire to be independent of these. Christianity thus came to believe in a three-tiered universe—a flat disc-shaped earth floating on water, heaven above, and the underworld (hell) below.

As for the afterlife, it is generally believed that once a person dies, his soul undergoes the 'particular' judgement and is sent to heaven, purgatory, or hell, depending on his deeds. Purgatory is where one is purified through various punishments and torments, after which the soul is allowed to go to the heaven, but those sent to hell, have to stay there eternally.

Then there is the last judgement that would take place after the resurrection of the dead and the reuniting of a person's soul with his physical body. At that time, Christ will come in His glory, and all the angels will be with him. In the presence of Christ, the Saviour, who will intercede on behalf of each soul, one's relationship with God will be laid bare. Those believing in Christ will go to everlasting bliss, and those who reject Christ will be sent to everlasting condemnation.

At that time, those already in heaven (mostly saints) will continue to be in heaven, and those in hell will continue to be there, eternally. The residents of the purgatory, undergoing punishment, will be allowed to go to heaven by the merciful Jesus. In his final stay, in heaven or hell, a person's pleasure or pain will increase many times, where he will get back his physical body that was given a burial, and would be resurrected. After this last judgement, the universe will be renewed with a new heaven and a new earth in the world to come.

A word about the soul in Semitic religions and Indic traditions. The most commonly used word for soul in Indic religions is *atman*, which is generally accepted to be the conscious principle behind everything, which neither takes birth nor dies. Different Indic religions discuss the cause of its bondage and nature of its freedom variously.

Although loosely translated as soul, the atman and soul are not same. In Indic religions, the soul roughly corresponds to the subtle body, which leaves a body once a being dies. The atman is the reality behind every being. When someone dies in India, it is said that he gave up his body. So, there is no question of praying, 'May his soul rest in peace', nor the fear of 'torment of the soul'. In Christianity, on the other hand, one 'gives up his soul' (or Holy Ghost).

The idea of eternal damnation for the non-believers is alien to Hindus. Even an illiterate believes that God is one, no matter which religion one follows. They also believe in karma, which can be rectified through many births. To be sent to eternal hell for the acts of one's life does not seem appealing to them, rationally or emotionally.

In the present times, Christians have become more liberal when it comes to extreme ideas of exclusiveness. Religious leaders now do interact with members of other religions and do not have the condescending or condemning attitude towards them.

SATAN, DEVIL AND THE END OF TIME

There is a clear dividing line between some ideas of Christ and popular Christianity, particularly, when it comes to taking the blame on oneself. Jesus not only 'bore his own cross' before crucifixion, he is also believed to have taken the sins of the world on himself so that sinners could be saved. Good Christians, on the other hand, prefer to blame Satan or the Devil for their misdemeanour. Jesus mentions him in passing, but devilish that he is, he manages to acquire importance in later Christianity! Milton made him famous in his famous work *The Paradise Lost*. Another book of the same period, *Doctor Faustus* by Marlowe, put the Devil forever in the Christian consciousness.

The much-hyped views about Satan have their roots in the Old Testament where he is believed to belong to the human world, and not to inhabit or supervise the underworld, as is commonly believed now. He is not God's enemy but his minister with investigative and disciplinary powers. But the early Church, looking for a distinct identity, away from Judaism, identified him with the Serpent of the Garden of Eden. He then came to be seen as an angel who rebelled against God, and who wanted to derail the divine plan for mankind. The role of Satan, howsoever nefarious, will continue only till this universe exists. Once the Judgement Day comes, new heaven will be formed and Satan will cease to exist. This point being the start of eternity, time too will stop to exist. So, who knows? Time itself may be Satan. Interestingly, one fundamental principle in Hinduism is that time begins with maya—

God's inscrutable power that causes creation—and time ceases to exist when the creation ends.

PHILOSOPHY

The story of Christ did not end with his crucifixion, nor even with his ascension to the heaven. The question of who was responsible for the Saviour's death became an issue that continued to be discussed throughout the history of Christianity, and its deadly consequences could be seen even as late as Hitler's pogrom. This is because the general belief among the Christians was that the Jews had killed Jesus and it had to be avenged.

St. Luke wrote:

> The people of Israel were also complicit in the death of Jesus. They were the ones who shouted, 'Crucify Him! Crucify Him!' as He stood on trial... *(Luke.23.21)*

Later New Testament *(Thessalonians.2.15-16)* was to mention:

> Even as they did from the Jews, who both killed the Lord Jesus and the prophets, and drove us out. They are not pleasing to God, but hostile to all men, hindering us from speaking to the gentiles so that they may be saved; with the result that they always fill up the measure of their sins. But wrath has come upon them to the utmost.

Christians thus came to consider Jews their enemy, despite the fact that many Jews had remained true to Jesus during the dark days of crucifixion, and the fact that Jesus himself was born Jew, and all his disciples, friends, and admirers were Jews. The inner circle of Jesus might have been angry with the insane behaviour of the crowd, even while they had to remain true to their paternal religion too. Unfortunately, the hostility between the two religions continued to grow that resulted in the persecution of the Christians at the hands of the Romans, who were the masters of the then Israel. Also, the later generation of the Christians did not have their roots in Judaism, and so there was no love lost between the followers of the two religions.

By the 4th century, Christians started working on a distinct identity for themselves by rejecting, at least partly, the beliefs, customs, rituals, festivals, and philosophy of the Jews. And yet, Christianity shared their scripture with the Jews. The dichotomy born of this need - hate relationship of Christianity with Judaism has shaped its philosophy, to which was added Greek and Roman influences popular in those days.

Christianity faces the same dilemmas that every dualistic religion, particularly the Semitic religions, faces. Transcendence of God (in spite of the belief that He is Immanent too) implies acceptance of two independent realities, God and the world. God being all-knowing and all-powerful, the question of divine will and free will (of humans) automatically arise, and also the role of grace, faith, reason, etc. Also, God being sentient, He cannot create the universe without a purpose; hence, the search for a meaning and purpose in life. Add to these the problems raised by the scientific discoveries and developments. All these questions, along with the subsidiary and supplementary questions, keep propping up like the demons, born of the blood drops of Raktabeej. In Hindu mythology, Raktabeej, the *asura* (loosely translated as the demon) had a boon that whenever a drop of his blood fell on the ground, a duplicate Raktabeej would be born at that spot. Likewise, one gets rid of one cantankerous issue only to encounter many more fresh ones. Hundreds of best Christian brains have gone into handling these questions to come up with more and more incomprehensible solutions, leaving the faithful wary of philosophy.

Although a dualistic religion, Christianity is different from Judaism and Islam in its two major philosophical principles. The first one is the idea of sin, and the second one is the idea of Jesus as the Saviour. Jesus exhorted people to strive for the kingdom of heaven (spirituality) by giving up their sinfulness (worldliness). In no time his followers made a virtue of denouncing sin and making the list of sins longer. Entry into the kingdom of heaven became the responsibility of Jesus, while sin and sinners became the focus of Christianity. This kind of misplaced priority is seen in every religion—jihad in Islam, laws in Judaism, maya in Hinduism, non-violence in Buddhism, and austerity in Jainism are more famous examples in which God or self-realisation became secondary to the non-consequential issue.

As mentioned in the chapter on Judaism, the fall of Adam and Eve from the heaven is the original sin that the humanity carries on its head even today. This leads to transferability of sin to Jesus who through his death and resurrection took the sins of others on himself so that the faithful can go to the heaven.

Christian philosophy thus revolved around how to be good so that one becomes fit to be saved by Jesus. Different sects prescribe various paths to this end, of which two are more popular—performing good works, and, living a simple life. Some sects also believe that baptism is enough to save a person.

The subtler outlooks in Christianity came mostly from Greek philosophy. In its early years, Christianity was heavily influenced by

Plato's philosophy, particularly the Platonic view of heaven, which although not Biblical, came to be accepted as the heaven by the Christians. There were many Christians in those early days who believed that Plato was prepared by God so that the spiritual truth could later be revealed through the gospel. Saint Augustine (5th century), a great theologian, modelled the theological principles of Christianity entirely in line with the thinking of Plato.

Later, Thomas Aquinas (13th century) based his arguments and views based on the works of Aristotle, which became the official outlook of the Church in most matters, including its views on science. The influence of the guru-disciple duo, Plato and Aristotle on Christianity ultimately resulted in the now famous Dark Ages (5th to 15th century) that stifled the growth of free thinking and science.

ETHICS

The ideal of every religion is to make its follower spiritual. To be spiritual means to be established in divine oneness by going beyond the characteristics of the world. It also means going beyond good and bad, virtue and vice. To an untrained, this may sound strange, but this is one fact that differentiates spirituality from religion. To be religious means to be ethical, but to be spiritual means to go beyond ethics. Rabia, an early Sufi mystic, used to say that she was so full of God that she had no room left for hating the evil or Satan. In the fullness of divine love, one transcends not only the good but also the bad, since the distinguishing factor between them, the world, loses its defining significance. What remains is unalloyed love/presence of God. Explaining this, Jesus said:

> That ye may be the children of your Father which is in
> heaven: for He maketh His sun rise on the evil and on the
> good, and sendeth rain on the just and the unjust...Be ye
> therefore perfect, even as your Father, which is in heaven
> is perfect. *(Matthew.5.45-48)*

But not every devout is a man of God. For most people, the world
is real and God is a distant reality, if not a mere possibility. To keep
such persons on the right side of values, a religion has to work out
an ethical mould in which its follower must fit to get rid of the extra
baggage of worldliness, which is also known as sin.

Christians believe that Jesus was crucified because he took
the punishment deserved by others for their sins, particularly the
original sin committed by Adam and Eve. They had disobeyed
the instructions of God and got expelled from heaven. This original
sin manifests in humans in the form of their carnal desires, which
means that every baby born is a baby born in sin. But as discussed
in the section on Judaism, Adam's fall is not seen as something
serious by the Jews and the Muslims. This is 'forgetfulness' of one's
divine nature, according to the Hindus.

Jesus himself did not pay importance to the idea of sin the
way it has been propagated in Christianity. In the story of the
fallen woman, who was to be stoned, Jesus sent away the crowd,
embarrassed, and then told her, 'I do not condemn you, either. Go.
From now on sin no more.' It does not need much imagination to
think what a good Christian would have done to such a woman
a mere hundred years ago! In the same vein, when Jesus once ate
with publicans and sinners, the scribes and Pharisees raised their
eyebrows. At this, he said, 'They that are whole have no need of

the physician, but they that are sick: I have not come to call the righteous, but sinners.' There is no idea of condemnation in these.

The later thinkers and theologians of Christianity gave shape to the ethical system that was to define the dos and don'ts for the Christians. To do this, they took help from the Bible, and also from the Jewish ethical traditions, particularly the Ten Commandments. There is a story about a great Jewish saint, Hillel (100 BCE), who when asked to explain the central teaching of Torah, while standing on one leg, said, 'That which is hateful to you, do not do to your fellow. That is the whole Torah; the rest is the explanation; go and learn.' Christian ethics followed this same common-sense principle.

Values like non-violence, tolerance, honesty, forgiveness, etc. were central to the teachings of Jesus, and so these got special importance in Christian ethical works too. But these values soon became ornamental and were used mostly to condemn other religions for their practices, all the while focussing themselves on sin, sinner, and repentance.

Like Jewish commandments, Christian ethics is inseparable from theology and revolves around God. So, Christian ethics also reflects and determines what conforms to God's character and what does not, if it is not already mentioned in the Bible.

Thomas Aquinas, the great Catholic thinker, treated the whole range of ethics in a philosophical manner. His works have been used as the foundations by the later philosophers and theologians. But like any true Christian, Aquinas too discusses ethics within the limits set by the Bible. Even when he talks about natural law that can be discovered by humans through reflection, he stresses on how that too will be 'man's participation in the divine law.' This implies the existence of an absolute moral order outside

227

of human mind that regulates the world, and to which everyone must conform.

The idea of a universal moral order is present in other religions too in the form of God's will (Semitic religions), Dharma chakra (Buddhism), and Ritam (Hinduism).

RITUALS AND FESTIVALS

Christians made a clean break from their Jewish past and centred their mundane and spiritual life around Jesus. This resulted in new rituals and festivals, of which the chief ones are mentioned here.

Mention was earlier made of Greek and Roman influences on Christianity. One major influence came in the form of Mother Worship in the Roman Catholic Church that started worshipping Mother Mary as the mother of God, although no such tradition existed in Judaism, nor did Jesus referred to his mother as someone special. He rather refused to give her any special importance, as mentioned earlier. But, Mother Mary now finds a special place in the prayers of the devout Catholic Christians, who while telling the beads on their rosary also pray 'Hail Mary, full of grace'.

Altogether, there are six prayers that are told on the rosary. Along with them are twenty mysteries on which one is supposed to meditate for one's spiritual growth. These twenty mysteries are twenty episodes from the life of the Saviour, like the birth of Jesus, his turning water into wine, crucifixion, etc. The great Christian monks, including the famous desert fathers, who lived the life of hermits in complete seclusion, have achieved enlightenment through these prayers and meditations.

Then there are seven sacraments (lit. sign of the sacred)— Baptism, Confirmation, Eucharist, Penance, Anointing of the Sick,

Holy Orders, and Matrimony. These are also known as sacramental grace since they flow from God as His grace. It is through the purification by these sacramental graces that a Christian becomes fit to receive the mercy of God. It is believed that these were instituted by Jesus Christ himself. Each of these is treated as Lord Christ himself because he gave his life to take the sin of the world upon himself to save the devout. Without receiving the sacraments, one cannot hope to be saved.

The important thing about the sacraments is that they are independent of the powers of the person handing it out; rather they depend entirely on the receiving power of the devotee. In the individual's preparedness to receive the grace of God, the priest acts as a mere conduit.

Baptism is the act of purification by water by a priest usually associated with admission to Christianity.

Confirmation is the strengthening of the union between an individual and God. This is usually performed when a baptised person grows up to have his own power of judgement to accept God and the basic tenets of his religion.

Eucharist (also called Holy Communion or the Lord's Supper) consists of a ritual meal of consecrated bread and wine that is treated as the body and blood of the Saviour. It is something like the *prasad* in the Hindu tradition. This sacrament is a strong source of spiritual healing, renewal of faith, and strengthening of bondage among the Christians. After the Sunday mass in the church, Eucharist is taken to the sick so that they too may receive the grace.

Penance involves four elements—contrition (sincere remorse of the wrongdoer); confession to a priest; absolution by the priest; and satisfaction or penance.

Anointing of the sick is the sacrament in which a priest anoints the sick with oil that has been blessed specifically for that purpose.

Matrimony is sacred in Christianity and seen as a grace of God.

Holy Orders, or Ordination, is the sacrament in which the priest vows to lead a religious life in which poverty, chastity, and obedience play an important role. A priest thus ordained also takes the vow of leading other Christians towards a religious life.

Centring the Lord's life, Christians assemble for communal worship, usually at a church, on Sunday, the day of the resurrection. In the same vein, Christmas, the day of the Lord's birthday, and Easter, his resurrection day are celebrated as the main festivals.

SECTS AND THE CHURCH

Of all religions, Christianity alone happens to be centrally organised. Even the highly monastic Buddhism never had the idea of a central church that would decide the fate and philosophy of its followers. In Christianity, the Church came to be considered as the mystical body of Jesus, and hence the central authority for Christians. It is believed, even after giving up his human form, Jesus continued with his mission through a new physical body in the form of the Church, whose head is he himself, and the Holy Spirit is its soul. Individual Christians are its cells. Thus, Christianity came to be identified with the Church, practically, from the time of Jesus and later came to represent the official view of the Christian world, even though some of those views were not in consonance with the Bible. Even some core ideas were decided by the Church and rejected through voting, like the idea of rebirth.

After the death of Jesus, his followers formed the Jewish Christian movement in Jerusalem. The members regarded themselves as a reform movement within Judaism and continued to sacrifice at the temple, circumcise their male children, follow Jewish kosher food laws, etc. These were all given up with time to stick to the new identity of Christianity.

Saul of Tarsus, originally a persecutor of the Jewish Christians, had a vision of the risen Christ, in c. 34, while on the road to Damascus to persecute the Christians. The vision caused a sudden conversion in him, and from being a Christian baiter, he became its protector. Adopting the new name of Paul, he became the greatest theologian of the early Christian movement. His writings, along with those of the authors of the Gospel of John, provided much of the theological foundation for what has been called Pauline Christianity.

Another belief system prevalent in earlier times was Gnostic Christianity. They taught that Jesus was a spirit sent by God to impart knowledge to humans so that they can escape the miseries of life on earth.

In addition to Gnostic, Jewish, and Pauline Christianity, there are many other sects of Christianity. They all adhere to the core beliefs but differ in the details. Of these the most important sect is Protestants.

The absolute power over the Christian world, coupled with the lack of religious freedom, made the Church more concerned with the world than with God. By the power the Church had, it even started selling 'indulgence' by which one could get away by committing any crime and then paying to the church for forgiveness. Martin Luther (16th CE), became so upset at what was going on in the name of Jesus that he started a reformative movement known as Protestantism. This led to a split within the church.

According to one estimate, there are over 30,000 denominations (organised group) in Christianity these days, each claiming to be the correct path to God. These groups may broadly be classified into three: a) Roman Catholic, which is the largest single body; b) Eastern Orthodoxy, which includes the Greek Orthodox, Russian Orthodox, and Armenian Orthodoxy; c) Protestantism, which includes the Anglican, Lutherans, Evangelical, and others.

MONASTICISM

The life and teachings of Jesus are essentially monastic in nature, as that was of Buddha. Jesus himself stands as the ideal of giving up everything for God, and his teachings too are a reminder of that.

> No man can serve two masters; for either he will hate the one and love the other, or else he will hold to the one, and despise the other. Ye cannot serve God and mammon....

ೲ

> For there are some eunuchs, which were so born from their mother's womb: and there are some eunuchs, which were made eunuchs of men: and there be eunuchs, which have made themselves eunuchs for the kingdom of heaven's sake. He that is able to receive it, let him receive it.

ೲ

> The foxes have holes and the birds of the air have nests, but the Son of Man has nowhere to lay His head.

Monasticism began early in the church. Those who had similar spiritual disposition modelled upon scriptural examples and ideals, lived together to lead a life of complete dedication to God. With time these evolved into two types: a) Hermits, who live in solitude, b) monks, who live in a monastery. Originally, all Christian monks were hermits, but the need for some form of organised spiritual guidance lead to the building of the first monastery. Soon, similar institutions were established throughout the Egyptian desert and in the eastern half of the Roman Empire.

The Christian monks take up the vows of chastity, poverty, and obedience, and live by these virtues. This is in contrast with the Hindu monks who do not take up any vows; they rather give up the identifications that they had with their body, mind, and the world. A Christian monk wants to be perfect in the image of Christ, while a Hindu monk believes that he is perfect by nature but has accumulated the dirt of worldliness over the course of his existence.

THE LAST WORD

Christianity is vast and is as deep. More importantly, it has immense thought currents produced due to the conflict of ideas working within it. It talks about faith but has produced maximum number of thinkers and scientists; it talks about God's will, yet Christian world has been most assertive in its individuality; it talks about turning the other cheek but that has caused maximum bloodshed in the world; it talks about God and His children, and yet believes in sinners and their Saviour. The list goes on.

Faith is a defining trait of Abrahamic religions. Going strictly by it, one may think Christianity to be a hidebound religion. However, the freedom of thought that one sees today in philosophy, society, politics, literature, art, science, etc. is the contribution of the Christian world. In spite of the restrictions imposed by the theologians, the freedom preached by the Lord somehow ignited the higher minds that resulted in the freedom of the thought. The world can never be grateful enough for this.

The universal love and acceptance as preached by Jesus is, indeed, the highest state of inclusiveness. The greatness of the Saviour clearly shows that he was much more than a human being. He was a principle to live by.

Islam
Religion of Surrender

EARLY DAYS

The dry desert of Arabia, in the earlier times, could sustain only the nomadic tribes that travelled across its vast stretches of land with their camels and goats in search of food and fodder. They were divided into clans and tribes to which they owed their loyalty. With time, these nomads started settling down near springs, wells, or along the coast, where they lived as small-time farmers, harvesting date palms and tending camels and sheep. With the excess of what they produced, they took up the trade of camels, sheep, wool, etc. Looting of caravans was the other profitable enterprise. There is an interesting old saying about these Bedouin people that throws some light on their need for survival: 'I against my brother; my brothers and I against my cousins; then my cousins and I against strangers'.

It was in this land and among these people that Ishmael had reached some 4,000 years ago. He was the son of Abraham, from a slave girl, and was accepted as the forefather of Arab tribes from where Islam spread all over the world. The other son of Abraham was Isaac, whose descendants came to be known as Jews, from which Christianity sprang. Thus, Abraham is the common father of these three Abrahamic religions. It is also known as Semitic religions (from Shem, son of Noah) because of a common ancestry of the language and culture of the land.

According to Islamic traditions, Ishmael established a Kaaba a cube-shaped stone building, as the house of God at Mecca, which must have been an inconsequential oasis in those days. Because of the Kaaba, Mecca became a place of pilgrimage for those Arabs who considered themselves descendants of Abraham.

By the time Prophet Muhammad was born in Mecca, the fortune of the city-state had brightened further, and it had become a commercial centre by 600 CE by gaining control of the caravan trade, passing up and down the west coast of Arabia. This change had taken place due to a rapid rise of pirates on the more convenient sea route. Mecca thus became a place for trade, pilgrimage, and also for tribal gatherings. This caused a cross-current of thoughts that had their origin in Arab, Iran, and Israel.

Being of Abrahamic stock, people of Arabia were religious in their own way. However, they felt bad that they did not have a revealed religion, nor had they been lucky to have a prophet amidst them, as Jews and Christians did. To add to their chagrin, the local Christians and Jews mocked at them for being left out like this by God. So, when God finally chose Prophet Muhammad as His messenger to end idolatry and to lead people towards Allah, the spiritually parched people of Arabia lapped up the new religion with a vigour that has not been seen in the world of religion ever. The excitement and enthusiasm caused in the hearts of the believers by the newfound spiritual liberty were too strong for the non-believers to withstand. The resulting wars, battles, and bloodshed between the two, and their consequences, were a foregone conclusion.

Muhammad was born around 570 CE in a poor family. His father, Abdullah, died before his birth, and he lost both his grandfather and his mother when he was still a child. The lack of any inheritance forced him to take up the job of a shepherd with his uncle, whose sheep and camels he tended. Jesus had talked of himself as a good shepherd, while Muhammad started the journey of his life literally as a shepherd.

Life in the desert is harsh, and its aridity can dry up the finer sensibilities of a person. But Muhammad was different. Unlike others, he was a sincere and honest person on whom one could depend. This earned him a commission from a wealthy widow, Khadija, who made him a steward of her trade to Syria, and on the successful accomplishment of the mission, she offered herself in marriage to him. She was forty at that time and had been widowed twice; Muhammad was twenty-five. The marriage was as successful as it could be, and Muhammad remained committed to her till her last. At the time of her death, Muhammad was fifty and had three sons and four daughters from her. Unfortunately, only his daughter, Fatima, survived him; the rest predeceased him. Muhammad had eleven wives after Khadija passed away, but it is said that he did not have any child with them.

Sometime after his marriage with Khadija, Muhammad began to devote time in contemplating on God in solitude. For this he often went to a mountain cave, Hira, on the outskirts of Mecca, where he spent long hours alone in the cave, praying to God. A time came when his prayers were answered and in the year c. 610 CE, the angel Gabriel appeared to him and commanded him to recite:

In the name of God, Most Gracious,
Most Merciful.

Proclaim! (or read)

In the name

Of thy Lord and Cherisher,

who created—

Created man, out of

A (mere) clot

of congealed blood:

Proclaim! And thy Lord

is most bountiful—

He who taught

(the use of) the pen—

This was the first revelation that Muhammad heard. For the rest of his life, he was to hear a large number of revelations that were collected in the sacred book, Quran. This particular revelation was incorporated in Surah-96 of the holy book.

Gabriel, the angel also told Muhammad that he was to be the Messenger of God (Paigambar, Prophet) on this earth. As the Prophet of God, he was to stop his people from idolatry and had to lead them to the worship of the one God, Allah. The tradition goes that after some ten years of this spiritual experience, Gabriel took Muhammad on the heavenly horse, Buraq, to the 'farthest mosque', possibly in Jerusalem, from there they travelled through various heavens to meet the earlier prophets and then they presented themselves before Allah. There, in the presence of Moses, Muhammad was instructed by God to pray five times daily—a practice that became one of the pillars of Islam.

From that first revelation onward, Muhammad's life was to become a long story of divine revelations and visions through which he was to act as the conduit between God and His people. What he heard from God and how he lived and behaved became the filter through which devout Muslims strained themselves to become perfect by giving up worldliness.

One may wonder whether one can hear God the way it has just been described. Or better still, does God even talk? The answer is a resounding, 'Yes'. The entire history of religions is full of great personalities who heard God—Noah, Abraham, Moses, Jesus, Muhammad, and Zarathustra—they all heard God speak to them. Indian religions firmly believe in this. Sri Ramakrishna specifically said that when one realises God, He talks directly to that person, and this is one sign of true God-realisation.

Since many emotionally unstable people hear voices as well, the sceptics like to tick off even the genuine spiritual cases. To judge whether a person indeed hears the words of God, one only needs to see if the claimant has the character, commitment, and compassion centring God.

Muhammad first talked about his spiritual experiences to his wife, who was convinced of his greatness, and she became his first converted disciple. He then started communicating these messages to his close friends, and finally by 612 CE onwards he started proclaiming the message freely. This drew many people, especially the younger ones, towards the new faith, Islam (submission to God) as the way of life (*deen*), in which one prayed five times daily:

Allaahu Akbar: God is great.

Ashhadu anna lah ilaaha illa-Lah: I bear witness that there is none worthy of worship except God.

Ash Hadu anna Muhamadar Rasulullah: I bear witness that Muhammad is the Messenger of God.

Hayya' alas Salaah: Come to prayer.

Hayya' ala Falaah: Come to Felicity (blissful state)

Allaahu Akbar: God is great.

Laa ilaaha illa-Lah: There is none worthy of worship except God.

This simple but profound prayer, as revealed to the Prophet, touched the hearts of the believers, who felt spiritually uplifted, and gained a sense of unity with all those who accepted the faith.

The important thing to note in this prayer is its assertion of the greatness of God above everything else in this world and heaven, which is preached by every religion. But unlike the Indic religions, Abrahamic religions, particularly Islam, interpret the greatness of God above everything to mean the supremacy of one's religion above others. In Islam, the ethos of Arab people to sort out the differences through fight leaves an additional imprint on it, the consequences of which have not always been peaceful.

ALLAH, THE ONE GOD

Before the advent of Prophet Muhammad, Arabs had the tribal concept of gods and djinns, according to which people were ruled by fate, over which no single power had complete control. The gods of nature, represented by idols, were the movers of the forces of nature, controlling local destinies. Greek gods were like this, and so were the gods of early Jewish people till Abraham changed all that for his people.

The Kaaba at Mecca where the Arabs of the period came to worship, had three hundred and sixty idols, same as the number of days of their lunar calendar. These idols, representing various facets of internal and external nature, were worshipped in anticipation of favours. When Muhammad began his spiritual journey, he was blessed by the words of Allah as described above. Many historians believe that Allah was one of the deities of the Kaaba, while traditionalists deny that, stressing the fact that 'Allah' in Arabic is derived from *al* and *ilah*, meaning 'the God'. Whatever the historicity, the ultimate result was that Arabia finally came to experience monotheism, expressed as Allah, the one God in exclusion to all the deities and djinns whom they earlier worshipped.

When God is perceived as infinite, it becomes difficult to contemplate on Him or to think of Him. An object causes sensations in the mind and thus produces mental impressions known as knowledge. But God, call it by any name, is neither an object nor finite to be captured as a mental impression. So, the mystics say that it is impossible to know God in His infinite aspect unless a person's consciousness merges completely in Him; for the rest, God can be known only by some pointer that can be grasped by the mind. Allah is that term by which God, the infinite, can be hinted at; It is not a name as is used for an object or a person.

Monotheism by its very definition is exclusive in nature. It means that it does not allow room for any other principle concerning God beyond what it believes. In extreme cases, religious exclusiveness extends to their prophets too. Thus, Christians believe that Jesus is the only Saviour, and Islam believes that Muhammad is Allah's last and the best Prophet in the series of His prophets (that he sent for Judaism and Christianity) on this earth.

A closer look at the concept of God in Islam reveals that Allah is not much different from the God of Christians and Jews. As mentioned in the earlier chapter, if the names of these gods were interchanged, it would be difficult for a common man to distinguish between the traits of the God of these three religions. The relative difference between these religions belongs to their respective prophets and their characteristics. Thus, while Islam claims to be the superior religion because it has the last and the best prophet, Christians and Jews reject the idea, and also reject the idea that Allah is same as their God.

The idea of God in Islam has come solely from what Prophet Muhammad uttered on the subject. This has resulted in a coherent idea about the Lord's nature unlike what one gets in other religions. For example, the unlimited variety and facets of God, the infinite, as seen in Hinduism, is replaced in Islam by a unified principle, which makes it easy for the simple folks to grasp the idea. The majesty of the infinite is thus replaced by simplicity.

God, according to Islam, exists but cannot be described, comprehended, or seen. He is stern but also forgiving and compassionate. The sacred books teach that God responds to anyone who prays to Him in distress, and He provides guidance to humanity to follow the path of righteousness.

> God is the light of the heavens and the earth. The example of His light is like a niche, wherein is a lamp; the lamp is in a crystal, and the crystal, shining as if a pearl-like radiant star, lit from the oil of a blessed olive tree that is neither of the east nor of the west. The oil would almost give light of itself though no fire touches it. Light upon light! God guides to His light whom He wills. God strikes parables for people. God has full knowledge of all things. *(Quran.24.35)*

Although God has revealed His will through the prophets, His actual nature remains unknowable. He is the all-powerful creator of a perfect, ordered universe. He is transcendent and is not part of His creation (unlike the Christian belief). He does not exist in anything, nor does anything exist in Him. He is above the Seven Heavens, mounted on His throne in the manner that suits His grandeur and majesty. He is also present everywhere and is 'as close to a man as the vein in his neck', without being one with it.

The nature of God in Islam can be best understood by the ninety-nine names, representing His qualities, by which Muslims pray. Some of these names are Allah (The Greatest Name), Ar-Rahman (The All-Compassionate), Ar-Rahim (The All-Merciful), Al-Malik (The Absolute Ruler), Al-Quddus (The Pure One), As-Salam (The Source of Peace), Al-Mu'min (The Inspirer of Faith) … Ar-Rashid (The Righteous Teacher), As-Sabur (The Patient One).

Allah, the divine dispenser of justice, expects righteous behaviour and submission to the divine will from His people. He is the *Rubb* who gets things done by mere will. Nothing happens without His will. He is merciful but He does punish unrighteousness.

Say, [O Muhammad], 'If you should love Allah, then follow me, [so] Allah will love you and forgive you your sins. And Allah is Forgiving and Merciful. *(3.31)*

He loves not creatures ungrateful or wicked *(2.276)*

Allah loves not the arrogant, the vainglorious *(4.36)*

God will not forgive the disbelievers, nor will He spare those who give up faith once they have taken it up, 'As to those who reject faith, I will punish them with terrible agony in this world and in the Hereafter, nor will they have anyone to help. *(3.56)*

THE PROPHET

From the day that Khadija accepted Muhammad as her spiritual master, he came to be adored as the Prophet who had a spiritual message to give and also to set things right for his people. His life is shrouded in a mass of legends and traditions contained mostly in the *Hadith*, the secondary scriptures. In general, Islamic scholars have stressed upon his human nature, while presenting him as infallible on matters of prophecy since those were the words of God.

In the first ethical steps, Prophet unified the Arabs in a community to stop the bloodshed that was common in those days. He stopped the idea of might is right and replaced it with noble qualities like humility and peace. He also instilled the idea of considering the community as one's own. These led to the reorientation of the then Arabic society as regards to their identity, belief, world view, and values. He preached against the social evils in areas of social security, family structure, slavery, rights of women, rights of ethnic minorities, female foeticide, exploitation, murder, etc. He also made it the responsibility of the Islamic government to provide food and clothing to captives, regardless of their religion. Islam also brought major changes to ancient slavery system. Slaves were now treated as human beings with a certain religious and social status and with certain quasi-legal rights.

The assertion of the equality of all, in the eyes of Allah, resulted in a kind of ethical advancement for the Arabs comparable to the advanced culture of Greco-Roman and the ancient Persian world. It is indeed amazing how one person could infuse a soft culture for its members, who otherwise knew only revenge and plunder. This transformation must be treated as the greatest miracle by Prophet Muhammad.

Prophet Muhammad experienced life in its many hues. He had been a shepherd, merchant, soldier, sage, hermit, mystic, exile, lawmaker, and prophet-priest-king. On the personal side, he had been an orphan, a king, a dedicated husband, and finally a husband of many wives. In all these roles he proved exemplary. He married twelve times, but only after the death of Khadija, his first wife. They were done mostly to save the concerned women from destitution. Most of them were widows of the martyrs of the Islamic cause.

Prophet Muhammad was aware that it would be necessary to expand beyond Arabia. Since tribes allied to him could not raid other allies, hence their energies needed to be directed elsewhere. He thus devoted special attention to the tribes on the route to Syria and to a lesser extent on the route to Iraq. He also won over his chief Meccan opponents, and their administrative skills later proved invaluable in conquering and ruling numerous provinces. The growth of the Arab Empire and Islam was made possible by favourable circumstances also; but the opportunity would not have been grasped without Muhammad's gifts of being a visionary statesman and administrator.

At a popular level, Muslims venerate him by expressing their love and devotion to him through poems, folk songs, and prayers invoking God's blessings. Many believe that he will intercede on their behalf on the Day of Judgement, the way Jesus is expected to do for the Christians. Prophet Muhammad is also considered sinless, and no act of his, howsoever trivial or serious, can be judged or reviewed by anyone in this world. Whatever a man of God does, is beyond the parameters of the world; the sins of the world do not touch him

Prophet Muhammad is thus viewed by Muslims as the spiritual guide and also as an exemplar in social, ethical, and political terms.

Islamic law grew from the impersonal spiritual principles of Quran, and also from the understanding of Muhammad's day-to-day manner of handling temporal issues. Of course, that creates certain emotional torque for people who have to balance the practices of seventh-century Arabia with today's changing world.

TO MEDINA WITH THE NEW RELIGION

The message of Allah and the new way of life preached by Muhammad annoyed many in Mecca, who felt socially, morally, and financially threatened by it. The monotheistic preaching by Muhammad stopped the income for those connected with the religious business at Kaaba. The moral teaching of Islam, the new faith, restricted the wild behaviour of the citizens of Mecca, who lacked finer sensitivities and were mired in a life of pleasure. Also, the moral responsibilities of the higher way of life preached by Prophet hit at the unjust social order of the period. These outcomes of the new teachings were indeed sufficient to put the old order into unease. Soon, opposition to Muhammad and his preaching spread among the leading merchants of Mecca, who started persecuting him and his followers. To escape these persecutions, including a threat to his life, Muhammad had to emigrate to Medina with some of his trusted followers in September 622 CE. This 'holy emigration' (rather than 'flight') is known as Hijrah, on which the Islamic era is based.

When Muhammad reached Medina from Mecca (around 400 km), he was welcomed by the Arab clans of the town who entered into an alliance with him and his followers. At first, the emigrants depended on the hospitality of people of Medina, but soon small groups, including the new converts from Medina, began to raid the

Meccan caravans to create their own wealth. This was a normal practice in those days. However, in this case, these were no tribal groups taking revenge but those united in the name of Islam, the religion of peace.

The word *Islam* is derived from the Arabic *aslama*, which primarily means 'peace'. It also means, 'to accept, surrender, or submit'. Thus, Islam means 'peace that comes when one surrenders to God'. Believers must demonstrate this by worshipping Him, following His commands, and surrendering oneself completely to Him.

The importance of prayer and surrender to God is best exemplified in one story of Fatima, the beloved daughter of Prophet. She was married to Ali, a deeply religious man. Once the couple was passing through severe financial strain at Medina, like many others. To seek help from her father, Fatima went to the Prophet one day, but he politely refused. He said that the money with him belonged to the community. That night, the Prophet visited them, and said, 'Let me tell you of something better than that which you asked of me. You should say *Subhaan Allah*—Glory be to God' ten times after every prayer, and ten times *Al hamdu lillah*—Praise be to God,' and ten times *Allahu Akbar*—God is Great. And that when you go to bed you should say them thirty-three times each.' The idea is that one must pray to God and depend on Him for everything.

This story, simple in its form but profound in its implications, reveal how Islam touched the hearts of people all over the world. The strength of a religion lies in its God-centredness, and not in wordplay or rationality. Akbar, the Moghul king, started a new religion, Deen-e Ilahi, by taking great concepts from different religions. But it proved to be a colossal failure even while he was alive. To arouse the dormant divine within a person, it has to be touched directly by the divine or through a tradition handed down from the divine.

The success and greatness of Islam lie in its core spirituality, which was handed to Prophet Muhammad, who in turn passed it on to all through his successors and followers. It is a fact of life that the spirit touches the spirit, and matter touches only matter. The spiritual need of people varies widely. The land of Arabia, as also of many other parts of the world, was in need of the spiritual message conveyed by Prophet Muhammad. The essence of that message was similar to what other religions preached, but the format was different, which suited the need of a particular class of people.

During the time of Muhammad, Medina had a large Jewish population that controlled most of the wealth of the city. As Muhammad believed firmly in his position as last of the prophets and as the successor of Jesus, he expected that the Jews and Christians would welcome him and accept his revelations, but he was disappointed in that. The Jews accepted Muhammad's administration but refused to offer him any religious allegiance. The same happened with the Christians too. Then there were some betrayals and let downs by both religions that made him distrustful of Christians as well as Jews. Thus, Islam developed a certain distinct identity from both the religions, while maintaining certain common threads because of their common ancestry.

In the meanwhile, the raids from Medina by the Islamic groups continued on the unprotected traders. At first, those raids did not have much success, but once a small band of attackers led by Muhammad himself decisively defeated a much larger force of Meccans. This caused a serious blow to Meccan prestige but gave a great boost to the faith of believers, who felt that God was vindicating Muhammad. This battle came to be known as the Battle of Badr.

To teach Muhammad a lesson, the Meccans then invaded Medina with a large force. Muhammad fought bravely but was defeated and had to beat a retreat. Fortunately, the Meccan army did not pursue the advantage, so not much harm was done, but the reverse in the battle shook the belief of the followers that God was vindicating him. But devoted as they were to the Prophet, their confidence in the Prophet was restored soon enough.

One wonders as to how Prophet Muhammad conducted raids that led to bloody battles. The answer is that every Prophet follows the norms of his society. None of the prophets in the history of humankind has ever adopted abrupt and drastic means to change the ways of his people. They all lead their people gently towards God by allowing some licences and taking away many more. For the Arab people, raiding and retribution was the norm by which they lived.

Thus, the Muslim groups, protected by the Prophet, started making several attacks each year with success. This annoyed the Meccans, who laid a siege of Medina with a strong army in April 627 CE. Muhammad himself protected the central part of the oasis by a trench that foiled the Meccan cavalry. For various reasons, the Meccan alliance broke up after a fortnight and the siege was raised. This was a major boost for Muhammad and his followers. When he went to perform traditional pilgrimage rites next year to Mecca, where he was prohibited from entering, the Meccans did turn him back as expected. However, they concluded a treaty with him. This was a triumph for Muhammad.

In the following months, many nomadic tribesmen and a few leading Meccans went to Medina to join Muhammad to become Muslims. This gave the new converts the protection that was important in those lawless days of the Arabian desert. The general opinion about Muhammad was now improving rapidly.

In January 630 CE, the treaty between Meccan and Medina people was denounced due to an incident involving allies of both sides. Muhammad then marched to Mecca with an army of 10,000 men who virtually faced no resistance in the city. He then entered Mecca in triumph, the city of his birth from where he had to once flee to live in exile. A fortnight later another 2,000 joined Muhammad's army in opposing a concentration of tribesmen east of Mecca and shared another victory. Muhammad was now the strongest leader in Arabia, and when he died on 8 June 632, he was in effective control of a large part of Arabia.

Muhammad's achievements have captivating similarities with other spiritual masters of the Abrahamic religions. In his attack on idol worship, he is like Abraham; as the codifier of the Islamic law, he is like Moses; in his political leadership, he has the appeal of David; and in conveying the message of God's love, he is like Jesus. The great unifier that he was, Prophet Muhammad united the ever-quarrelling tribes, bordering the urban and sophisticated empires of the vast desert into a single social unit under the banner of a monotheistic belief.

SACRED TEXT

It was described earlier how Gabriel first recited divine words to Muhammad, and how Prophet continued to hear and then re-recite them to his followers. It is described in the sacred books that whenever messages came to him from God, they used to sound like the 'reverberating of bells' which gradually used to get condensed into a single voice. Those messages of God (revelations) used to take a complete control of Muhammad's personality, appearance and voice. The words seemed to weigh upon him as if they were solid and heavy. Once, he was on a camel when these voices came. The camel tried to adjust the increased weight but finally collapsed under it, with its belly pressed against the earth and legs spread wide.

Comparing the spiritual agony of Muhammad with the shallowness of a common mind, Swami Vivekananda said:

> Some people find it really difficult to understand the frenzy of religious fervour which moved the heart of Muhammad. He would grovel in the dust and writhe in agony. Holy men who have experienced these extreme emotions have been called epileptic. The absence of the thought of self is the essential characteristic of the love of God. Religion nowadays has become a mere hobby and fashion. People go to church like a flock of sheep. They do not embrace God because they need Him. Most persons are unconscious atheists who self-complacently think that they are devout believers. *(CW.8.202)*

What the Prophet uttered in those moments of trance, were collected to form the sacred Quran, which literally means recitation. The first words of the Quran came to Muhammad in the month of Ramadan in 610 CE, and he continued to receive messages in various contexts for the next twenty-three years, until his death in 632 CE. These were collected and organised into chapters, or *surah*s, partly during Muhammad's lifetime and definitively about

650 CE. Over the centuries, it has proved to be the most recited and memorised book in the world. So great was Muhammad's regard for its contents that he considered it the only major miracle of God, worked through him. Prophet himself was unlettered, and yet the book is grammatically perfect and poetically marvellous! This is the chief argument in favour of the divine origin of the book. The beauty and the poetry of the language are so captivating that no translation can do a justice to it. Muslims all over the world strive to learn Arabic just to read the holy book.

There are 114 surahs in the Quran, arranged in order of decreasing length. The first surah has 286 verses, whereas the last has only six. Coincidentally, Rigveda is also arranged in the same style. The content of Quran has a comprehensive outlook towards life, which provides its followers with spirituality, rituals, social conduct, history, legal considerations, and other issues that a person may have to face in his journey of life.

The opening chapter of Quran, 'Al-Fatihah', has seven verses and is considered to be the central message of Quran:

> In the name of God, most gracious, most merciful.
> Praise be to God, the cherisher and sustainer of the worlds;
> Most Gracious, most merciful;
> Master of the Day of Judgement.
> Him we worship, and His aid we seek.
> Show us the straight way,
> The way of those on whom Thou hast bestowed Thy Grace, those whose (portion) is not wrath, and who go not astray.

The second surah (chapter), 'Al-Baqarah' (The Heifer), is considered to be the gist of the whole Quran. The Quran is treated as a perfect copy of an eternal book—the *umm al-Kitab*, or Mother of the Book—that has existed forever with Allah. Thus, the words in the Quran, though spoken out by Muhammad as revelation, are not Muhammad's. This book is not only sacred for the Muslims but is also venerated as divine, next only to God,

Although it is the word of God, Quran is not treated as His essence or nature. Allah Himself is the speaker nearly throughout the Quran (there are occasional mention of 'if Allah wills' (*Surah 48.27*). Most often Allah addresses Muhammad directly, frequently telling him what to say about various matters, and legislates by giving him instructions on what laws to lay down.

The message and teachings of this sacred book are tiered, which helps differently-evolved persons take up various teachings according to their disposition. On the higher side are the spiritual truths that assert God's greatness and power, as taught by every religion. The next tier belongs to the religiously inclined, who are repeatedly reminded of the importance of Day of Judgement when they would be called to justice and will then be assigned to paradise or hell in accordance with their righteous living. The assertion to be charitable, noble, religious, and pious is central to this tier. The third aspect of Quranic teachings is when they exhort believers to defend themselves against the non-believers, and also attack the idolatrous, blasphemous, and the wicked.

These three tiers bring out the divide between the spiritual, religious, and the fanatic. Depending on which verse one prefers to adopt, a person gets the choice of moulding his personality on the lines of one of these three. It is due to this that Islam has produced great mystics, along with the not-so tolerant.

SECONDARY SCRIPTURES

Early Muslims elaborated two sources to provide the context for the Quran: Tafsir (commentary on the Quran) and Hadith, traditions of the Prophet Muhammad.

Tafsir literally means to explain and expound. In Islamic tradition, it implies understanding and uncovering the inner meaning of the Quranic text. This demands a thorough knowledge of classical Arabic language, particularly the language current in the Prophet's time. In addition to this, one has to know the laws, rulings, finer shades of language for metaphors, and an understanding of the parables. The first Tafsir came from Prophet himself. Later, the sacred work was taken up by his successors and then by the scholars.

Hadith is the collection Prophet Muhammad's sayings as opposed to what he uttered in a trance and has been recorded in the Quran. When Prophet died, many people came up with claims to have heard many things from him, and seen him doing certain things. However, not all of these could be substantiated. So, the oral traditions were collected, cross-checked, and only those were accepted that seemed to be authentic. These came to be known as Hadith.

Unlike Quran, which was compiled under the official direction of the early Islamic state in Medina, Hadith was not a compilation by a central authority. In fact, the process of compilation began generations after the death of Prophet. Of the many Hadiths, six are considered to be authentic, of which the most authentic one is by Muhammad al-Bukhari, who was born in 810 CE, well after Prophet had passed away.

A significant amount of a Hadith is Tafsir itself. They give the circumstances of revelation for various Quranic verses, which can have important implications on how the verse is to be applied in the modern age. Most *fatwah*s (diktats by the Muslim religious body) are issued based on a Hadith, although different sects of Islam rely on different Hadiths. There are some that are not even accepted as authentic.

In addition to these, there is the *Sira*, or biography of Prophet. The first full-length biography of the Prophet did not appear until 150 years after his death. The Prophet's first biographer was Muhammad Ibn Ishaq Ibn Yasar, generally known as Ibn Ishaq (704–773 CE). While many biographical nuggets are contained in other sources, Ibn Ishaq's *Sirat Rasul Allah* (Biography of the Prophet of Allah) was the first attempt to provide a continuous narrative of Muhammad's life.

The Quran, Hadith and *Sira* make up *Sunnah*, which defines the way of life for a Muslim. It is the model that has to be followed by every practising Muslim.

PHILOSOPHY

The land of Arabia was parched of spirituality and philosophy before the advent of the Prophet. Once the floodgates of Islam were opened by him, not just Arabia but countries after countries were flooded with Islamic philosophy, religion, and culture, all over the world in a very short time. Incidentally, during this period of flooding of Islamic philosophy, the rest of the world seemed arid due to reasons of their own—Christian Europe world had entered the Dark Ages, Buddhism was decaying towards irrelevance in India, and Hinduism was lost in spiritual ennui. Of the four chief philosophical forces of the world, only Islam remained vibrant, acting as the channel for the East-West linkage of thought process.

The spiritual upheaval caused by the Prophet resulted in a torrential outpouring of philosophical and scientific work by the Islamic minds for centuries. A lot of advancements in the world of ideas at present times, like popularising the use of zero which was invented in India, are directly linked to the rise of Islamic scholarship during the period. The love for learning among the Muslims of that period was so great that scholars went everywhere to learn the science of that land, even if that be an enemy land.

Every religious philosophy discusses the nature of God, man (soul), and the world. Along with these, it discusses the methods by which knowledge is acquired and the parameters within which the discussions are made. Islamic philosophy discusses the nature of God and soul strictly from the standpoint of Quran. Its content is nearer to Judaism than any other religion while its idea of the world builds on Greek philosophy. It is believed that in its early days, Islamic scholars looked at Greek philosophy with suspicion, but slowly they adopted it well.

God in Islam is monotheistic, as described earlier, and His prophets are all men who act as His messengers. Islam does not accept that a prophet can be His begotten son as in Christianity or Himself as in Hinduism. Although Muslims believe that Jesus was a prophet, they reject the Christian doctrine of the Trinity, comparing it to polytheism (many gods). Prophets are considered closest to perfection of all humans and are the unique recipients of divine grace, either directly from God or through angels. Islamic theology says that all of God's messengers since Adam preached the message of Islam—submission to the will of the one God, and Prophet Muhammad was the last of this series.

Islam does not believe in the immanence of God, nor does it accept the idea of God being everything, as in Hinduism. The idea that Allah can appear in any other form than what He is, is unacceptable in Islam. Nor can Allah be seen or experienced by anyone. The very idea that one may physically see God is held to be a sort of polytheism and idolatry. Only Moses and Muhammad were capable to see the Lord.

The uniqueness attributed to Allah is the stand-alone outlook of Islam. So much so, it does not even accept the words of Quran as being one with God, as Bible believes, or as Hindus accept. There were periods in Islam when scholars were beheaded by the kings for holding the belief that Allah and His words are non-different. Many devout find it easier to settle a philosophical debate with the help of a sword than through reasoning even today.

Islam does not believe in a go-between an individual and Allah. So, there is no need for a church, clergy, rituals, or a priest for saying one's prayers to the Lord.

The concept of 'original sin' of Adam and Eve of Christianity is replaced by *gaflah*, negligence. People on this earth are not weighed down by sin but have forgotten their divine origin due to negligence. Islam that way is nearer to Hinduism than Christianity.

The concept of evil is also different in Islam. Iblis is considered evil in Islam, but it is not because of his evil deeds. He loved God so much that he refused to bow down before Adam, a man, whom God considered to be His highest creation. This actually implies that the greatest evil for a religious person is to apply his free will against the Divine command. Surrender to the will of God being primary in Islam, anyone who tries to assert himself beyond what has been commanded, is sinful, and it is a punishable act by God. This approach is central to Judaism too.

The world is God's creation and hence very much real, important, and good. Unlike many other religions, there is no inherent dualism between the physical world and the world of the spirit in Islam. Here there is no struggle to annihilate the world of the flesh to reach the other world. If one follows the basic tenets of Islam and stays pure during the time of prayer, a devout is guaranteed the access to the heaven. So, one can expect to move towards God not by giving up the world, but by a complete sense of attraction for Him.

Allah does not discriminate between His devotees, so Islam is based on the principle of equality of all human beings who are Muslims. The sense of brotherhood implied in this outlook indeed makes Islam great. Once a person accepts Islam as his religion, he does not remain inferior to anyone anymore. This has attracted a large number of underprivileged races and people to accept Islam whenever they found the going tough in their own society. A large many Indians accepted Islam simply because of the social discrimination that they were facing in the Hindu society.

There is nothing universal in Islam. All life is individual, the soul is individual, and God Himself is an individual, though unique. Islam stresses on the self's individuality; its uniqueness, and the responsibility that devolves on it. The individuality of the soul is everlasting. Once created, it never dies.

This, however, creates a philosophical contradiction. The soul is supposed to have its freedom, which implies a freedom of will. On the other hand, God is all-knowing, which points to predestination. Islamic theologians have tried to resolve this contradiction rationally since the earliest days of Islam without much success. They finally concluded that the workings of the Divine Decree remain a mystery to humans, who should rather focus on the freedom that they have in their hands, and stay away from sin and other wrong activities.

One important aspect of Islam is its forays in every area of an individual's life. Thus, apart from religion, it also guides its followers in the matters of the society, politics, and economics. Due to this, Islam ends up being not only a religion but a state too.

WORLD VIEW

According to the Quran, Allah created the Earth and Seven Heavens for his creatures. He then created Adam, Eve, and the Garden of Eden for their stay and was so pleased with His creation that He ordered the angels to prostrate before them. Iblis (Satan), an angel, loved God so much that he refused to bow down to anyone other than Allah. This annoyed God who exiled him from Paradise. Since then Iblis is out to waylay God's people.

When Adam and Eve were expelled from the Eden, they were given the promise that those of their descendants who believe in God and are righteous will return to Paradise to dwell there for eternity.

> Yes, whoever earns evil and his sin has encompassed him—those are the companions of the fire; they will abide therein eternally. But they who believe and do righteous deeds—those are the companions of Paradise; they will abide therein eternally.' *(Quran.2.81–82)*

An individual's lifespan is determined by God, although one has the freedom of choice in most other matters. After death, one has to wait in the grave until the Day of Judgement (*al-Qiayamah*) when everyone will be raised from the dead and called to answer for their thoughts and actions. Only Allah knows the date for this. He will resurrect all, even if they have turned to stone, etc. Once woken, they will feel as if only a short time has passed between their life on the earth and their new birth.

The Judgement Day will start thirty years before the end of the earth. The coming of the Mahadi (the divinely guided one), which would precede the second coming of Jesus, would trigger the redemption of Islam and the defeat of its enemies. Isa (Jesus) and the Mahadi would work together to fight evil in the world to bring justice on earth, and to unite the Muslims and true Christians under true Islam. According to some traditions Isa will marry and have a family, and then die.

After the arrival of the Mahdi—

> The ground will cave in; fog or smoke will cover the skies for forty days. A night, three-nights long will follow the fog. After the night of three nights, the sun will rise in the west. The beast of the earth shall emerge. The beast will talk to people and mark the faces of people. A breeze from the south shall cause all the believers to die. The Quran will be lifted from the hearts of the people...When the sun shall be folded up, and the stars shall fall, and when the mountains shall be set in motion... and the seas shall boil...Then shall every soul know what it has done.

During judgement, a person's own 'book of deeds' will be opened, and he will be apprised of every action he did and every word he spoke. The Quran states that some sins will surely condemn one to hell. The wicked will then be separated from the righteous, where they (the wicked) will 'burn in a blaze.' The hell will burn with such fury that it will nearly burst. It will be surrounded by scalding water, and whenever the fires begin to abate, '...we shall increase for them the blaze.' (*Quran.17:97*).

Over the centuries, a strong belief in the terrifying possibilities arising out of the Judgement Day has helped the preachers portray these vividly to put the fear of God in the hearts of the simple folk. Thus, the religion of peace and self-surrender took up the ideas of fear and divine punishment more and more as the time passed.

The underlying principle of Judgement Day, however, is that of a complete and perfect justice administered by Allah. The accounts of judgement are also replete with the emphasis that Allah is merciful and forgiving, and that mercy and forgiveness will be granted on that day to the deserving.

The righteous, if they are believers too, will go to the heaven, *jannah*, which is a shortened version meaning simply 'garden'. Paradise is described as surrounded by eight principal gates, each level generally superior to the previous by a factor of hundred. The highest level is known as *firdaws* (sometimes called Eden). It will be entered first by Prophet Muhammad, then by those who lived in poverty, and finally, by the most pious. Entrants will be greeted by angels with salutations of peace.

The Islamic texts describe life for its immortal inhabitants, one that is happy—without hurt, sorrow, fear or shame—where every wish is fulfilled. Traditions relate that inhabitants will be of the same age (33 years), and of the same stature. Their life would be one of bliss, which includes: wearing costly robes, bracelets, perfumes; partaking in exquisite banquets, served in priceless vessels by immortal youths; reclining on couches inlaid with gold or precious stones. The food offered there includes meats, scented wine and clear drinks bringing neither drunkenness nor rousing quarrelling. Inhabitants will rejoice in the company of their parents, wives, and children (provided they were admitted to Paradise)—

conversing and recalling the past. Texts also relate 'pure consorts' (*houri*s), created in perfection, with whom carnal joys are shared— 'a hundred times greater than earthly pleasure'. Female inhabitants admitted to Paradise will rank 70,000 times greater than houris through the merit of their good deeds.

It should be mentioned here that much is made out of this description of heaven by some believers, and the same is discredited by the detractors. But the fact is that every religion uses figures of speech to describe the good and the bad to create strong impressions in the minds of the crude to make them pious. The spiritually enlightened never take these figures of speeches literally; for them love for God alone matters above everything.

In spite of the goodly dwellings given to the inhabitants of Paradise, the approval of God and nearness to him is considered greater in Islam. God will bring the elect few near to his throne (*arsh*) on a day on which 'some faces shall be shining in contemplating their Lord.' The vision of God is regarded as the greatest of all rewards, surpassing all other joys.

ETHICS

Ethics in Islam is strictly dictated by what Prophet uttered in Quran as the word of God, and by what he himself did, or said in his non-trance state, in that order of importance. Since the ethical principle in Islam is centred on Prophet Muhammad, the followers of Islam are also known as Mohammedans. In Judaism, ethics flows out from the revelations to prophets, particularly the Ten Commandments; Christianity grounds morality in God's essential character and defines good and bad based on those qualities; Hindu ethics follows the principle of unselfishness; but in Islam, ethics is entirely Prophet Muhammad centric.

The Islamic view of ethics, like the other two Abrahamic religions, affirms ethical absolutes, without any scope for licences. But there is a major difference between the moral absolute of Islam and Christianity. Holy Quran teaches that God cannot be known. Hence, His virtues cannot be a model for deciding what is good. So, an act is considered good because God chose to call it good, and not because it derives its rightness from God's character or any other principle. God could have decreed a different set of moral principles, in which case the parameters of morality would have been different.

The simple underlying principle of ethics in Islam is to submit oneself to the will of God to keep Him satisfied by one's acts, and also to be loyal to the community.

> Worship Allah and associate nothing with Him, and to parents do good, and to relatives, orphans, the needy, the near neighbour, the neighbour farther away, the companion at your side, the traveller, and those whom your right hands possess. Indeed, Allah does not like those who are self-deluding and boastful. *(Quran.4.36)*

The important thing to note in this quotation is the assertion of one's freedom to act, and also the importance of community life (or, tribal unity, as practised by the then Arabs). It also values the importance of the role of Prophet Muhammad in facilitating one's submission to God. The Prophet was sent by God to remind human beings of their moral responsibility, and challenge those ideas in society that opposed submission to God.

Unlike the Christian belief that man is evil by nature, Islam holds that man is born with a morally good nature that responds to faith and ethical values. Over time, it may get contaminated due to temptations and one's inability to exercise control over his desires. So, in spite of there being universal equality among mankind, people differ in matters of moral strength.

Islam believes that to be ethical one's intention must be good, and his action too must be according to what Quran says. One must have qualities like truthfulness, honesty, kindness, integrity, sincerity, etc. to be beloved of God, but at the same time, a devout must practise these in his daily life. Prophet Muhammad himself was the personification of all the noble qualities. Hence, he is the mould in which every true Muslim has to cast himself to be perfect. He is the one and the only model of religiosity. Morality does not determine Prophet's actions, but his actions determine and define morality. This makes Muslims unflinchingly loyal to what they do even if these be considered outdated by others.

Along with the general virtues, the five pillars of practice, discussed in the next section, form the core of Islamic ethics.

RITUALS AND PRACTICES

Islam has five pillars of virtue that every devout Muslim must practice. These practices distinguish a Muslim from a non-Muslim.

* Shahadah (Acceptance): Every Muslim must repeat, 'There is no God other than Allah; and, Muhammad is His prophet,' correctly, slowly, thoughtfully, aloud, with conviction and understanding at least once in his lifetime. This is not only a re-affirmation of the sacred belief but also the central prayer for Muslims which is supposed to bring spiritual enlightenment to the practitioner. In its subtle aspect, it is like a mantra of the Hindus that convey an idea, which when meditated upon reveals palpably the knowledge contained in those words.

* Salat (Practice of prayer): Muslims are asked to be in constant prayer to keep one's life in perspective, and to see it objectively. The story goes that God asked Muhammad to pray fifty times a day, but he got the permission for the believers to pray only five times a day. Since then the number remains fixed. This praying must be done facing the Kaaba at Mecca. During prayer, they are not expected to visualise God but to worship and adore him as a protector.

* Zakaat (Charity): Islam being a community religion, it is mandatory for every Muslim to pay 2.5% of his wealth to specified categories in society when their annual wealth exceeds a minimum level. Also, one must give alms to the needy.

* Hajj (Pilgrimage to Mecca): Every Muslim is supposed to go visit Mecca on pilgrimage at least once in his lifetime. A person returning from Hajj is called haji and is treated with respect in his community.

* Sawm (The fast of Ramadan): The first words of the Quran came to Prophet in the month of Ramadan. The holy emigration also took place in the same month. Hence the religious importance of that month in which every devout Muslim observes a month-long fast and prays religiously in a congregation.

Apart from these rituals, there are other beliefs that one must have to be a true Muslim:

* Belief in God (Allah), the one and only one worthy of all worship (*tawhid*).
* Belief in the angels (*mala'ika*).
* Belief in the books (*kutub*) sent by God (including the Quran).
* Belief in all the prophets (*nabi*) and messengers (*rusul*) sent by God.

* Belief in the Day of Judgement (al-*qiamah*) and in the Resurrection.
* Belief in destiny (*qadar*).

There are many more beliefs and customs like encouraging people to perform good deeds, discouraging people from committing sin, to love the family of Prophet Muhammad, and to disassociate oneself from the enemies of the Prophet.

JIHAD

Jihad means the struggle to earn the favour of God, which is of two kinds: the greater jihad, 'al-Jihad al-Akbar'—the struggle against the evil within one's own soul; and the lesser jihad, 'al-jihad al-Asghar'—the fight on the battlefield in defence of Islam. The spiritually inclined Muslims prefer to accept jihad in its higher aspect, and thus strive to become spiritually perfect. But it is the lesser aspect of jihad that attracts the common minds, and in turn, affects the world of the non-Muslims, and in many cases, even the sects and sub-sects of Islam.

Islam divides the world into two categories of people, those who follow the book (*al-kitab*), and those who do not (*jahiliyyah*). In Judaism, 'People of the Book' means the Jewish people who had Torah and the Talmud. Christians claim themselves to belong to the 'religion of the Word of God', since it includes the words of Jesus, along with the Torah and Talmud. Islam, on the other hand, treats the Quran as the completion of the Old and New Testament, and also to synthesise them as God's true, final, and eternal message to humanity. These three religions, according to Islam, are adherents of *al-Kitab* (People of the Book), and those who are not adherents of *al-Kitab* are *jahiliyyah* (ignorant of divine guidance). It is the duty of the devout to bring light to the ignorant. To begin with, those who do not belong to *al-Kitab* are to be enlightened, and those who have not yet got the true light (i.e. Judaism and Christianity) are to be shown the light. Unfortunately, the battle extends to the sects of Islam too, and thus Sunnis battle with Shia, while they both fight against Ahamadiya. The list goes on, staying true to the Arabic proverb mentioned in the beginning of the section.

In a more comprehensive division, Islam accepts the idea of *millat* (believers) and *kufr* or *kafir* (non-believers), according to which every Muslim is a brother of every other Muslim around the world, and all kafirs are enemies of the Muslims. This results in two kinds of land all over the world: *dar-ul-Islam* and *dar-ul-harb*.

Dar-ul-Islam means those countries which have already come under the domination of Islam, whereas dar-ul-harb are those countries which have not yet been conquered by Islam, but where the Muslims are fighting with the kafirs to bring them under their control. Many in Islam consider it their duty to bring dar-ul-harb land under an Islamic state. This requires jihad, the holy war.

> Go on fighting against them till the rule of Allah is not established *(8.39)*

> Jihad is better for you than your sitting back at home and if you do so, He will forgive you your sins, your foulest deeds and admit you into the gardens of eternity (the Paradise) *(Quran.61.12)*.

Also, there is no place for disbelievers in Allah's graciousness.

> I will cast terror into the hearts of those who disbelieve. Therefore, strike off their heads and strike off every fingertip of them. *(Quran.8.12)*

> Fight those who do not believe in Allah or in the Last
> Day and who do not consider unlawful what Allah and
> His Messenger have made unlawful and who do not
> adopt the religion of truth from those who were given the
> Scripture—[fight] until they give the jizyah willingly while
> they are humbled.' *(Quran.9.29)*

Jizyah is the tax levied by the Muslims on the non-Muslim subjects if they refuse to convert to Islam.

To implement these wishes of Allah, one needs jihad. Jihad affects the fighters (*jihadi/mujahidin*) in two ways—firstly, if they are victorious, they get to enjoy the booty earned by doing jihad. Quran commands to reserve one-fifth of war booty as the 'holy khum' for the Prophet during his lifetime and to divide the rest equally among the mujahidin (fighters). If the jihadi dies, he becomes a martyr in the cause of Islam and thus becomes a favourite of Allah, who is supposed to receive him in Paradise even before the Judgement Day and provide him with profuse sensual enjoyments. His sins will be forgiven, he will be able to intercede with Allah on the Day of Judgement for seventy of his relatives and friends, and he will enjoy the highest bliss of the Paradise.

Interestingly, during the period that Prophet lived in Mecca in his first phase of revelations, fighting was forbidden for the Muslims. But after his migration to Medina, Allah at first gave them permission to fight and subsequently made fighting obligatory for every able Muslim.

> Hence when you meet them who disbelieve, smite them
> on their necks till when you have killed or wounded many
> of them.' *(Quran.47.4)*

SUFISM

The Sufis were those dedicated Muslims during the time of Prophet who wore simple monastic cloaks of *suf* (coarse wool). Another derivation of the word is from the *ahl-e-suffa* (the people of the bench), a group of early Muslims, who lived in the first mosque at Medina in close proximity to Prophet Muhammad. Yet another derivation of the word is from *safa* or purity. Whatever the root of the word, Sufis are accepted to be the mystics of Islamic tradition who do not care much for the simplistic beliefs of a common Muslim.

Sufis trace their origins to Prophet Muhammad, who is believed to have instructed his successor in mystical teachings and practices, in addition to the Quran or hidden within the Quran. Sufis strictly adhere to a teacher-student relationship that forms a link in the spiritual chain that connects any authentic Sufi order back to the Prophet Muhammad. This relationship is known as *silsila* and is considered sacrosanct in Sufi tradition.

As mentioned earlier, Islamic outlook is tiered that allows room for different mindsets to pursue their spiritual disposition, although that may not be acceptable to the majority, and may ultimately end up in bloodshed. Sufism is a classic example of this. Symbolism, as the science of relationship between multiple levels of reality, is the foundation of Sufism. Sufis believe that Quran conceals a minimum of seven hidden significations, and at times this number can reach up to seventy. They believe that the revelation of God could come only through and during ecstasy, and that ecstasy was impossible without love. Neither a person's will nor his curiosity was enough to take one to God. Love requires the performance of good works for the beloved. Thus, the prime themes of Sufism are the doctrine of light, union with the Divine, love, and service.

The first great Sufi, Hallaj (9th century) declared *Ana el Haq* (I am He, I am Truth). This was entirely counter to Muslim doctrine as discussed in the earlier sections. He was beheaded for his assertion, which was nothing less than a sacrilege for the conservative Muslims.

However, his life and words were simple, creating immense appeal in later times. He explained that since God created everything, He dwelled in all things, from a tree to a man. This implied that there was an essential unity throughout the universe. This approach is quite similar to that of the Vedantic approach, *Aham Brahma asmi* (I am Brahman, the supreme reality).

It was left to El Ghazzali (d. 1111 AD), who synthesised reason and faith to make Sufism respectable. He was a great scholar and a mystic, but because he advocated Sufism, he was thrown into the jail many times. He utilised that period in deep meditation, and whenever he was out of the jail, he studied, went around gathering spiritual information and writing books. It is through his writings that we know a lot about the process of spiritual enlightenment of a spiritual aspirant.

Jalaluddin Rumi (13th century), a great poet and a mystic founded a special sect of Sufis called *Dervishes*, who used to dance round and round to stun their minds away from material goals. The mystic poems of Rumi are famous even today. Here is one to give an idea of mysticism practised by the Sufis:

> There is a community of the spirit.
> Join it, and feel the delight
> of walking in the noisy street
> and being the noise.

Drink all your passion,
and be a disgrace.
Close both eyes
to see with the other eye.

Sufism presented a new kind of mysticism in which there was only positive, characterised by '*fana* in *fana*,' i.e., extinction of extinction. Instead of rooting out the evil (a popular concept in Christianity and then in Islam), they treated the individual ego as something false, since it was not divine. This meant that once a person achieved the union with the Divine, the extinct (the false ego) automatically became extinct. Rabia, an early Sufi mystic used to say that she was so full of God that she had no room left for hating the evil or Satan.

Sufis felt that it was impossible for a man to conceive of God, who was unknowable and limitless. People need something concrete, to begin with, in religion. So, some Sufis began to treat Muhammad as an incarnation of God, calling him the Light of Light. With time, the idea of Muhammad being an incarnation became more concretised. Although centred at Quran, it incorporated the elements of Christian desert fathers, Buddhistic meditations, and Hindu *pranayama* as time passed. The focus was on seeing the divine light in a meditative state.

All this made the orthodox Muslims annoyed with the Sufis and finally left them to their own fate, disowning them, and treating them as non-Muslims.

SECTS

Medina continued to be the capital of the Islamic state, although Mecca, after the destruction of the idols around the Kaaba, became the spiritual centre of Islam. In 632 CE, soon after completing his pilgrimage at Mecca and setting out again for Medina, Prophet fell mortally ill from a fever. In his final days, he made no specific arrangements for succession.

With illness preventing him from leading the prayers, he asked Abu Bakr to lead the community in prayers. Abu Bakr had been Prophet's senior companion and the father of Ayesha, Prophet's favourite wife. Ayesha is respected so much by the Sunnis that her name is reverentially prefixed with 'Mother of the Believers'. This gesture by Prophet towards Abu Bakr was later interpreted in Sunni Islam as a recommendation for a political succession of Islam by him. Thus, Abu Bakr became the first Caliph of the Islamic world.

But this was not acceptable to many others, who pointed at the prophet's praise for Ali as a reflection of the Prophet's general designation of Ali as his successor. Ali was also Prophet's son-in-law through his marriage to Fatima, and he was thus the father of Prophet's two grandchildren, al-Hasan and al-Husayn.

Soon battles and wars broke out between Prophet's Father-in-law's followers, and the followers of Prophet's son-in-law, who came to be known as Shi'ite. The first battles left such deep wounds in the psyche of the respective followers of both the groups that these two sects look at each other suspiciously even today; they continue to kill each other, whenever provoked.

In spite of all the fighting, the two sects do not differ at the core level of their religious beliefs; the difference is mostly regarding the branches and elaboration of creed related beliefs. In general, Sunnis are considered more strict and orthodox, with a strong adherence to exact words of the Quran, whereas the Shia are more liberal with a freer spirit. Shias have a strong Persian culture behind them, whereas Sunnis are backed by the Arabic culture. The sect of Sufis, the mystics of Islam, evolved from the Shia sect.

There are many other sects that differ with each other in their secondary beliefs.

THE TRADITION GOES ON

There can be no doubt that the religion of Prophet was the great boon for the then tribe people of Arabia, which in turn spread all over the world. The brotherhood, as preached in Islam, has no parallel in the history of religions. In the process, Islam has done much to raise the conditions of the spiritually underprivileged. No wonder it continues to thrive.

Religion in the E-age

The preceding chapters give a fairly good idea of what religion truly means. The world of religion is qualitatively different from the world of matter, as also from the world of thoughts. True religion, i.e. spirituality, has no frame of reference in the world that we live in. This makes many believe that religion is a sham and an opiate and that it is antiquated and useless. However, as can be seen in the previous chapters, religion is not a misadventure of the human race, nor is it a pseudoscience, and definitely not bogus. It is the highest achievement by the finest faculties of the human mind, which has brought solace and hope to all who lived by its ideals and aspirations.

The prophets were born in different ages and different lands. So, no country or race can ever claim absolute right over spiritual wisdom, nor can any religion claim to be exclusively right. The masters never had issues with past masters; they only gave impetus to core spirituality, away from the externals of religion. The fight among the followers is not because their masters would have fought over it but because the followers do not have a good grasp of spiritual matters. In their limited understanding, the followers claim superiority over others.

Religion, as usually understood, is the outcome of the dynamics of spirituality, playing freely in a society. But unlike the world of matter, where the outcome of various forces working on an object can be predicted to precision, the forces of the society, working out the application of spirituality cannot be predicted to satisfaction. The human mind is free, and therefore it has different levels of purity and unselfishness. Just as the purity of a religion depends on the nature and character of its followers, the not-so-noble minds invariably add dross to a religion due to their incompetence and greed. The onlookers blame religion for the dirt it carries, but the fault lies somewhere else.

A look at the history of human civilisation shows how when religion (the practical aspect of spirituality) becomes hollow, materialism takes over it. When both create hollowness in the social psyche, a spiritual force descends in the society. These three, spirituality—religion–materialism, coexist and also tend to impact each other, although their timings cannot be ascertained in advance.

Life runs on the twin realities of the collective external world and the individual inner world. Of these two, the inner world is more important, since it dictates one's behaviour in the external world. A rich inner life results in a fulfilling external life, as can be seen from the lives of the prophets and saints. Thus, a powerful inner moral sense makes a person ethical in the external world.

The present age, and possibly the coming years, belongs to materialism. Superficiality in the name of rationality, licentiousness in the name of freedom, greed in the name of free market, and bloodbath in the name of ideology, has grown to monstrous proportions. Today, when every other young person believes in the truism 'religion is irrelevant' its standing in this e-age looks shaky. Will the high-tech generation of the future have anything to do with religion? Will they throng places of worship as their ancestors did?

The answer is an emphatic 'yes'. After all, the folks of the cyber age are in no way different from those belonging to the earlier ages; the human template is same as it was thousands of years ago. Driven by greed and fear, people continue to run after wealth, sex, fame, and power, as their ancestors had wanted. The desire to gorge on excellent food, have grand dresses, live in large houses, move in impressive vehicles, etc., often without even toiling for it, is as common today as it was yesterday.

As materialism increases, misery and desire are bound to increase. The consequences of an impoverished inner life are visible all over the world today. A phenomenal rise in cases of suicides, molestations, killings, exploitation, etc. is a pointer to the bankruptcy of the inner wealth. To save oneself from being fractured by the sledgehammers of the world, one needs the inner strength that can be consolidated only through a moral force, usually dictated well only by a religion. Inner paucity makes one brittle like iron ore that can be forged into steel most easily through the fires of spirituality.

Religion was never for all, nor will it ever be for everyone. There will always be people who would love the trinkets of the world and will remain content with it trivialities. As any grown-up mind knows, these are the people who suffer and make others suffer in the long run. But blessed are those who can think of the permanence underlying the impermanence all around, and then strive to attain that. There can be no doubt that the coming ages too will have such blessed souls.

Also, the possibility of some noble minds being handpicked by the Divine to express Himself through them is always there. There are countless examples from the past when an ordinary person like Saul has been chosen by the Lord to become St. Paul. If the Divine is indeed all-powerful, as the previous chapters show, then that possibility always remains.

A spiritual search is akin to a search for perfection. However, there can be no perfection in the world and definitely not in any kind of knowledge that is based on this world. Religion being applied spirituality in the world, no religion can ever be perfect either. For the same reason, there can never be one single universal religion. Two minds are not identical. Hence, the choice to cast oneself into one or the other mould will always depend on the mental makeup of a person.

The intensive and extensive reach of knowledge has changed the human race from being ignorant to well-informed. It may so happen in the future that people will move away from the non-essentials of religion and take up spirituality as a way of life. In essence it means that people may move away from the forms of religion, as they are today, and look only for core spirituality. The struggle of the human race to be what it is—divine—appears quite natural and fair.

Acknowledgements

It is impossible for anyone to work on a project like this without the support of great minds and heart. It was God's grace and the kind support of many friends and well-wishers that helped me complete this mammoth task. A big thank you to all of them. They went patiently through every word of this manuscript and helped me perfect the papers. Many of them do not want to be named.

The manuscript of this book was read and re-read many times by a number of my good friends, who also helped me with invaluable suggestions and corrections. Of them, the more involved ones were Sri Rusi C. Mithawala (Mumbai), Sri Pradipto Chakraborty, Dr Gurmeet S. Narang (Tavleen Foundation, Indore), Sri Dripta (Dublin), Sri Rajshekhar (Chandigarh), Sri Biswanath Bose, Sri Hersh Bharadwaj, and Sri Avinash Singh. Thank you all, for bearing with me. A book of this intensity could not have been possible without your support.

I take this opportunity to thank Dr Assim Derweesh (Oman), who wrote to me after reading the manuscript, 'Finally, I have finished reading your article about Islam...It was so full of information and quality analysis that even I, a Muslim with good knowledge of history, found several new information and deep education.' His words were highly encouraging.

Prof. S. Makbul Islam, Kolkata, was kind enough to write the foreword for this book. He also went through the entire manuscript meticulously. His sheer intensity and speed on this project were awe inspiring. Thank you, Prof. Islam. I cherish your friendship.

Sri Nripendra Prasanna Acharya, USA, is a great scholar, and a perfect gentleman. In spite of his advanced age, and busy schedule, he was kind enough to go through the manuscript, and suggest changes.

Sri Dibyojyoti Chatterjee, Mumbai, leads a hectic professional life. In spite of his busy schedule, he helped me immensely in preparing this manuscript. Dr Alok Bajpayee, a professional psychiatrist and a scholar, very kindly went through the entire manuscript and made suggestions. Thank you, my good friend. Mr Pranav Kumar Singh, a great friend of mine and a great editor, deserves very special thanks. It was he who first conceptualised this book for publication. Thank you, Pranav ji.

Sri Ajey Ranade, IPS, loved the manuscript and encouraged me in various ways to complete the project on time. He has been a great support to me in numerous ways.

Mr Shyam Anad Jha, Muzaffarpur, who is associated with management teaching, has been a great help in innumerable ways. Without his active support, even my monastic life would not have been possible. Thank you, sir.

My good friend Sri Parmil Mittal, and Sri Manish Jain are from the publishing world. They have been extremely supportive of my ventures over the years, both personally and professionally. Thank you, sirs.

I take this opportunity to thank Sri Nirmal Kanti Bhattacharjee, Publisher, Niyogi Books for kindly consenting to bring out the book. And, special thanks to Ms Jayalakshmi Sengupta, the editor of this book whose contribution has been invaluable.

My friends, Sri Amit Ray Chowdhury, Sri G. Sreenivas, Sri Nabin Chandra Ghosh, Sri Amit Kumar Chatterjee, Sri Anibrata Sen, Sri Anupam Mukherjee, Ari Arup Kar, and Sri Buddhadev Das have been supporting me unflinchingly for years. Thanks to you all.

Work of this stature requires care for a long time by a supportive group. I wish to thank Sri Swarup Mukherjee, Sri Siddharth Baskhor,

Sri Ganesh Mallick, Sri Ramesh Rana, Sri Surya Biswakarma, Sri Mangal Biswakarma, Sri Jagadish Thakur, Sri Shantimani Roy, Sri Paradip Das, Sri Prashanta (Madhav) Kumar Das, Sri Gour Chand Mandal, Sri Dinesh Mallick, Sri Soumyadeep Roy Chowdhury, Sri Samir Roy, Sri Panchugopal and above all Dinu da, who took care of me during all hours. Their love and support have been unbound.

To end it, I wish to thank Sri Ajay Nayak, IAS, who has been a great inspiration behind all my works. It was he who kept prodding me to write. I doubt if I would have ever been a writer without his constant pushes.

Thank you, readers, for going through this work patiently.

Samarpan

Select Bibliography

- Augustine, Saint. 'On the Trinity, trans.' E. Hill, Brooklyn, NY,1991.
- *Bhagavad Gita: the song celestial.* Heritage Press, 1965.
- Bhattacharya, Harisatya. *The Jaina Prayer.* University of Calcutta, 1964.
- Bhattacharyya, Haridas, ed. *The Cultural Heritage of India: The philosophies.* Vol. 3. Ramakrishna Mission, Institute of Culture, 1953.
- Bhikkhu, Thanissaro. 'The Dhammapada, a Translation.' 1997.
- Bible. English. New International Version. *The Holy Bible: new international version.* Hodder & Stoughton, 1996.
- Bose, Abinash Chandra. *Call of the Vedas.* Vol. 25. Bharatiya Vidya Bhavan, 1988.
- Britannica, Encyclopaedia. 'Chicago: Encyclopaedia Britannica.' 1985.
- Burke, Marie Louise. *Swami Vivekananda in the West: new discoveries.* Vol. 6. Advaita Ashrama, 1987.
- Chanchreek, Kanhaiyalal, ed. *Jaina Sutras: Sutrakritanga.* Shree Publ., 2006.
- Chatterji, Kshitish Chandra, ed. *Vedic selections.* Calcutta University, 1944.
- Dhalla, Maneckji Nusservanji. *Homage unto Ahura Mazda.* Victoria Printing Works, 1970.

- Gnanarama, Pategama. 'Essentials of Buddhism.' *Principal Buddhist and Pali College in Singapore*. 2000.

- Griffith, Ralph TH. *The Rig Veda*. Vol. 1. Library of Alexandria, 2009.

- *Illustrated World of Proverbs* (n.d). http://www.worldofproverbs.com.

- Jacobi, Hermann. trans. Jaina Sutras: The Acaranga Sutra. 1884.

- Kaul, Kadambari. 'The Dhammapada: with an Introduction to the Life and Times of Lord Buddha And His Philosophy.' 2007

- Keay, John. *India: A History. Revised and Updated*. Grove/Atlantic, Inc., 2011.

- Khalsa, Sardar Dr Sant Singh, trans. *Sri Guru Granth Sahib*. SikhNet, 2016.

- Khushwant Singh, Nanak. *Hymns of Guru Nanak*. Orient Blackswan, 1991.

- Majumdar, Ramesh Chandra, Bharatiya Vidya Bhavan, and Bharatiya Itihasa Samiti. *The history and culture of the Indian people*. G. Allen & Unwin, 1969.

- Masani, Rustom Pestonji. *The religion of the good life: Zoroastrianism*. G. Allen & Unwin, Limited,1938.

- Mirza, Hormazdyar Dastur Kayoji. *Outlines of Parsi history*. Mirza, 1974.

- Müller, Max, ed. 1879. *The Sacred Books of the East*. Oxford University Press, 1910.

- Pendergast III, Michael S. *Children of Abraham: Jesus and Mohammed*. Author House, 2012.

- Pesala, Bhikkhu. *Debate of King Milinda*. Delhi: Motilal Banarsidass, 1991.

- Renou, Louis. *Vedic India*. Susil Gupta, 1957.

- Sachau, Edward C. *Alberuni's India: An Account of the Religion, Philosophy, Literature, Geography, Chronology, Astronomy, Customs, Laws and Astrology of India*. Vol. 2. Routledge, 2013.

- Sayanacharya, and Pandit Baladeva Upadhyaya. *The Veda Bhasya Bhumika Samgraha: a collection of all available Sayana's introduction to Vedic commentaries*. Chowkhamba Sanskrit Series Office, 1958.
- Sewell, Dennis. *The Political Gene: How Darwin's Ideas Changed Politics*. Pan Macmillan, 2009.
- Shollenberger, George D. *God and His Coexistent Relations to the Universe*. Author House, 2014.
- Spiegelberg, Frederic. *Living Religions of the World*. Thames and Hudson, 1957.
- Steinsaltz, Adin. *The thirteen petalled rose*. New York: Basic Books, 1980.
- Swarup, Ram. *Understanding Islam Through Hadis*. Exposition Press, 1983.
- Swarup, Ram. *Understanding Islam through Hadis*. Voice of Dharma, 1982.
- *The Meaning of the Holy Qur'an : complete translation with selected notes*. Kube Publishing Ltd, 2015.
- Thomas, Cleary, trans. *Essential Koran: The Heart of Islam*. Booksales, 1998.
- Torwesten, Hans. *Ramakrishna and Christ, or, The paradox of the incarnation*. Ramakrishna Mission Institute of Culture, 1999.
- Vivekananda, Swami. *Christ, the Messenger*. Advaita Ashrama (Publication House of Ramakrishna Math, Belur Math), 2016.
- Vivekananda, Swami. *Complete works*. Vol. 1–9. 1962.
- *Words of Master*. (n.d.). Indore: Tavleen Foundation.
- Zaehner, Robert Charles. *Hindu Scriptures: Edited with New Translations*. University of California Press, 1996.